Care and Repair of Lawn and Garden Tools

Homer L. Davidson

TAB BOOKS
Blue Ridge Summit, PA

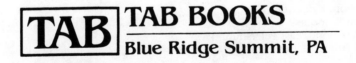

FIRST EDITION
FIRST PRINTING

Library of Congress Cataloging-in-Publication Data

Davidson, Homer L.
Care and repair of lawn and garden tools / by Homer L. Davidson.
p. cm.
Includes index.
ISBN 0-8306-3898-9 ISBN 0-8306-3897-0 (pbk.)
1. Lawns—Equipment and supplies—Maintenance and repair.
2. Garden tools—Maintenance and repair. I. Title.
SB433.2.D39 1992 91-36105
635—dc20 CIP

TAB Books offers software for sale. For information and a catalog, please contact TAB Software Department, Blue Ridge Summit, PA 17294-0850.

Acquisitions Editor: Kimberly Tabor
Director of Production: Katherine G. Brown
Book Design: Jaclyn J. Boone
Cover Design: Denny Bond, East Petersburg, PA
Cover Photograph: Homer L. Davidson TAB1

To my father, Chester, who raised ten children,
and who worked a garden patch every year—
without power tools or equipment.

Contents

Acknowledgments ix

Introduction xi

PART ONE
MAINTAINING TOOLS AND EQUIPMENT

1 Safety 3
Grounding power tools *5*
Extension cords *7*
Weather conditions *7*
Lawn mowers *8*
Snowblowers *8*
Rototillers *10*
Shredders and chippers *10*
A word about tools *10*

2 Cleanup and Lubrication 15
Cleanup *15*
Lubrication *20*
Fuel requirements *22*

3 Servicing Small Hand Tools 23
Replacing handles *23*
Sharpening tools *24*
Repairing rusty tools *25*
Maintenance *27*

4 Servicing Small Power Lawn and Garden Equipment **43**

Periodic inspection *43*
Chain saws *44*
Compost tumblers *55*
Cultivators *58*
Electric edgers *60*
Hedgers *60*
Leaf blowers *61*
Leaf shredders *63*
Weed and grass trimmers *63*
Sharpening tools *77*

5 Servicing Medium Power Garden and Lawn Equipment **81**

Periodic inspection *81*
Lawn mowers *82*
Shredders/chippers *91*
Snowblowers *101*
Tillers *108*

6 Large Power Mowing and Weed-Cutting Equipment **117**

Power weed cutters *117*
Rear-end mowers *125*
BCS 700 power unit *129*
Riding mower *132*

PART TWO
SERVICING ENGINES

7 Briggs & Stratton Engines **155**

Fuel and lubrication requirements *155*
Control adjustments *155*
Maintenance *158*

8 Clinton Engines **163**

Fuel and lubrication requirements *168*
Maintenance *170*
Minor and major tune-ups *172*

9 Jacobsen Engines **185**
123V two-cycle engines *185*
A984H two-cycle engines *191*

10 Tecumseh Engines **205**
TVS/TVXL840 two-cycle engines *205*
Four-cycle engines *214*
OVM four-cycle engines *224*

Glossary **241**

Resources **245**

Index **247**

Acknowledgments

Without the help of several power mechanics and repairpersons, and service and general managers, this book would never have been written. A great deal of thanks goes to the manufacturers who provided service data and illustrations for this book. These include:

Amerind MacKissic Inc.
BCS Corporation
Briggs & Stratton Corporation
Clinton Engines Corporation
Crary Bear Cat Company
Deere & Company
Homelite Division of Textron Inc.
Inertia Dynamics Corporation
Jacobsen Division of Textron Inc.
Kinco Manufacturing
Mainline of North America
McCulloch Corporation
Poulan/Weed Eater
Solo Incorporated
Tecumseh Products Company
Woods (Division of Hesston Corp).

Introduction

Troubleshooting and repairing your own small hand tools and lawn and garden power equipment can be a lot of fun and quite rewarding. You can also quickly finish the job without waiting weeks for someone else to repair it. You can say, "I did it!" Well-maintained lawn and garden tools keep the lawn and garden neat and in tip-top shape. There is nothing greater than a neighbor or visitor complimenting you on your nice clean yard or garden.

Repairing and maintaining small gasoline engines or small electrical tools is not as difficult as you might think. Before starting any job, check chapter 1 on safety. Even the smallest hand or power tool can be dangerous if it isn't operated correctly. Part 1 covers how to properly care for your tools, including lubrication and fuel requirements, checking and troubleshooting small and medium-sized garden equipment, as well as sharpening blades and tines, rustproofing equipment and tools, and much more.

Part 2 of the book covers how to maintain, repair, service, and lubricate four different engines, beginning alphabetically with Briggs & Stratton engines, then Clinton, Jacobsen, and Tecumseh engines. These are the most common engines found on lawn and garden equipment, and knowing how to take care of these engines is more important than the garden or lawn tool itself.

For some, working in the garden or putting the finishing touches on the lawn provides a different means of relaxation away from the work week. Taking care of Mother Earth makes us forget everyday stress, provides a healthy lawn and garden, and in some cases, helps place food on the table every day of the year. So let's take care of those tools out there—and have some fun doing it.

Introduction

Part 1

Maintaining Tools and Equipment

Chapter 1

Safety

Lawn and garden tools are easy to operate and can last a lifetime if properly handled, operated, and maintained. Before operating or assembling power tools, be sure to read the owner's manual several times. Know how to operate small hand tools to prevent breakage or possible personal damage. Follow all safety rules found in the service manual.

Power tools should be operated with the correct oil and fuel requirements and receive proper maintenance. Chapter 2 covers general fuel and lubrication requirements for a variety of tools and power equipment. Where appropriate, specific fuel and lubrication information is provided for a particular unit. Other hand tools should be lubricated and sharpened regularly.

Gasoline is extremely flammable. It can explode from combustion or ignite near an open flame. Always stop the engine and allow it to cool before filling the fuel tank. Do not smoke, and keep sparks and open flames away when filling the tank. Pressure can build up inside fuel tanks, so loosen fuel tank cap slowly to relieve any pressure in the tank.

The follow are safety guidelines that you should adhere to when operating any tool:

1. Thoroughly inspect all power units for loose or damaged parts before each use. Do not use until adjustments and repairs are made.
2. Avoid accidental starting.
3. Keep all bystanders, especially children and pets, away from the area. Never allow children to ride with you on a riding lawn mower or allow pets to roam free.
4. Wear safety glasses or goggles at all times when operating any type of equipment. Do not rely on eyeglasses. Rocks, pebbles, and twigs can be thrown against the glasses, ruining expensive prescription glasses and possibly damaging eyes.

5. Dress properly and wear proper footwear. Do not operate any power tool with loose clothing.
6. Keep hands, face, and feet away from moving parts. Do not touch mufflers or cylinders. These parts can stay warm for a short time after equipment is turned off.
7. Operate units in well-ventilated areas—outdoors. Do not operate engines faster than the speed necessary. Do not run the engine at high speed when cultivating.
8. If you strike or become entangled with a foreign object, stop the engine immediately and check for damage. Make necessary repairs. Do not operate with loose or damaged parts.
9. Always stop the engine when walking from one location to another.
10. Keep tines and guards clear of debris. Never attempt to clear tines and guard of debris with the engine running.
11. Allow equipment to cool before storing.
12. Wear gloves when cleaning blades and tines because they become sharp from use. Never put your finger between blade openings or grasp blades, even if the machine is not running. The blades are very sharp.
13. Always first inspect areas to be cut, trimmed, or cultivated. Remove wire, string, tin cans, twigs or material that can be thrown by a power tool.
14. Keep proper balance at all times. Do not overreach to get at a small area while trimmer is operating.
15. Disengage clutches and remove spark plug wire before attempting any maintenance or adjustments on a machine.
16. Never try to clear or work on the blade with the engine running.
17. Always try to mow uphill, sideways or diagonally—never straight down a hill.

Heed all manufacturer's danger signs when operating a lawn mower, snowblower, tiller, tractor, or chipper/shredder. These power units can be dangerous if not operated or serviced properly. All power equipment should be operated with extreme care. Although the preceding safety guidelines apply to engines as well, the following safety warnings are specifically for engines:

1. Do not run engine in an enclosed area. Exhaust contains carbon monoxide, an odorless and deadly poison.
2. Do not check for spark with spark plug or spark plug wire removed. Use an approved tester.
3. Do not crank engine with a spark plug removed. If engine is flooded, place throttle in fast position and crank engine until it starts.

4. Do not operate engine when an odor of gasoline is present or other explosive conditions exist.
5. Do not operate engine if gasoline is spilled. Move machine away from the spill and avoid creating any ignition until the gasoline has evaporated.
6. Do not refuel indoors where area is not well ventilated.
7. Do not operate engine without a muffler. Inspect periodically and replace if necessary.
8. Do not operate engine with an accumulation of grass, leaves, dirt or other combustible material in the muffler area.
9. Do not use the engine on any forest-covered, brush-covered, or grass-covered unimproved land unless a spark arrester is installed on the muffler.
10. Do not run engine with air cleaner or air cleaner cover removed.
11. Do not run engine at excessive speeds; this can result in injury.
12. Do not tamper with governor springs, governor links, or other parts that might increase the governed engine speed.
13. Do not tamper with the engine speed selected by the original equipment manufacturer.
14. Do not touch hot muffler, cylinder or fins as contact might cause burns.
15. Do keep cylinder fins and governor parts free of grass and other debris as this can affect engine speed.
16. Do pull starter cord slowly until resistance is felt. Then, pull cord rapidly to avoid kickback and prevent hand or arm injury.
17. To prevent accidental starting when servicing the engine or equipment, always remove the spark plug or wire from the spark plug. Disconnect the negative wire from the battery terminal if it is equipped with a 12-volt starting system.
18. Do use fresh gasoline. Stale fuel can cause leakage.

GROUNDING POWER TOOLS

All power tools fastened to a workbench should be grounded at a power receptacle box and metal base plate. Use at least #10 or #12 copper wire. Portable AC power tools are grounded with a three-prong plug (FIG. 1-1). Do not cut off the grounding pin to plug in an ungrounded receptacle or extension cord. Use a grounding adaptor instead.

Improper connections on any power tool could result in electrical shock. Usually, the grounded wire conductor is green, with or without yellow stripes. Use an ohmmeter to identify the ground wire. Check the continuity between the ground wire or large brass plug to the motor bell or power equipment (FIG. 1-2). A high-resistance measurement indicates a poor ground.

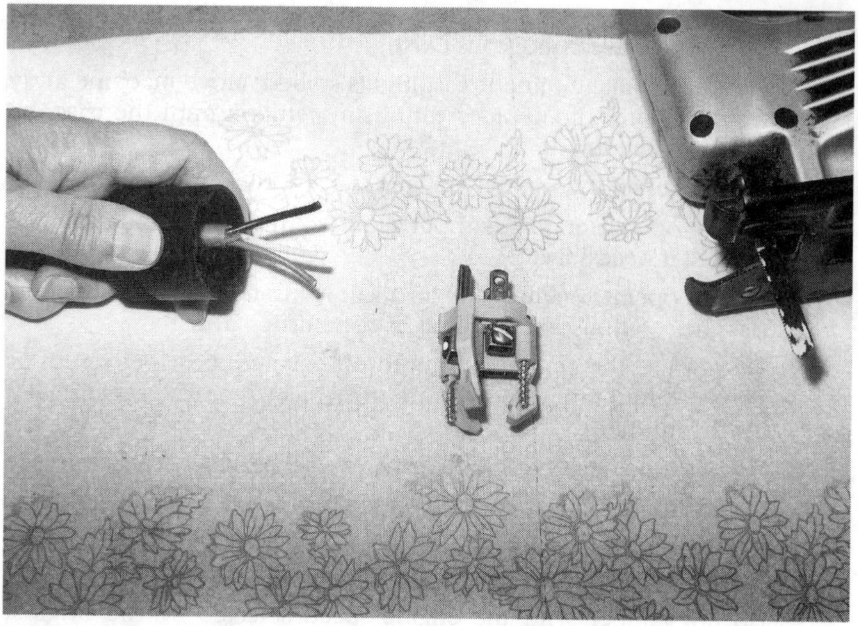

1-1 All power tools should be grounded with a three-prong plug and rubber three-wire cable.

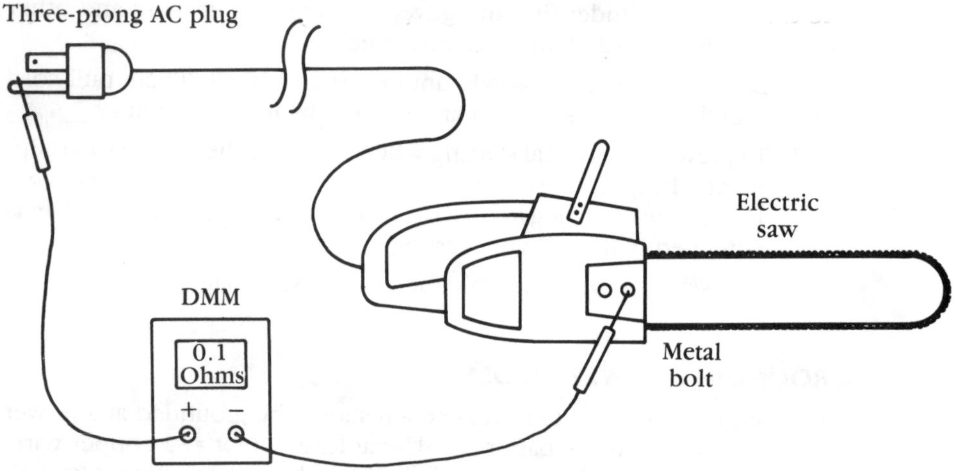

1-2 Check the ground wire of power tools at the long brass prong and on the metal body.

All power outlets should be grounded outlets for AC outdoor equipment. Don't take chances—check the grounded equipment and the receptacle. Use only three-wire extension cords that have a three-prong plug to prevent electrical shock. Make sure that AC lawn mower and trimmer tools are grounded with a three-prong plug.

EXTENSION CORDS

If you must use an extension cord, select only a three-wire cord with a three-prong plug and socket. All extension cords should be recommended by Underwriters Laboratories (UL) and have a UL rating. The letters WA on the cord jacket indicate that the cord can be used outdoors.

A rough estimate of extension cord length with power tool amperage should be #16 for 15 feet or less; #14 for 50 feet or less; and #12 for 100 feet or less. This might depend on the amperage of the power tool, however. The smaller the size of the wire, the greater carrying capacity of the extension cord. For instance, #12 gauge wire is larger and carries a higher amperage than #18 wire. It's best not to use two or three different power cords to cover the same distance as one long extension cord. The plug-in connections might become overheated with poor contacts and cause the extension cord to overheat and burn.

All extension cords should be repaired or replaced if cut, worn, or damaged. If an extension cord must be repaired in the middle area, make a telephone splice, solder all connections, and place a layer of rubber and thin plastic tape over the entire connection (FIG. 1-3).

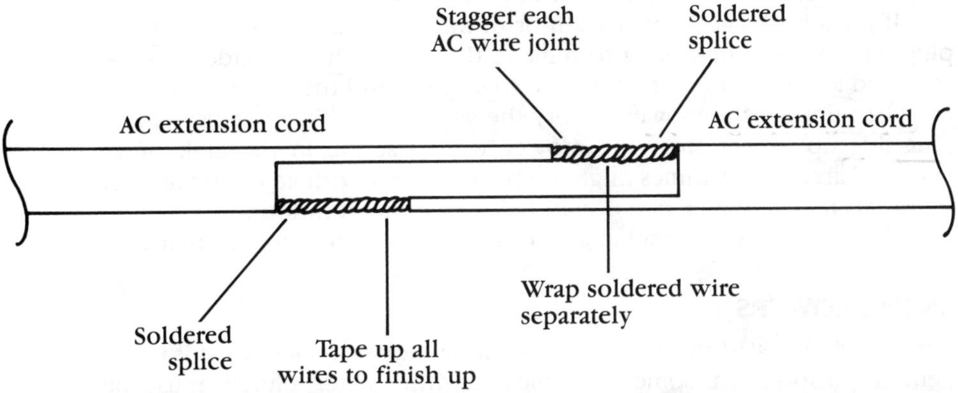

1-3 If an extension cord is cut or broken, repair with a good telephone-type splice.

Never use extension cords outdoors in rain, sleet, or snow. Make sure the grass is not wet when using an electric lawn mower, edger, or clippers. Wait until the dew or rain dries up before working with electric extension cords outdoors. Keep the extension cord out of the blades of lawn mowers or edgers when making sharp turns.

WEATHER CONDITIONS

Do not mow the grass immediately after a rain or early in the morning when dew is heavy. The danger of slipping and losing your footing it too great. Wet grass will also stick to the underside of the mower, preventing proper discharge of grass clippings. If a bag catcher is used, the wet grass will clog up the chute and the motor can become bogged down. Wet grass and dirt must then be cleaned from the discharge chute and undercarriage before you can finish mowing the grass.

Do not use an extension cord with a trimmer, electric lawn mower, or any power tool in the rain or under wet conditions. Besides clogging up the machine, it's possible to be electrocuted or receive extensive shock with a wet extension cord. Inspect extension cords even under dry conditions for cuts, breaks, or frayed cords.

LAWN MOWERS

Do not operate a mower with the chute door open unless the grass bag, if there is one, is properly mounted. Make sure the mower clutch drive, levers, and speed controls are operating properly. Do not make any adjustments to the motor without stopping the engine. Disengage all clutches and blades if any adjustments are made, such as to the carburetor, while the engine is running. Keep away from all moving parts. Be careful of heated motor and exhaust or muffler. Do not wash down a hot motor with a hose or you could damage the engine. Keep feet and hands from under mower carriage at all times. Place foot on top of motor carriage, if necessary, to pull or start a stubborn motor.

If grass is clogged underneath or in the chute, disconnect the spark plug wire before attempting to remove the debris. If the blade must be removed for sharpening, remove the spark plug and the ground. Be careful when tipping the mower; empty the gas tank and keep engine spark-plug-side up. Never store the mower with gasoline in the tank of an enclosed area where fumes might come in contact with an open flame or spark. Make sure the engine is cool before moving it indoors.

Do not change the engine governor settings or overspeed engine.

SNOWBLOWERS

Before trying to start the engine of your snowblower, make sure it is in the neutral position. In some snowblowers, the auger clutch must be engaged. The 7½ HP snowblower shown in FIG. 1-4 must have the auger clutch raised and locked down before starting the motor. When the temperature is below zero, it's difficult to start the engine with a heavy rotating load.

Always keep the snow chute rotated away from yourself and in the direction of discharging snow. Do not try to clean out a clogged chute of wet snow while the motor or auger clutch is engaged (FIG. 1-5). Do not try to remove clogged wet snow with your hands. Shut off the motor and pull the plug wire. Dislodge the wet snow with a stick or small board.

Be very careful when going over ice or slick spots. You could fall down, and with larger snowblowers, the unit will keep moving. Keep hands on the shifting lever and handlebars under difficult walkways, roads, or terrain. Pick up all limbs, litter, and rocks before a snow so they are not picked up and thrown out with the snowblower.

1-4 Before starting the engine on this 7 1/2 HP Montgomery Ward snowblower, disengage the auger clutch.

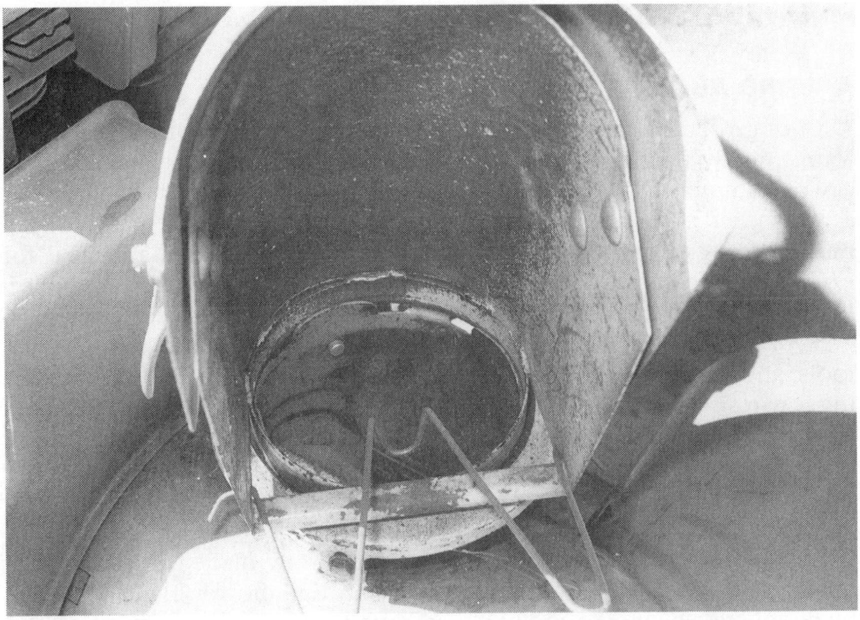

1-5 Never clear the chute of a snowblower when the engine is operating. Disengage the auger and shut off the engine.

ROTOTILLERS

Keep the Rototiller's rotating thongs disengaged when moving the tiller or when the tiller is inactive. Keep all drive belts and chain drive covers and shields on at all times. Do not remove and forget to replace shields and covers. Before removing brush, wires, and twine from rotating blades, shut off the engine and remove the spark plug wire.

SHREDDERS AND CHIPPERS

Before starting the motor of a shredder or chipper, shut off shredder blades from rotating. Keep in mind, however, that some models do not have a separate shutoff for blades; the blades start to rotate when the motor operates. Keep hands, face, clothing, children, and pets away from the intake hopper discharge area and moving parts. Obey the danger signs on the side of the shredder, and never place hands below a feed line.

Do not use hands to clear the discharge area. If the unit jams, shut off the motor and use a wooden stick to clear the area. Do not use hands to install rods, screen, or adjust for service with the shredder operating. Do not operate the grinder with the feed slide gate open.

Do not try to remove the chipper gate while operating. Keep hands above the caution line. If the metal shield is removed, large pieces can be thrown causing injury.

Place the shredder/chipper on level ground because it vibrates and moves. Never operate a shredder/chipper in an enclosed area. Heed all safety signs on the unit to prevent personal injury. Finally, always wear safety glasses and gloves when operating a power shredder/chipper.

A WORD ABOUT TOOLS

A lot of garden and lawn tools can be repaired with just a few hand tools found around the home or in the garage. A standard pair of pliers, a screwdriver, hammer, and a soldering iron can repair a lot of tools. Of course, a set of socket wrenches, a cordless power screwdriver, and a DMM (digital multimeter) can quickly aid any repairs. Socket wrenches are ideal for reaching those hard-to-get-at areas to remove bolts and nuts, and a cordless screwdriver can quickly remove Phillips-head and slotted screws.

A DMM or VOM can solve open cords, check the continuity of power tools, and pinpoint improper grounding problems. In addition to providing low-resistance measurements, a DMM can check the AC and DC voltages of motors, extension cords, and batteries. A DMM can also check open or leaky diodes with a diode test. Purchase a low-priced digital multimeter if you don't already have a VOM, because it's more accurate with voltage and resistance measurements (FIG. 1-6).

Keeping blades sharp is important. A dull saw blade can cause burn marks, slow feeding, and rough-cut edges. A dull mower blade can leave blades of grass bent over and half torn—white ends. Improper cutting and tearing of vines can result from a dull power trimmer blade. Most tools

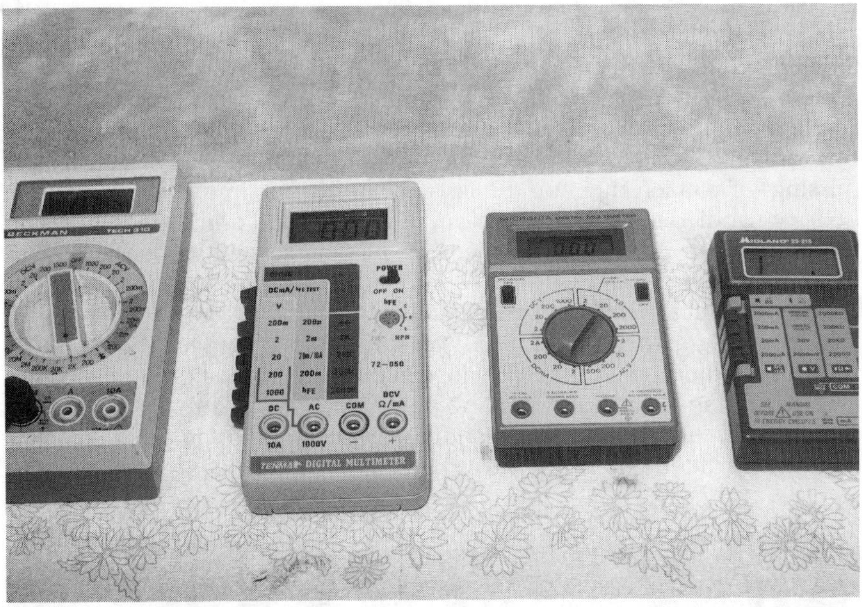

1-6 Digital multimeters (DMM) are more accurate in small resistance and voltage tests.

can be sharpened with a flat file, stones, or a grinder (FIG. 1-7). A grinder is particularly useful for larger surfaces. You might also want to have a good honing kit and whetstone.

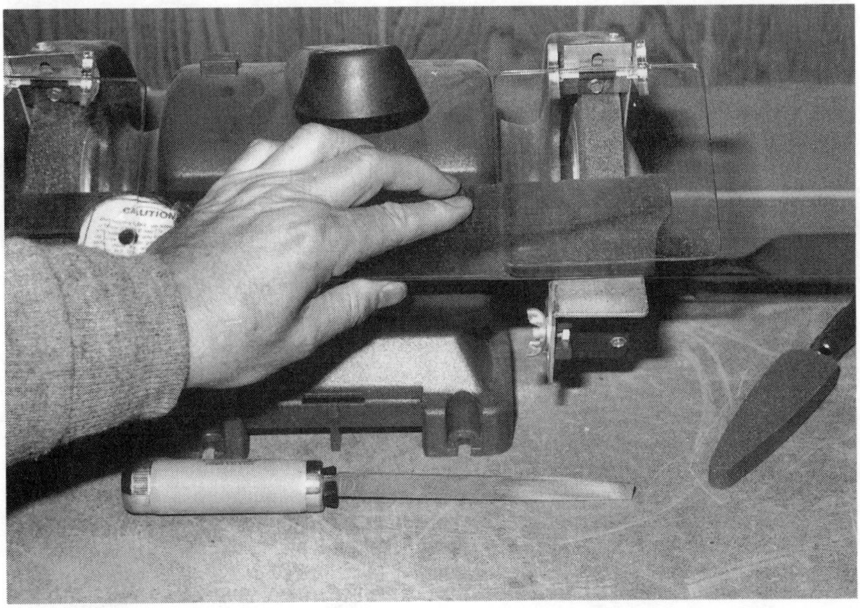

1-7 Most tools can be sharpened on a grinder, whetstone, or file.

Organizing tools

Small hand tools are often left on a workbench or covered up with other equipment. When you need them, they are no where to be found. Why not keep those small tools in a drawer, hung on pegboard, or in the toolbox? If you have a regular place to keep them, you'll know what tools are missing—if you left them on the last job, or outside in the weather. Hang up long-handled tools so they are out of the way and don't get stepped on or driven over. Protect sharp edges by placing several garden and lawn tools on shaker pegs.

To hold all the shaker pegs, cut a long piece of oak molding or board. Lay each long garden or lawn tool on the board and space them so that they don't touch (FIG. 1-8). For instance, place two shaker pegs close together for spade and shovel handles. Space two shaker pegs at least 10 inches apart for a rake. A long-handle shovel can be hung on two shaker pegs under the top lip of the shovel area.

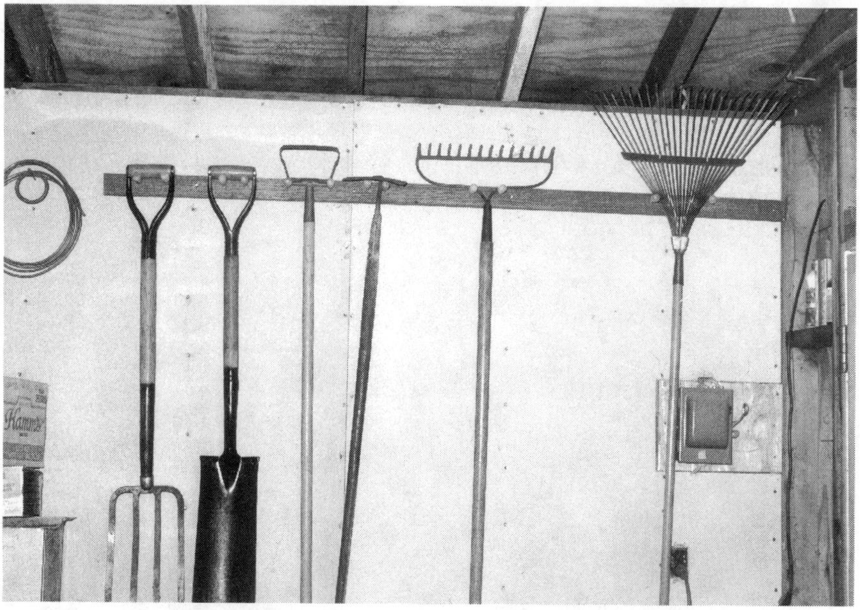

1-8 A shaker peg assembly to keep tools up off the garage or shed floor.

Use wood screws on 16-inch centers of the garage or work shed's 2×4s for long tool hangers. Countersink 2-inch wood screws into the oak support. After all holes are drilled, apply wood glue and insert each shaker in the right hole. Now, when one space is blank, go hunt up that lawn or garden tool you left outdoors.

Using VOMs or DMMs

A volt-ohmmeter (VOM) or a digital multimeter (DMM) can help locate defective parts in lawn and garden equipment. Choose a digital DMM if you need to purchase a new test instrument because it can do a wide variety of different tests. Choose one with an audible readout for making continuity measurements. In addition to providing a readout, you will be able to hear a tone if continuity is present.

A low-resistance ohmmeter scale can be used to determine continuity across AC plug terminals if coil and armature winding, cord, or AC switch is open (FIG. 1-9). Just take a continuity of the AC terminals to determine if a DC or AC motor is open. Continuity of an AC extension cord can indicate a break or intermittent connection.

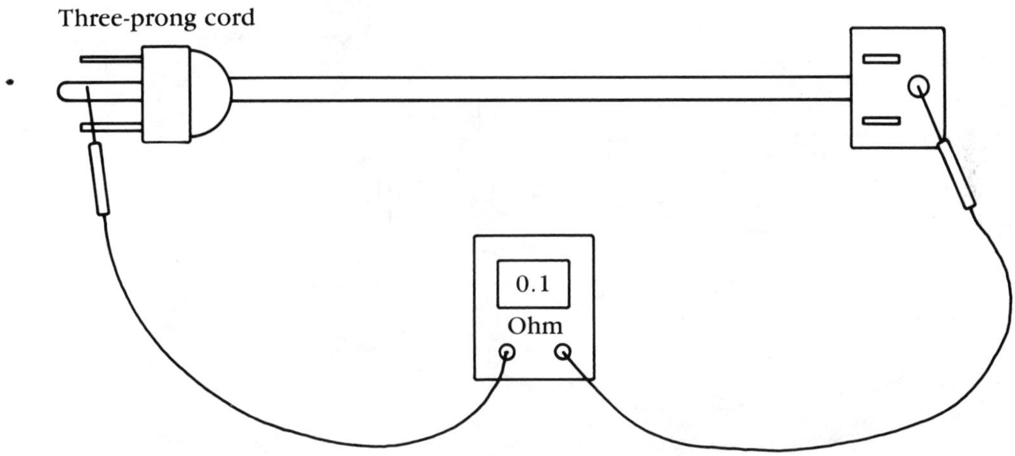

1-9 Checking the continuity resistance measurements of power cords and motor cords might find a broken or open AC cord.

A battery ignition system can be checked with the volt and ohmmeter range. Simply check the DC voltage of the battery. An ignition switch and spark coil continuity can also be checked with an ohmmeter. The ohmmeter can also be used to check breaker points when they are opened or closed. Likewise, the ohmmeter can check a magnet wiring system (FIG. 1-10). Finally, Zener and regulator diodes can be checked in a typical capacitor discharge ignition system.

Voltage measurements on cordless tools can determine if a battery is weak and needs charging or must be replaced. Likewise, an AC voltage measurement on larger AC motor terminals can determine whether motor or voltage is reaching the motor terminals. An AC voltage measurement on an electric lawn mower might indicate whether the motor is defective.

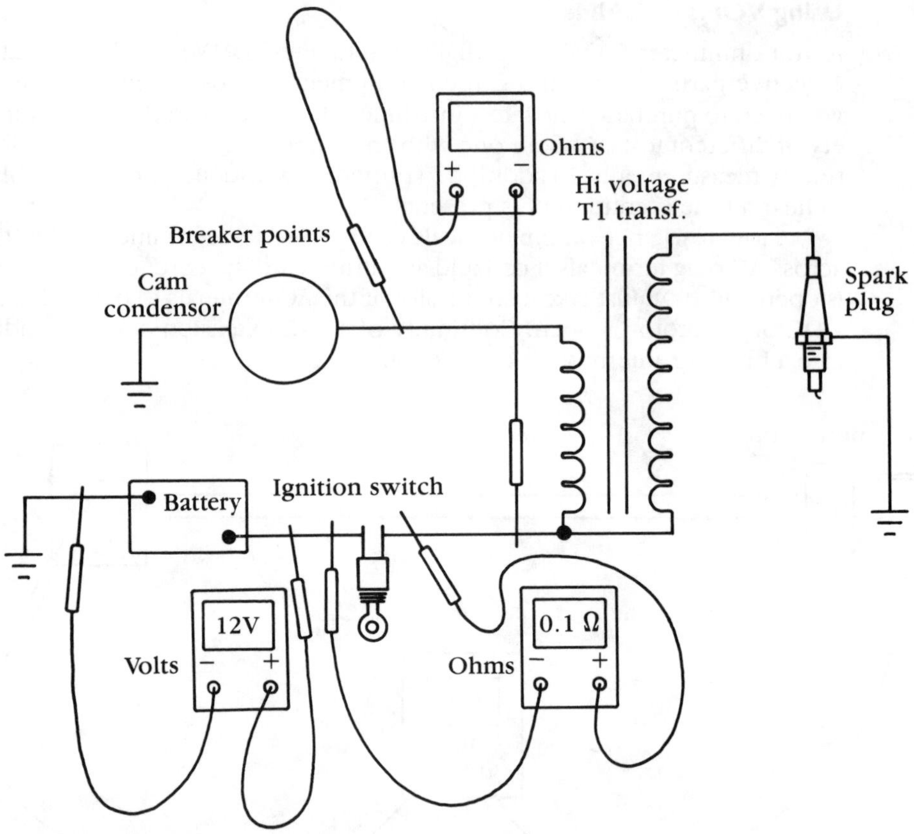

1-10 Use a DMM to check battery voltage, switch continuity, points, and high-voltage coil resistance.

Chapter 2

Cleanup and lubrication

Your power tool will operate for many years if properly maintained. Keeping lawn and garden equipment cleaned up and properly lubricated extends the life and adds years to each tool. A good wash or cleanup also prevents damage. Proper lubrication eliminates bearing, engine, and rod damage. This chapter only covers the basics of engine lubrication. For specific instructions for your unit, consult the owner's manual. Part 2 covers engine service and maintenance by engine type in more detail and, where appropriate, information on fuel and lubrication is included. You will also find specific lubrication recommendations and lubrication for some power equipment throughout the book.

CLEANUP

Nothing beats good old soap and water for cleaning up power equipment. Wash out filters with soap and water. Clean up oily surfaces with degreaser solvents. Wash out the carburetor with carburetor solvent. Clean up engine parts with kerosene or solvent and paint thinner. Wash out gummed up bearings with cleaning solvent or kerosene.

Besides scraping off mud and dirt, wash up the engine and body of large lawn and garden equipment. Clean off that old grease and dirt that has built up over the years. Because oil, grease, and grime clings to the engine and machine body, spray on some auto degreaser and then hose it off. Often, engine degreasers will not only clean the engine, but also a grimy battery, fire wall, hoses, and solid tire wheels. Make sure the equipment or engine is warm. Cover up spark plug and high tension wires. Allow to penetrate for 10 minutes. Rinse off with a high-pressure water jet.

Air filters

Inspect air filters when the fuel and oil levels are checked. Remove air cleaners and wash out dust and dirt to prevent loss of power within the engine. Wash out oil-foam filter elements in soap and water or detergent (FIG. 2-1). Dry thoroughly and dip foam element in light motor oil and squeeze out surplus before replacing.

2-1 Clean out foam air cleaners with detergent and water, apply motor oil, and squeeze out excess oil before replacing.

For dry-element cleaners, tap out dust and blow out dirt. Wash out the element with water. Dry thoroughly. Do not use oil on the dry air cleaner.

Wash out metallic air cleaners with soap and water or mild solvent. Most metallic cleaners can be used over and over again if properly washed and not damaged.

Clean polyurethane air cleaners with soap and water. Dry thoroughly. Cover the face of the polyurethane element with light oil. Always replace air cleaner before starting engine.

Ignition system

Cleaning the spark plug, high-tension wire, capacitor, coil, and breaker points might solve a defective ignition system (FIG. 2-2). Most ignition components, with the exception of the capacitor and breaker points, are easy to locate. Usually, the flywheel has to be removed to get at these parts.

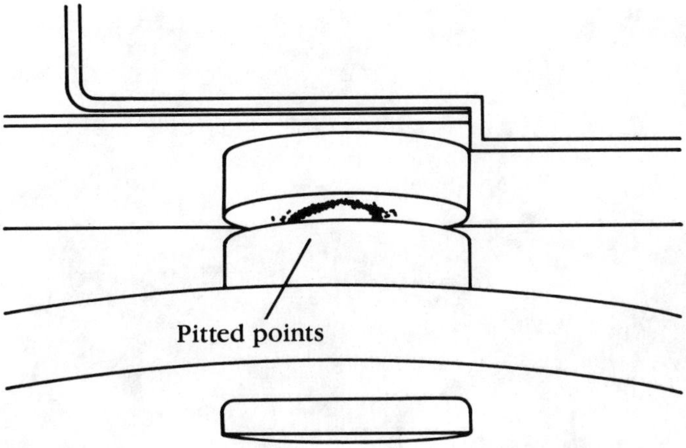

2-2 Pitted or bad breaker points can prevent an engine from starting or running properly.

Blades and belts

Before removing any blades, remember to remove the spark plug wire and wear gloves to protect from cuts. Remove all cutting blades and clean them up with solvent, kerosene, or paint thinner. Scrape off all hard residue with a putty knife. Sharpen mower blades with a file, grinder, and Carborundum file. Use a Diafold rod on curved edges. A round rotary mower sharpener can fit in a 1/4-inch drill for sharpening mower and tiller blades.

Inspect the drive belts for loose, broken, or slipping areas. Shiny belt surface indicates some slippage (FIG. 2-3). Clean off with soap and water. Check the belt for breaks and check marks. Temporarily apply wax to belt surface when all tension is applied and belt slips a little. Check take-up tension on all belt drive assemblies.

Spark plug

To clean the spark plug, remove the high-tension cable and brush off all dirt around the plug. Secure a spark plug wrench or socket to remove the plug. Clean off all carbon deposits on end electrodes and wipe off the porcelain section. Inspect for a cracked porcelain insulator. Check for pitted or burned points (FIG. 2-4). After cleanup, reset gap of the electrodes (FIG. 2-5). Replace if points are burned too badly.

Bearings

Clean bearings with a solvent then lubricate with light grease. Most electric motors have sleeve or ball bearings. Use light oil on sleeve bearings and light grease on ball bearings. Lubricate axle bearings, steering spindler, and idler sprockets with lithium-based grease or light motor grease. Apply grease fittings with required grease gun (FIGS. 2-6 and 2-7).

2-3 A shiny pulley can indicate that a belt-driven clutch or drive mechanism is slipping.

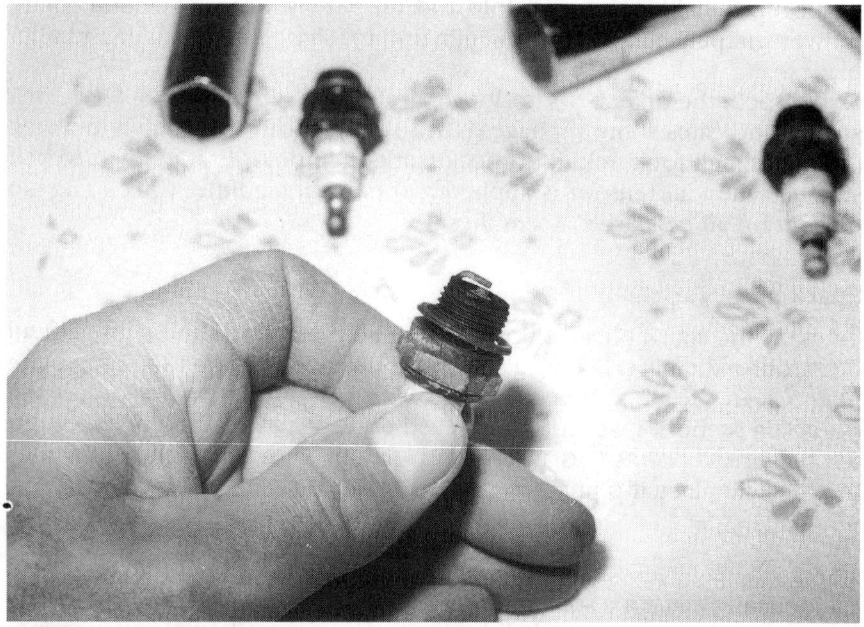

2-4 Inspect spark plugs for burned points or pitted marks.

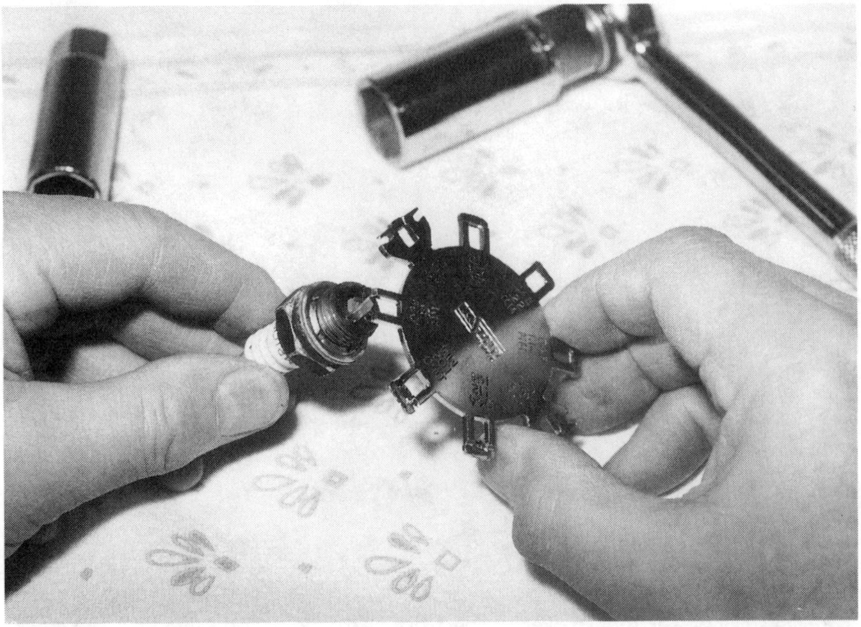

2-5 Adjust spark plugs with a feeler gauge.

2-6 Dry or frozen bearings can cause clutch or drive belts to slip and possibly smoke.

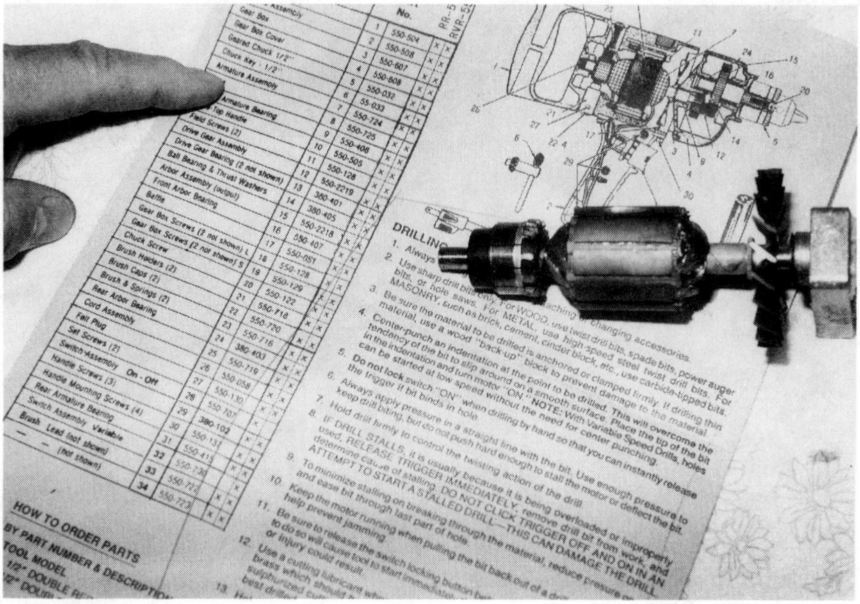

2-7 If a small power tool smokes, suspect dry or frozen bearings.

High-tension lead

Wipe off all dirt and grime from the high-tension cable. Inspect and clean up the spark plug connection if it's corroded. Check the cable for cracks or areas that might need attention. Look for evidence of the insulation chafing where the lead is running close to the various housings and shields. After cleanup, measure the resistance between plug connector and ground. Use a metal ground post on the engine head for a good ground.

Rusty areas

Clean off rusty spots and areas with sandpaper, scraper, and steel wool. On large rusty areas, use a wire brush in a 1/4-inch drill or a rotary sander. Although you might not be able to get the exact color of paint, small scratched areas can be filled in with auto enamel.

LUBRICATION

Remove and lubricate all wheel bearings and axles with light grease. Spray a lithium-based grease on sprockets, gear teeth, drive chains, and moving rods. For smooth operation, use light oil on rotating chutes, bolt bearings, knuckles, and spindles.

Fill snowblower gearboxes with the grease mandated in the owner's manual. Check all fittings with light grease from the grease gun of a tiller. Double check transmission and differential fluid levels at least once a month. Lubricate the chipper/shredder main bearings with light grease.

Engine

Before mowing or tilling, check the oil level. If the engine is hot, let it set for a few minutes before checking the oil level. Keep the oil level at the right level. Too much oil can make an engine smoke. If equipment needs oil each time it is used, make sure the oil is not leaking out. On some engines equipped with an extended oil fill tube, vibrate and work upwards, letting oil seep out and down over the engine and mower (FIG. 2-8).

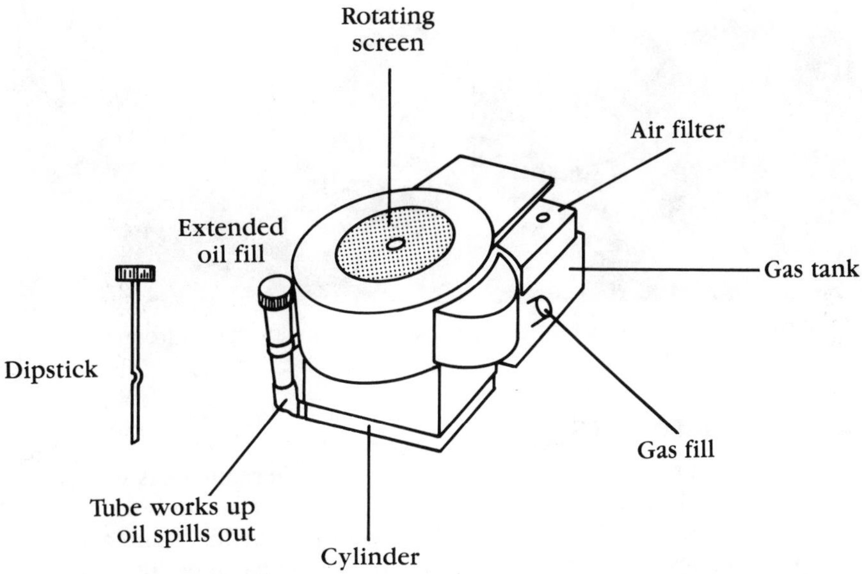

2-8 Check for a loose filling tube that might spill out oil when oil is added.

Most engines require SAE 10W 30 or 10W 30 motor oil. In hot climates, use 10W 40. In winter, use a 10W 30 or 10W 20 motor oil. Read the owners manual for correct oil requirements. Change the oil at least twice a season if you have more than an acre to mow or till. Most engine manufacturers require that oil be changed after every 25 hours of use. Use any high-detergent oil that is marked SF, SE, SD, or SC. Clean and reoil the air cleaner when the oil is changed.

Change the oil after each season. Always remove the spark plug wire before changing the oil. Check for the oil drain hole on the base of the engine or underneath the rotating blade (FIG. 2-9). Once the drain plug is found, drain the oil through the oil-filled hole or oil-external fill tube. When tipping an engine up for drainage, empty the fuel tank and keep the spark plug on the muffler side up. Clean up all excess oil with a rag and deposit old oil where it can be recycled safely.

Check the owner's manual for the correct oil mixture in two-cycle chain saw, weeder, and trimmer engines.

2-9 A small oil plug at the bottom of the motor mount to drain the oil from the motor.

FUEL REQUIREMENTS

Most engines burn regular or unleaded gas. Because regular gas will eventually be phased out, most new mowers and tillers burn unleaded gasoline. Lead-free gasoline results in fewer combustion deposits and a longer life. Most engines will operate satisfactorily on any gasoline intended for automotive use except gasohol, but a minimum of 77 octane is recommended. Do not use gasoline containing methanol.

Do not purchase more than 2 gallons of gas at one time unless, of course, you have an acre of land to mow or till. Gasoline sometimes contains deposits of varnish that can settle on valves, causing carburetor needles and fuel lines to clog up. If gasoline is more than three to six-months-old, discard it in a safe and environmentally friendly way. It is a good idea not to use fuel older than 30 days. If the extra gasoline is the right blend, you might be able to place it in the car.

Always clean around the fuel cap before removing it. Be careful not to let gas overflow. If it does, wipe it off at once. Do not fill fuel tanks to overflowing. Allow a $^1/_4$-inch tank space for fuel expansion. Do not remove foam elements from fuel tanks, if so equipped. Do not remove fuel tank caps while an engine is still running.

Chapter 3

Servicing small hand tools

Small hand tools keep the lawn, shrubs, trees, and garden in tip-top shape. Many of these hand tools can last a lifetime if they are properly cared for. All small tools should be cleaned up after each use and properly lubricated. Tools should also be hung up after each use to prevent rust and possible injury.

REPLACING HANDLES

Wooden handles often break in the middle or right where they enter the tool. Repair handles cost about a third of the price of a new tool. To make a temporary repair, place two layers of plastic tape around the split handle. Remove metal rivets by grinding them off on a portable or bench grinder. Either replace metal rivets or install bolts and nuts to hold the wooden handle in the tool.

Wooden handles can also be repaired with a good cleanup and cement. Sand down all rough spots and place a coat of wood glue between broken areas. Spray on a coat of paint or clear varnish to brighten.

Handles that turn within a hand trowel or cultivator can be repaired with epoxy. Mix up a batch of epoxy and fill up the holes around the metal handle. Let set up for a whole day. Grind off any surplus epoxy. Also, rubber silicon cement can be worked down inside the handle area to keep the handle from turning.

Handles that will not stay on lopping shears can be repaired in the same manner. When the wooden or metal handle keeps dropping off the metal shear end, place epoxy on the long handle piece before inserting it into the handle. Fill up the handle area with epoxy. Work the epoxy down into the hole by pulling out the metal rod half way and scraping epoxy down into the hole. Sometimes, filling the hole half full of epoxy and then inserting the metal rod works best. Wipe off all excess. Let large epoxy areas set up for at least 24 hours.

SHARPENING TOOLS

Keep blades sharp and rust-free with a coat of wax or light oil. Often, spades, shovels, and hoes might have a V-type blade. In this case, both sides of the blade must be sharpened. Some hand tools are sharpened with a tapered point, including the hoe. Sharpen the hole edge on the inside of the blade. The tapered-pointed blade can be touched up with a file or grinder. If a blade is worn or has nicks, they can be removed on a grinder. A round Carborundum stone placed in the small hand drill can be used to touch up edges, although, at times, uneven cuts might result.

Spades, shovels, and scoop shovels should have a sharp edge for removing dirt, snow, and ice. Keep hand hoes sharp for weeding, cultivating, and grubbing with a large file. Fine, sharp edges should be placed on knives and axes. Grind down dull edges on an axe or hatchet and finish up on a whetstone for a fine cutting edge (FIG. 3-1). An electric augur and regular wood bits can be sharpened with a three-corner file. Place large bits in a vise with a cloth wrapped around it and file down the lip and bottom cutting edges. File even cuts on the bottom cutting edge (FIG. 3-2).

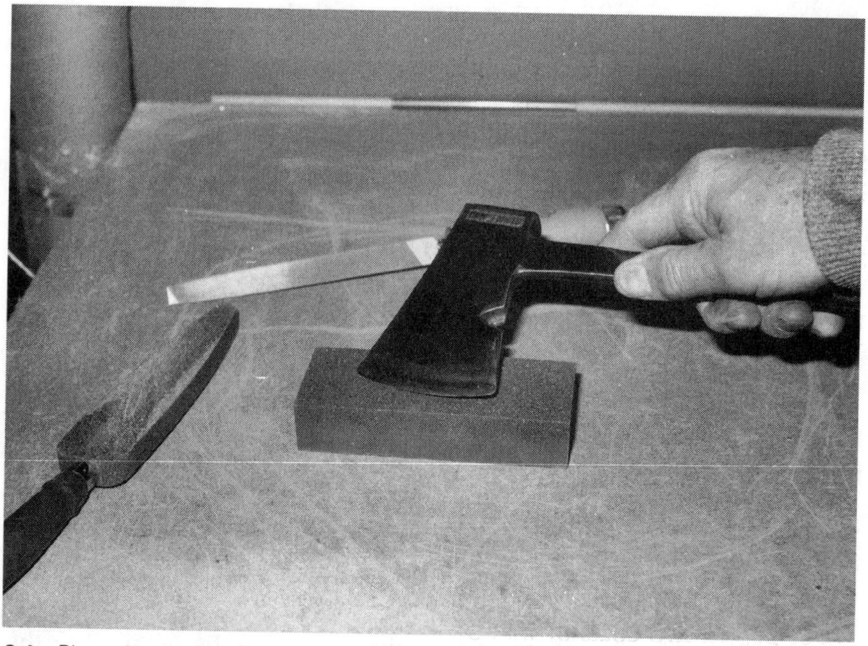

3-1 Place sharp edges on axes or hatchets with a whetstone and some cutting oil.

3-2 Clamp the wood bit into a vise with a rag wrapped around it. Sharpen both cutting edges with a three-corner or small, flat file.

REPAIRING RUSTY TOOLS

Excessive rust builds up on large metal surfaces when they are not properly taken care of. Placing a spade or hoe in a corner until the next use without any cleanup or leaving an axe on a damp garage floor will cause rust to accumulate.

Excessive rust can be removed from any tool with a little time and muscle. Start by scraping or brushing off all excess rust with a scraper or steel brush. Steel wool also works, but is much slower. If you have a lot of rust to remove, place a round rotary-wire brush in a hand drill (FIG. 3-3). Steel wool dipped in turpentine or paint thinner eliminates small rust spots.

Wipe metal areas with light oil. Sometimes, a coat of Naval Jelly on both sides of a metal shovel or spade can remove all signs of rust. Let it set on the blade for a half hour before wiping and washing off. Thoroughly wash off with a scrub brush or sponge several times. Wear plastic glasses as this is a toxic cleaner.

Although the blade will turn blue, the surface is clean of rust. Wipe up the metal surface with an old towel or paper towel. Spray on a coat of oil or put on two coats of wax over the cleaned metal area. Now, all you have to do is to clean up the blade each time you use it and lubricate it

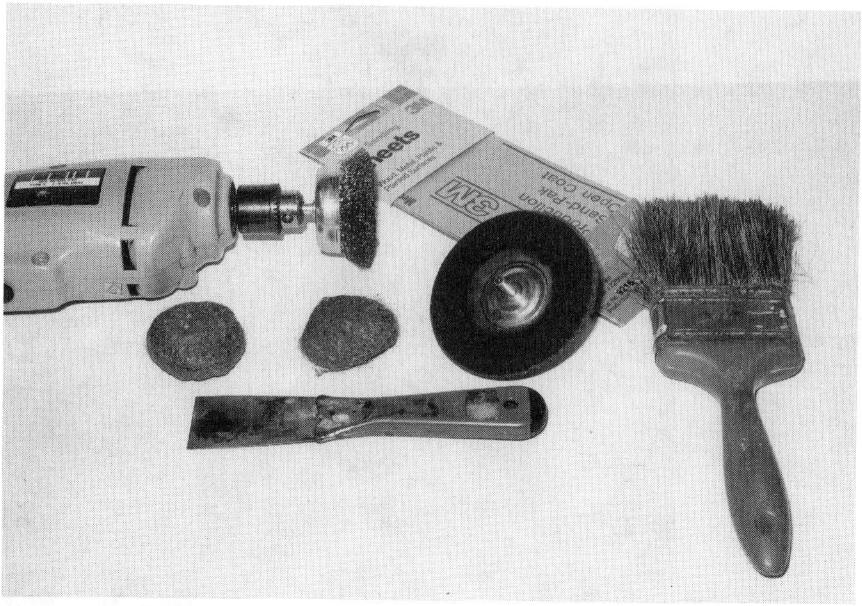

3-3 A round circular wire brush in a drill can remove large areas of rust.

with an oily rag or sock. Figures 3-4 and 3-5 show some of the many types of files available.

To make that tool look like new once again, repaint areas that were painted before with a couple coats of rustproof spray enamel. Spray with a final coat of silicon oil or a coat of wax to make them shine.

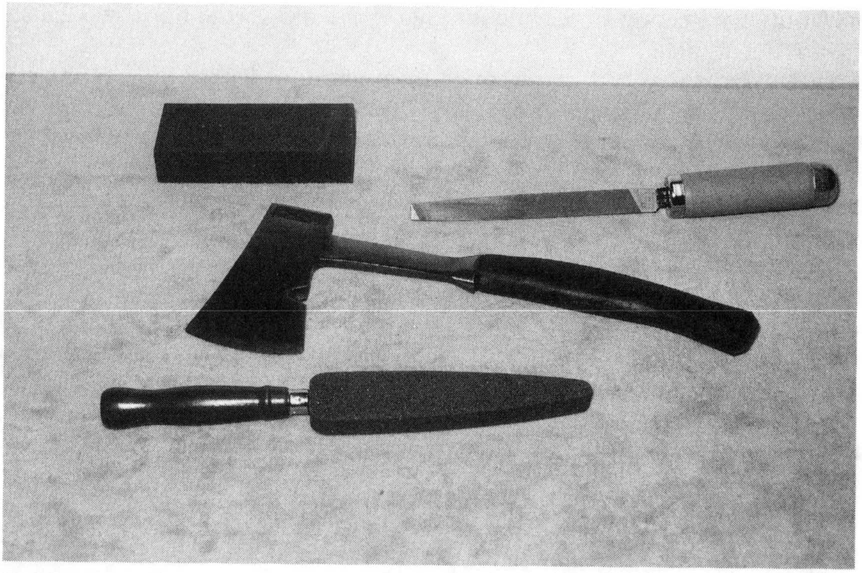

3-4 Many types of files can be used to sharpen lawn and garden tools.

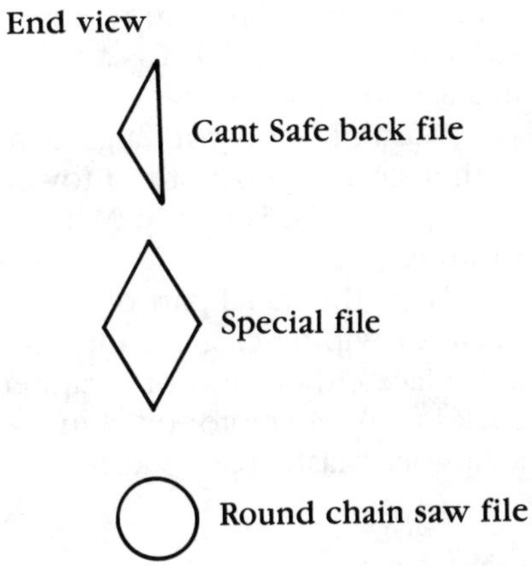

3-5 The Cant Safe back file, special file, chain saw file, and mill bastard files have different-type surfaces.

Hand tools

Spades, shovels, and scoop shovels should have a sharp edge for removing dirt, snow, and ice. Keep hand hoes sharp for weeding, cultivating, and grubbing with a large file. Fine, sharp edges should be placed on knives, axes, and other blades with oilstones, silicon carbide, Carborundum, and diamond-sharpening whetstones.

Clean up tools after use and wipe off with an oil sock. Keep blades sharp and rust-free with a coat of wax or light oil. Grind down dull edges on an axe or hatchet and finish up on a whetstone for a fine cutting edge. An electric augur and regular wood bits can be sharpened with a three-corner file. Place the large bit in a vise with a cloth wrapped around it and file down the lip and bottom cutting edges. File even cuts on the bottom cutting edge.

A honing kit with Arkansas hard and soft stones and honing oil can be purchased. The Carborundum file is ideal for sharpening spades, hoes, and axes. The ceramic sharpening stick, coated with a non-rust aluminum shaft, is recommended for all type edges, straight or serrated knives, shears, and other hands tools. With a little care, these stones will last a lifetime. The flat steel Mil Bastard file is also used in hoes, spades, and saws.

Choose a Cant Safe back file for sharpening crosscut saws, circular saws, and saws with a 60-degree angle. An 8-inch round with a tapered body file is ideal for sharpening chain saws. Choose an ABF file to sharpen bits.

MAINTENANCE

This section contains an alphabetical listing of small hand tools that should receive some type of regular maintenance. Remember to wear gloves when handling sharp blades and safety glasses when sanding or grinding. Clean off all dirt and dust with an old brush. For stubborn dirt, use a wire brush, hardwood paddle, Brillo pad, putty knife, or steel wool.

A hardwood paddle can remove most dirt without scratching the tool's surface. Small hand tools can also be cleaned by repeatedly sticking them in a sandbox.

Wash off tools with a garden hose or wet rag. Wipe off excess water with a small sponge or old towel. Lay it in the sun for a few hours if no wiping material is handy. Make sure the tool is dry to prevent rust from forming.

Wipe the metal part of tools with an oily cloth or rag. An oil sock is ideal for wiping clean spades, saws, and metal shears. Take an old sock and place either sand or wrapped cloth inside. Tie a knot and soak the sock in 10W 30 motor oil. Squeeze out the excess oil. Keep the oil sock in a zip-lock plastic bag to keep the sock from collecting dust.

Axes

Hand axes can be single bit or double bit. A double-bit axe might have a $2^1/_2$ to $3^1/_2$-pound head with a 28 to 36-inch-long handle. A single-bit axe might have a forged head with a 36-inch handle (FIG. 3-6). Sharpen the axe blade with a grinder or a large file, then just touch it up with a whetstone for a razor-sharp edge.

3-6 Keep single or double-edged axes sharp with a grinder, file, or whetstone.

Branch loppers (tree saws)

Most lopping shears have long handles and a curved blade with extending metal or wood poles to remove tree limbs that can't be reached from the ground. Some loppers have a serrated cutting edge (FIG. 3-7).

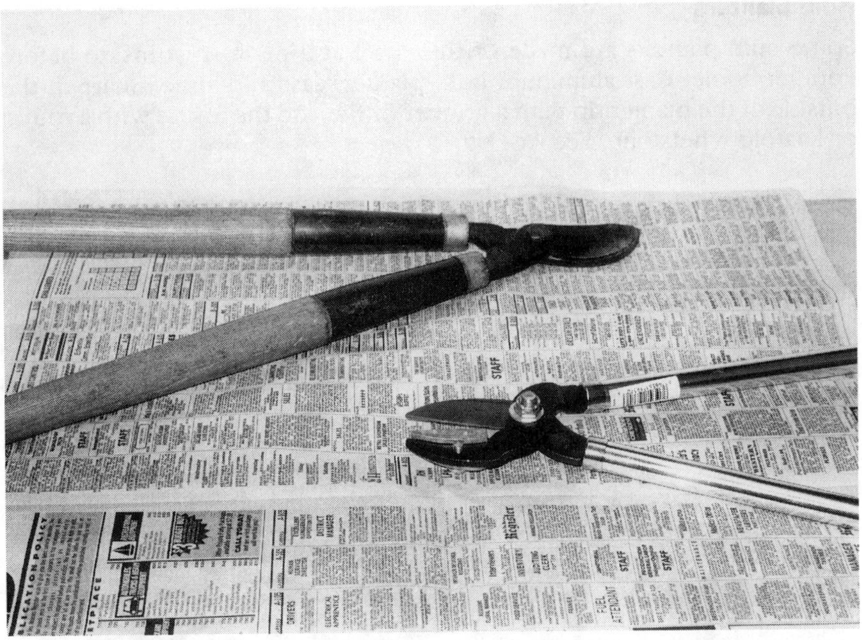

3-7 This branch lopper has long blades on wooden handles.

Keep blades sharp with a whetstone for quick clean cuts. Some lopping shears have removable handles. Loose or broken handles can be repaired with epoxy (FIG 3-8). Sand wooden handles and spray on clear varnish or a lacquer finish at least every five years.

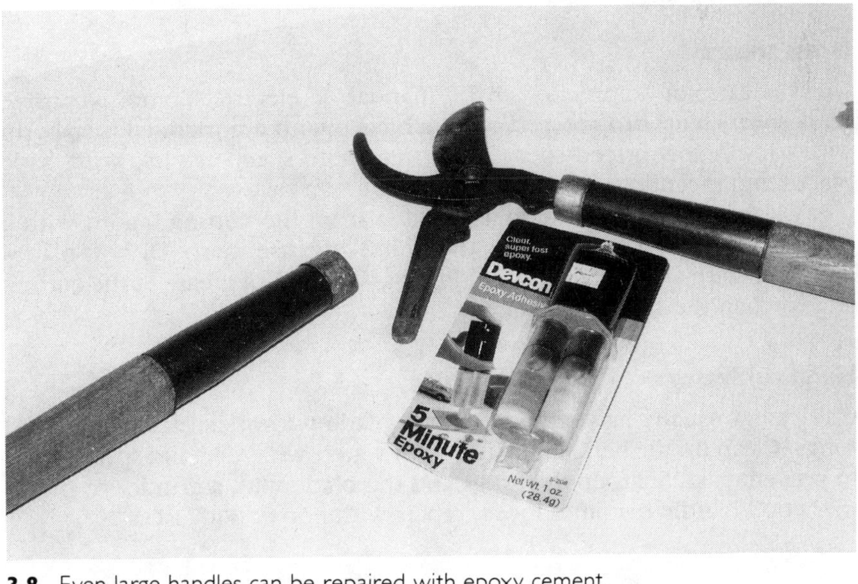

3-8 Even large handles can be repaired with epoxy cement.

Bulb planters

Some bulb planters are made of thin steel and might rust inside before you get home. Cast aluminum bulb planters last a lifetime. Sharpen the outside of the planter tip with a grinder or file and the inside with a round or Diafold whetstone. See FIG. 3-9.

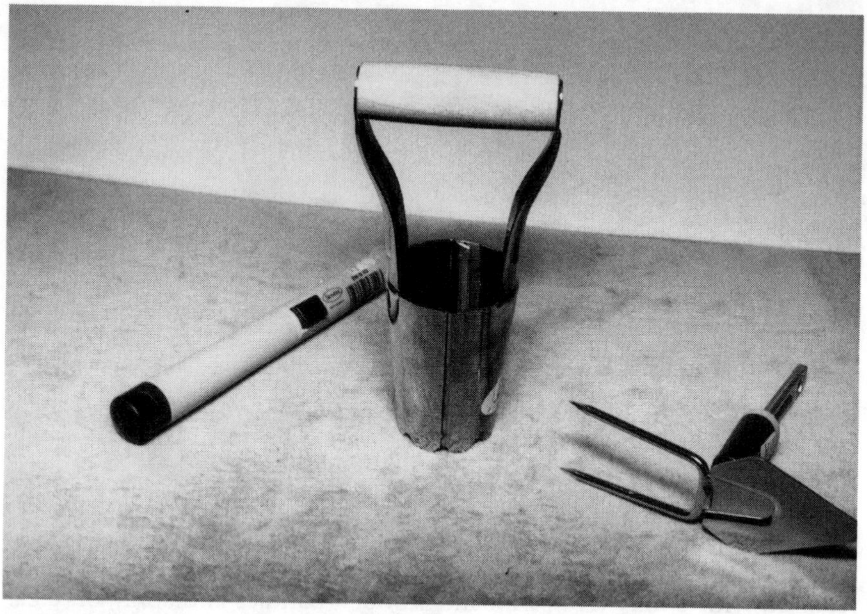

3-9 Inexpensive bulb planters can be made of light sheet metal or with a cast-type body.

Grass shears

Grass shears, or trimmers, can be manual or electric. Some expensive grass shears have drop-forged cutting blades with a horizontal metal grip (FIG. 3-10). A low-priced shear might resemble sheep shears, with wide blades and metal logs at the rear.

Clean off all weed and grass residue from the cutting blades with a cleaning solvent or soapy water. Careful! Blades are sharp. Dry off blades and wipe with an oily rag or sock. Place a thin coat of grease in the cutting edges when the season is over.

Hand cultivators

Cultivators usually have a wide, 5-inch blade with metal tapered-curved tongs. Clean up the hand cultivator with water; wipe dry, and spray on oil to prevent rust. Sharpen the tongs and the blade with a grinder or file. If the wood handle becomes loose, repair with epoxy (FIG. 3-11).

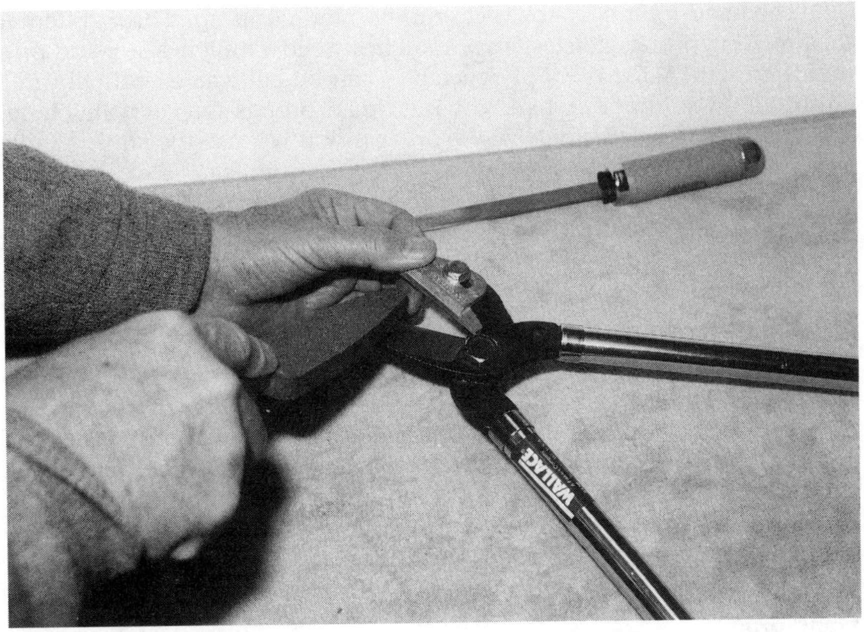

3-10 Grass shears can be electric or hand-operated.

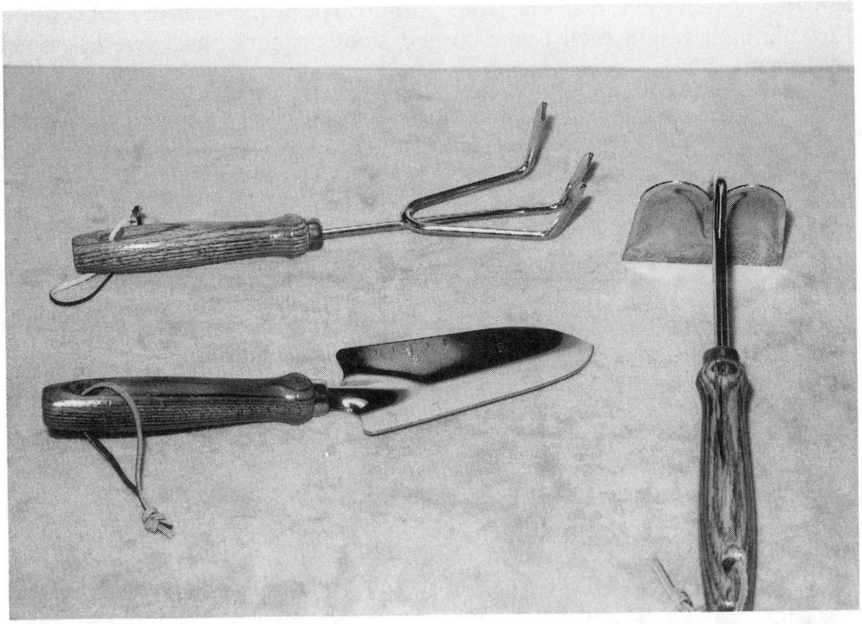

3-11 Hand cultivators get down in and around plants where large machines can't reach.

The hand roll cultivator is easy to use and clean up. Three different dual rotating prongs aerates lawn, mulches weeds, mulches soil and promotes growth. Wide rows of vegetables can be cultivated with all three cultivators. Use the long handle with 2-dual prongs for easy mulching, and cultivation over a single row. For narrow rows, use the short handle and a single prong.

The rotating prongs are cast of rustproof material. Cleanup is quick and easy—just rinse under the faucet, dirt and debris washes away. Wipe off handle and holder with rag or old towel.

Hand lawn mowers

Although the power mower has replaced the hand mower in popularity, hand mowers are still used on small lawns. Experts suggest sharpening the blades four to eight times a year. Dull mower blades tear grass instead of cutting it, causing a yellowish, disease-prone lawn. Take the blades to a professional or use a sharpener that allows you to do a professional job. Lubricate end wheels and rollers with light motor oil, and lightly grease blades before storing the mower for the season.

Hand pruners

Hand pruners are used to eliminate vines and branches from grape vines, trees, and rose bushes (FIG. 3-12). The heavy-duty pruner might have hollow, ground-hardened steel blades and a carbon-fiber handle for a comfortable lightweight feel. Some forged steel pruners have Swedish steel replaceable blades.

3-12 Hand pruners easily trim up vines, branches, and bush twigs.

Some of the blades can be removed for sharpening. Take the nicks out with a grinder and file. Finish up with a whetstone for a razor-sharp edge. Use a Diafold rod for sharpening curved-edge pruners. Place in a pouch or hang up until used.

Hand forks

Wash off hand fork tines and body with a hose and scrape off flat tines with a hard wooden paddle. Dry off the fork with an old towel and spray a light oil on the tines to prevent rusting. The ends of the tines can be sharpened with a flat file.

Hatchets

Hatchets are small, single-bit axes with a short handle. The hatchet is used in tight places or as a substitute for a large axe (FIG. 3-13). Sharpen the bit with a grinder, file, and then touch up on a whetstone.

3-13 Small hatchets and small, single-bladed axes can easily be carried or handled in a self-contained pouch.

Hedge shears

Long-handled hedge shears with metal or wooden handles can reach most hedges for trimming (FIG. 3-14). Remove large nicks on blades with a grinder or file. Sharpen edges with a whetstone. Use the Diafold whetstone on serrated steel blades. Repair wooden handles with epoxy. Hang up hedge shears after using.

3-14 Wipe off the metal of long-handled shears after use with an oil rag.

Hoes

Scrape off all dirt and residue from the blade and handle with a scraper or wooden paddle. Wash off blade and handle. Dry thoroughly. Keep the back edge sharp with a grinder or large file. If the handle brakes or cracks, replace it with a universal hoe handle at half the cost of a new hoe. Rivet or bolt the handle into position.

Lawn spreaders

Many small lawn spreaders have a self-cleaning, rustproof hopper. Larger spreaders might be pulled by a tractor. Keep spreaders up off the concrete or dirt floor to prevent rust at the bottom leg supports. Clean out hopper each time so it will not cake or harden up. Grease or oil wheels once every two years.

Lawn weeders

Lawn weeders or trimmers might be the same as those tools used to cut weeds in and along side the garden (FIG. 3-15). The dandelion digger is a sharp metal blade notched on a long rod with a wooden or metal handle. The asparagus knife is used to remove weeds or cut asparagus at ground level. The notched weeder might have come with an interchangeable handle. Wipe off cutter and rod with an oily cloth. Hang up off the garage or shed floor. If the wooden handle doesn't have a hole, drill a 1/4-inch hole and place on a metal nail or peg.

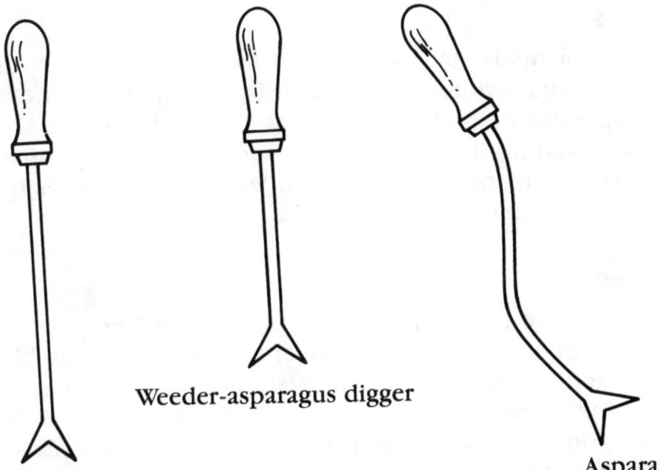

3-15 Lawn weeders consist of a long metal rod and handle with a sharp forked end.

Planting tools

Planting tools might consist of a planting dibble, soil knife, planting bar, and seeding bar (FIG. 3-16). Keep blade ends sharp with a grinder or file. Clean off with water and base after scraping down surplus dirt. Protect metal blades by wiping with an oily rag or sock.

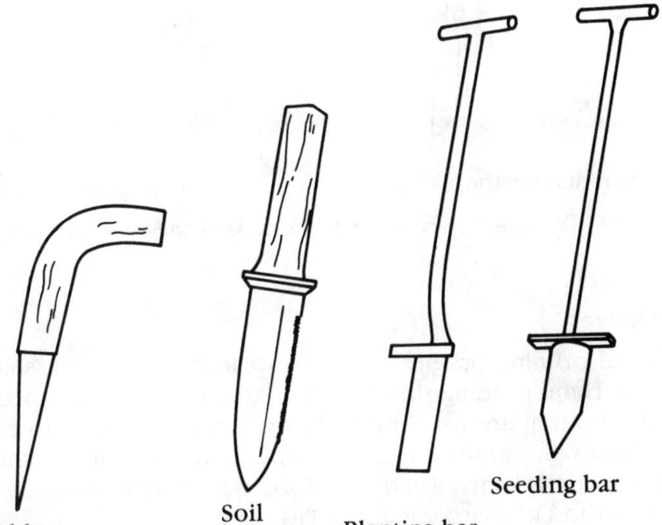

3-16 Different planting tools.

Pocketknives

Pocketknives, or utility knives, are used to graft or place buds on tree limbs. A double-bladed knife might consist of a budding and a grafting knife. The special rose budding knife has a 1/2-inch-serrated thumb support with a curved blade and top-back lifter. Grind down a broken tip or nick in the blade first on an electric grinder. Place a razor sharp-edge on blades with a whetstone.

Posthole diggers

Posthole diggers are the poor man's electric augur. The posthole digger might come with one metal bar and steel blades, steel screw blades, and two wood handles with metal blades (FIG. 3-17). To prevent rust, keep clean and wipe off with an oily rag. Sharpen the edge of blades with a large file or grinder. To keep the handle from getting misplaced, drill a hole in one end of the handle so it can be tied to the metal rod.

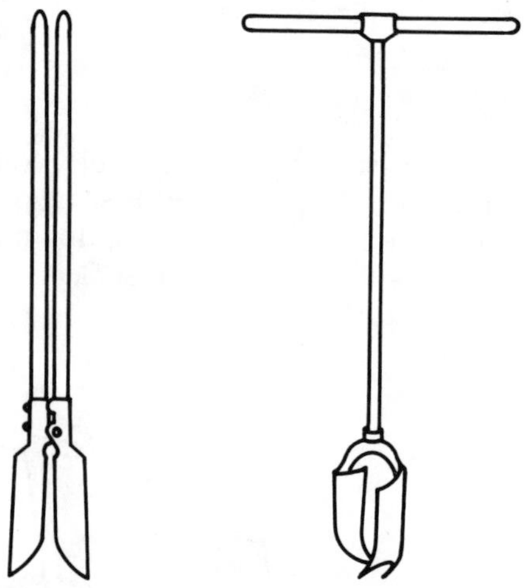

Wooden posthole digger — Metal bar posthole digger

3-17 Posthole diggers can be two wooden handles or one metal rod.

Pruner knives

Professional pruning or shearing knives can be kept razor-sharp with a whetstone. Hand pruning shears with a large blade at the top and a small one at the bottom are usually hand-forged metal alloy with razor-sharp blades. Use a whetstone or a DMT sharpener to keep blades sharp. A diamond-embedded electroplated nickel sharpener is the fastest, easiest, and cleanest method of sharpening. See FIG. 3-18.

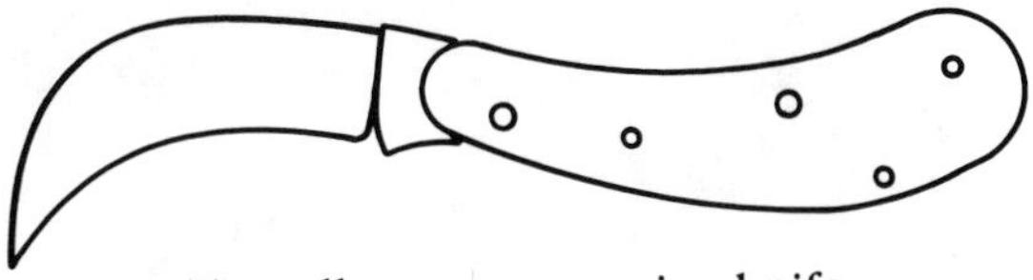

Tina all purpose pruning knife

3-18 There are many different types of pruning knives for grafting fruit trees and bushes.

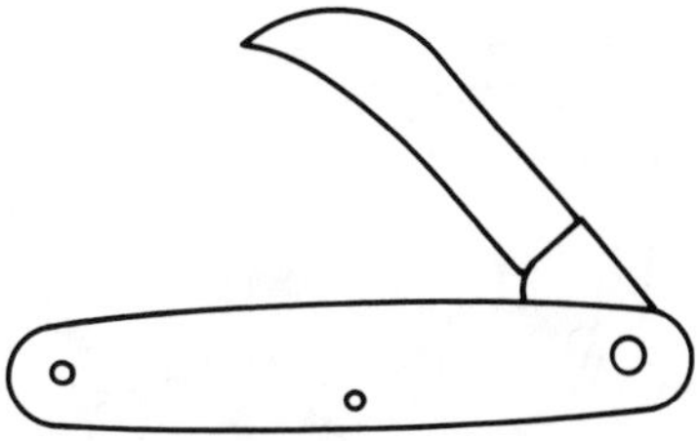

Victorinax pruning knife

Rakes

Ordinary garden rakes consist of metal teeth and a wooden handle. Aluminum grading rakes have a replaceable aluminum teeth assembly. Metal rakes consists of curved metal teeth with a wooden handle. If the metal teeth get out of line, place in a vise and bend in place. Sometimes, only one bent tooth can be bent back in shape with a large pair of pliers. Keep teeth clean by washing off with water. Dry thoroughly. Spray on several coats of oil to prevent rust. Hang up out of the way after cleaning up.

Scythes

Grandpa used the scythe to cut weeds around buildings, fences, and yard (FIG. 3-19). American scythe blades have a hand-hammered cutting edge with a polished point and edge. Sharpen the blade with a file, whetstone, or a special scythe stone that has an oval pattern. Oil the blade to prevent rusting.

Shovels

Keep shovel blades sharp with a grinder or large file. Always sharpen on the inside of the blade or topside of the shovel. Clean all debris with a scraping tool or hardwood paddle. Spray on oil to prevent rust or wipe blade off with an oily rag or oil sock. Place a layer of grease on a new ground edge to prevent rusting over the winter months.

Snow shovels can be made from aluminum, steel, poly, or plastic. Aluminum shovels require very little maintenance and will not rust. Regular steel shovels require a good cleaning up and should be wiped off with an oily rag to prevent rust.

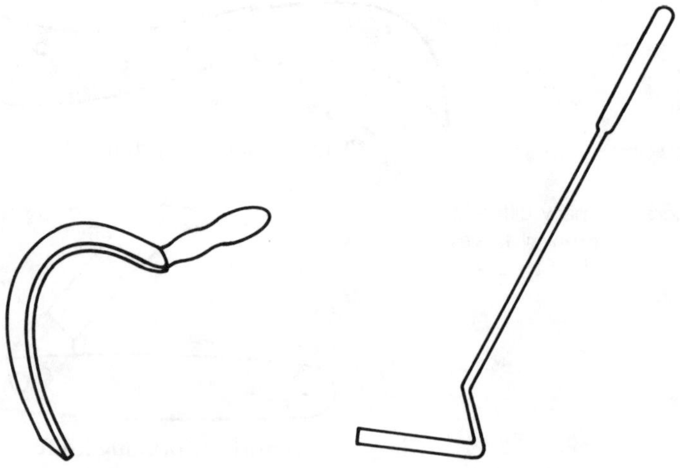

3-19 Clean off grass and dirt on cutters with soap and water before storing.

After several years use on cement walks and driveways, the ends of the scoop often turn up, tear, or become damaged. Round off both ends with a grinder. File down the front, top edge for easy loading. Spray paint metal shovels to prevent rusting. Hang up on a peg or nail to prevent injury or damage.

Sod planters

Sod planters restore lawn vitality by sod coring, sod planting, and lawn aerating, removing spikes of soil to allow air and water penetration. Sod planters are often used as an aerator in spring and fall in small lawns, highly troubled areas, hard to grow spots, and around tree roots. Clean off the metal cutter after each job. Sharpen round cutting edges with a round file. Wipe all metal with an oily rag.

Spades

The garden spade is used to dig deep trenches and plant trees and shrubs. Most spades and shovels will rust if not taken care of. Remove debris with wood scraper, wash off, and dry with a towel (FIG. 3-20). When blade corners curl up or become damaged, round off with a grinder. Hang up the spade when not in use. Replace broken handle with a spare repair handle at 1/3 the cost of a new spade. (See also *Shovels*.)

Tree trimmers

Tree trimmers can be attached to several lengths of wood, metal, or fiberglass poles with a bracket and rope-operated cutting blade to reach unaccessible tree limbs. Sharpen cutting blade with Diafold rod or whet-

3-20 Clean up rusty garden spades with a metal brush, sandpaper, steel wool, or an electric metal brush in an electric hand drill.

stone. Wipe off metal cutting head after use. Store poles where they will not get bent or accidentally broken. (See also *Branch loppers*.)

Trowels

Nursery or florist trowels usually have wooden handles and a one-piece blade and shank. Pick up all trowel and tools when finished in the garden. If left outdoors, the wooden handles will eventually crack and break off (FIG. 3-21). Wash off and dry thoroughly. Wipe metal parts with an oily rag or old sock. If rust forms, remove with sandpaper or an electric metal brush.

3-21 If the handle turns inside the trowel, repair with epoxy.

Weeders

The weed cutter for the garden looks and works like a small narrow hoe with a flat blade. The cutter is narrow enough to go down the center of a 14-inch garden row to cut out weeds and turn up surface soil. Keep the narrow blade sharp at both sides with a bastard file (FIG. 3-22). Use a ceramic sharpening stick on serrated edges or blades. Clean off all dirt and wipe metal with an oily rag or sock.

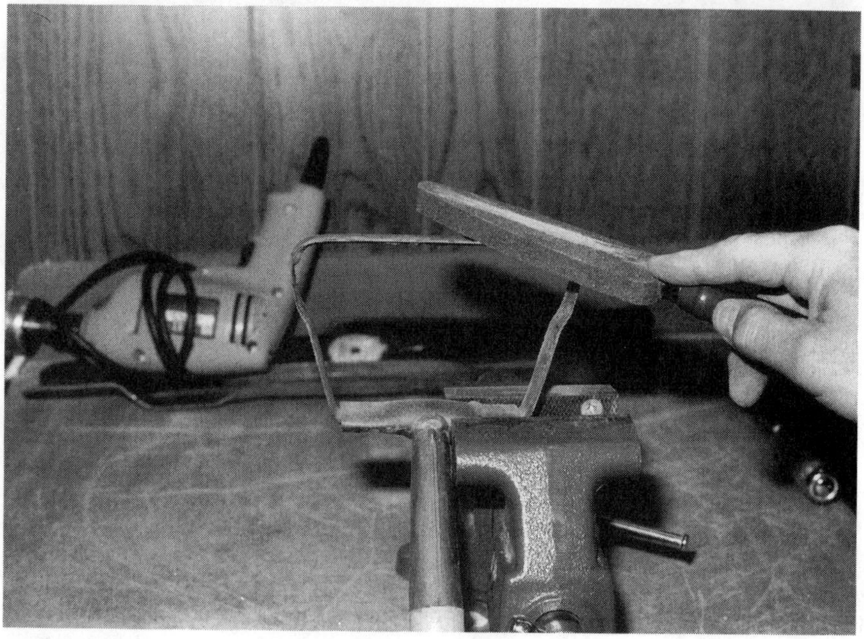

3-22 Garden weeders look and work like the garden hoe.

Wheelbarrows

The wheelbarrow is a must when hauling or moving soil or debris to another location. After several years usage, cracks or broken metal pins might leave holes around bolts and rivets at the bottom of the metal body. To patch rusty holes or torn spots, use a fiberglass or a muffler mending kit. Auto body fender repair kits can also be used.

Clean up the entire metal body with an electric metal brush and sandpaper. Clean off all stuck-on residue and rust. A large metal brush can help with this task. Wash out with solvent cleaner to remove grease or oil. Sand or brush to the clean metal around the area to be patched.

Place the fiberglass or muffler mend piece over the small area to be patched. Smooth out the cement over the entire patch (FIG. 3-23). Do not leave any of the fiberglass or plastic cloth in view. Let it set up for a whole day, then sand down with an auto or power sander. Brush and blow out all dust from the metal surface.

3-23 Patch metal cracks and holes in the bottom of wheelbarrows with fiberglass patches or a muffler mend kit.

Clean up and sand down the wooden handles. Remove the front wheel and lubricate. Remove any vinyl grips from the metal handles, then spray paint the underside of the wheelbarrow first. If the handles are wooden, mask with heavy-duty tape. Apply two coats of rustproof enamel on the topside of the wheelbarrow.

Whetstones

A honing kit might consist of a hard and soft oilstone plus honing oil and a storage box. The most popular pocket stone found around the home and workshop is Carborundum stones (FIG. 3-24). The silicon carbide bench stone might have one course side and one fine side. The Carborundum file is a diamond-shaped stone with a handle that can sharpen spades, hoes, and axes. Keep the whetstone up out of the way so it is not accidentally dropped on the cement floor.

DMT (Diamond Machine Technology) sharpeners use high-quality industrial diamonds embedded in the electroplated nickel to provide fast, easy and clean sharpening. These sharpeners can be used dry or lubricated with water. The Diafold whetstone is ideal for sharpening knives and hand or garden tools. The Diafold rod hones straight or curved edges, knives, and tools of any hard material.

Keep stones clean. If the stone is glazed, apply water or oil. Clean off with ammonia or kerosene if surface becomes gummy. To restore flat surface, rub with sandpaper on a smooth surface. Use entire surface of stone to reduce uneven wear.

3-24 Whetstones can be made of Carborundum, silicon carbide, oilstone, or diamond-embedded in electroplated nickel.

Yard carts

Yard carts are handy for hauling garden or lawn tools, brush, trash, or garden produce (FIG. 3-25). Check body and wheels for damage after hauling large loads. Repaint sides after five years of use. Check and grease the wheel bearings every two years. Store out of the way from cars and tractors.

3-25 Inspect the wheels and apply grease on bearings every two years.

Chapter 4

Servicing small power lawn and garden equipment

Small lawn and garden equipment would include small compost tumblers, leaf blowers, chain saws, and gasoline and electric weeders. Hand or power garden equipment can be dangerous if not operated properly. Always shut off the power equipment before removing clogged or jammed objects. Do not attempt any repairs until the unit is shut off. Avoid sharp tongs and blades by wearing a pair of gloves for safety. Always remove the spark plug or spark plug wire (if so equipped) from power equipment before attempting any service work. Read chapter 1 on safety before beginning any service work.

PERIODIC INSPECTION

All power tools and garden/lawn equipment should have an annual check up and regular maintenance. The engine oil in a new mower, shredder, or tiller should be changed after the first five hours of operation. After that, change the oil every 25 hours of operation. The engine air filter should be checked every 25 hours. The spark plug should be inspected once a year along with regular annual maintenance. Periodically tighten mounting bolts on both engine and equipment, tiller blades, shredder, and mower blades.

Check small portable power tools for excessive firing at the brushes. If brushes are worn down, drip oil down on the armature. Check the commutator for excessive dust. Inspect the AC cord for broken or bent prongs. Make sure that the grounding prong is still intact.

Periodic cleanup helps keep power tools running longer. Brush out all dirt and dust from the motor housing of power tools then suck it up with a shop vacuum. Wash the plastic housing of power tools with soap and water. Scrape off all old chipped paint. Scrub and clean off all rust areas. A touch up with spray paint prevents rust and can make a power tool look like new again.

Just about any lawn, garden, or power tool will rust if left in a damp basement, garage, or outdoors. The way to protect valuable equipment is by keeping them clean, lubricated and maintained.

CHAIN SAWS

This section covers two types of chain saws—The Homelite EL Model Series chain saw and the McCulloch 300 Series chain saw, which includes the MACCAT and Eager Beaver 2.1 two-cycle gasoline powered units.

The Homelite EL chain saw

The Homelite EL model series chain saw operate directly from a 120-volt AC power line. Chain saw models EL12 and EL14 are electric chain saws with a short AC cord (FIG. 4-1). Both units have safety kick back saw chains. If there is a drop in voltage at the saw, loss of power, or overheating, suspect an undersized cord. Examine the electric cord regularly and replace the cord immediately if damaged.

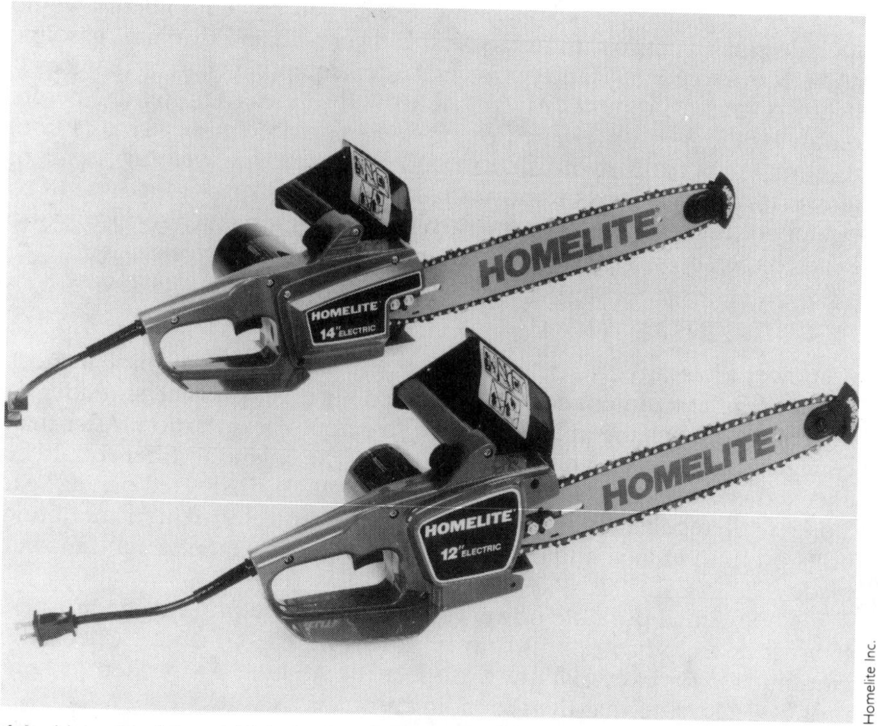

Homelite Inc.

4-1 Homelite 14- and 12-inch electric saws.

Brush dirt and oil from the housing. Wipe with a damp cloth using warm water and a mild detergent. Do not use products that contain ammonias, chlorine, or abrasives. Do not use chlorinated cleaning solvents, carbon tetrachloride, kerosene, or gasoline. Do not submerge the saw in any liquids.

Tension adjustment Failure to maintain proper chain saw tension will cause rapid saw chain, guide bar, and sprocket wear. Before adjusting chain saw tension, make sure the guide bar nuts are only finger tight. Turn the adjusting screw clockwise until all slack is out of the saw chain. Wear protective gloves and pull saw chain around the guide bar, it should move freely. If necessary, readjust the chain using adjusting screw (A). There should be no gap between the side links of the saw chain and the bottom of the guide bar. Tighten guide bar nuts securely using a wrench.

Guide bar Most guide bar problems are caused by uneven bar wear. Incorrect filing of cutter and depth gauge settings are the primary cause of uneven bar wear. When bars wear unevenly, the bar slot widens and causes chain chatter and sweat popping and makes it difficult to cut straight.

Periodically remove all sawdust from the guide bar with a putty knife or a wire. Clean oil holes after each use. Remove burrs and restore square edges to an uneven rail top by filing with a flat file. Replace the guide bar if it is bent or cracked.

Sharpening saw chain Shut down the saw for filing whenever sawdust turns chips to a fine powder and you have to bear down hard to make the saw cut. If you plan to do your own chain filing, be sure to use the correct file guide. Press the guide so it rides on both the cutter top plate and depth gauge with guide marks in line with the length of chain. File one cutter (from the inside cut) until it is sharp. File the remaining cutters on the same side of the chain. File all cutters identically. Move to the other side of the chain, and repeat the process.

The cutter depth gauge clearance is reduced as the cutting edges are sharpened. The cutter depth gauge clearance will need to be set after every second or third sharpening. Place the depth gauge set firmly across the top of two cutters so the depth gauge enters the slot in the gauge set. With a flat file, file the gauge level with the depth gauge set using a firm, forward pressure. Round off cutter gauge depth to maintain its original shape.

After several hard filings of the saw chain, have an authorized service center or sharpening service shop sharpen the saw chain on a sharpening machine to ensure uniform dimensions.

The term *skid-nose* describes the edge areas of teeth that have hit hard objects such as stones, nails, etc., or cut dirt, sand, etc. The skid-nose rides above the wood surface, keeping the sharp edges out of the wood. The friction of the skid-nose area overheats the cutter steel, and the chain gets soft. The only way to restore the chain to good condition is to file away all of the skid-nose steel, then adjust all cutters to the same length. This can be tedious to do by hand, so consider having it done by a service dealer.

Slight wear on the drive sprocket is normal. If a chain must be replaced, however, always include a new sprocket to maintain proper driving of the chain. The Homelite Models EL-12 and EL-14 electric chain saw parts layout is shown in FIG. 4-2.

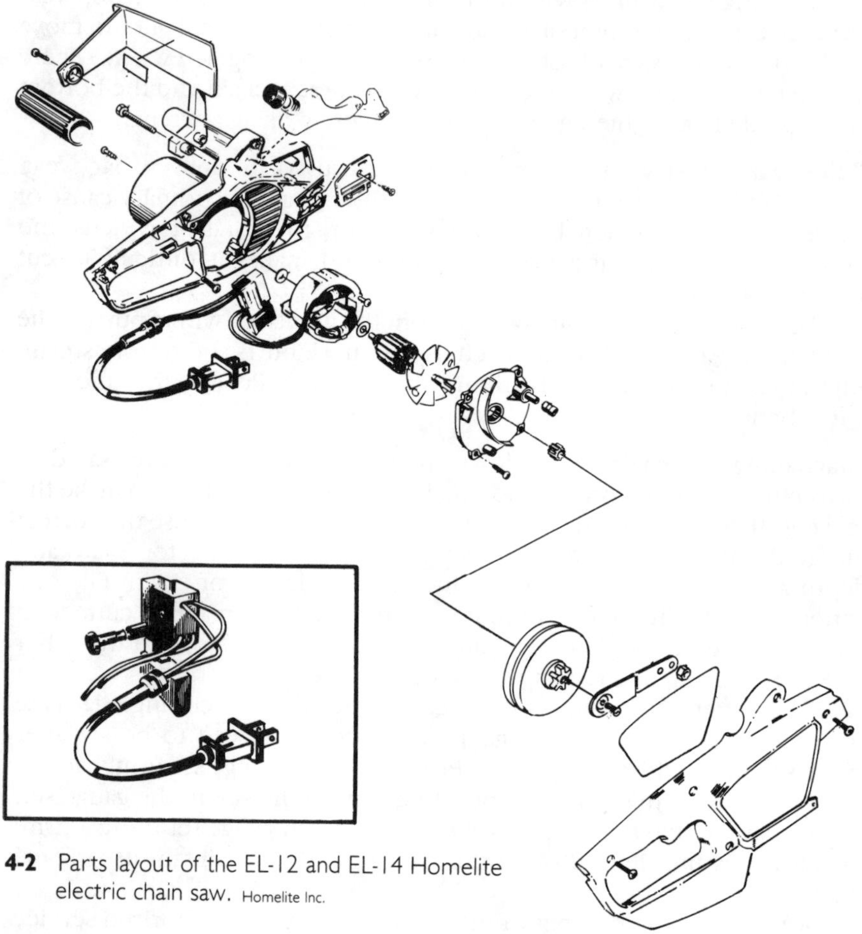

4-2 Parts layout of the EL-12 and EL-14 Homelite electric chain saw. Homelite Inc.

McCulloch 300 Series chain saws

McCulloch 300 Series chain saws include the MACCAT and Eager Beaver 2.1 two-cycle, gasoline-powered saws (FIG. 4-3). The general description and identification of operating parts are found in FIG. 4-4.

Check all symptoms before servicing the chain saw engine and carburetor—check the ignition detent switch for proper operation; inspect the fuel tank; make sure fuel is clean and not old; check the carburetor

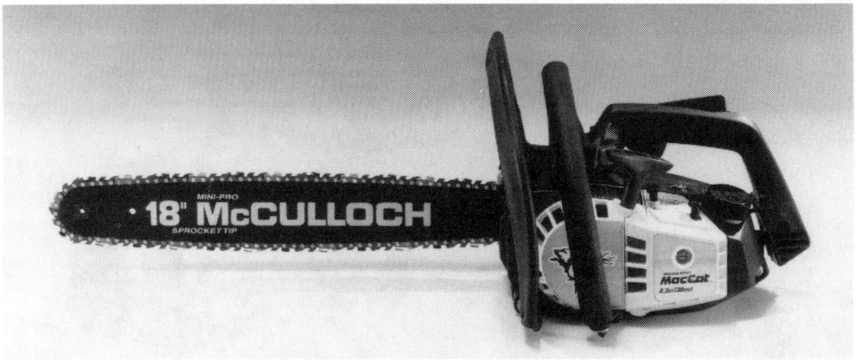

McCulloch Corp.

4-3 The McCulloch 18-inch 300 Series chain saw.

settings; inspect carburetor needle settings; check choke operation; and look for a plugged air filter or fire screen.

Servicing the starter assembly Before servicing any system, always drain the unit of all fuel and oil. Remove the air cleaner cover to get at the starter assembly. Remove the two starter housing fasteners and the 5/16-inch nut and washer that fastens the front handle link to the starter housing. The bottom starter housing screw threads into a nut that is glued in a nut pocket in the fan housing. Remove the starter assembly from the rear, pulling out and back.

Servicing the starter housing Pull 6 to 8 inches of rope off the starter pulley. Inspect the rope for breaks or worn areas. If the rope has pulled out, check the notch of the pulley. Hold tension on the rope in the notch and allow the pulley to rotate, relieving the spring tension from the pulley. Be careful when removing the starter pulley, as there is tension on the rewind spring.

Remove the pulley screw. Carefully lift the pulley while containing the spring with a screwdriver until the spring disengages. Check for a broken or pulled off rope, a broken or bent spring, or a jammed assembly from pulling on the rope trying to start the engine. Replace broken or damaged parts.

Before reassembling, check the required length of the rope—31.75 inches minimum—33.75 inches maximum and 120 inches in diameter. Rewind the starter rope clockwise on the pulley. Position the pulley so the ramp aligns with the inside loop of the spring. Push down and rotate back and forth until the pulley engages. Pull off enough rope to engage the notch and rotate the pulley one full turn, applying tension to the spring.

Be careful to prevent premature recoil spring failure, the recoil spring must never bottom out to its full length when the starter rope is pulled out. Hold the starter rope fully extended with one hand and turn the pulley with the other hand. The starter rope must have at least 1/4 turn of play remaining for correct recoil tension. If there is not at least 1/4 turn of play, remove one loop of rope from the starter pulley to ensure correct spring tension.

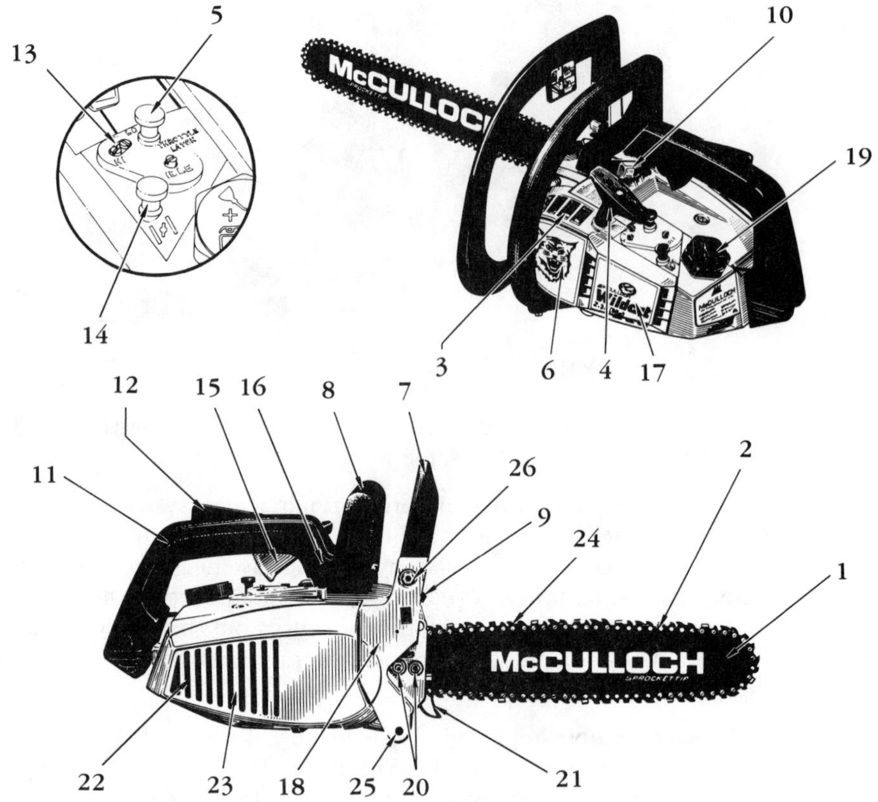

1. Guide bar
2. Saw chain
3. Fan housing
4. Starter handle
5. Throttle latch knob
6. Starter cover
7. Chain brake lever/hand guard
8. Front handle
9. Oil tank cap
10. Ignition/stop switch
11. Rear handle
12. Safety trigger
13. Carburetor adjustment screws
14. Choke knob
15. Throttle trigger
16. Manual oiler button
17. Air cleaner cover
18. Chain brake
19. Fuel tank cap
20. Bar bolt retaining nuts
21. Spike (optional equipment)
22. Spark plug
23. Muffler shield
24. Saw chain adjustment screw
25. Chain catcher
26. Chain brake lever retaining nut

4-4 The different components on the McCulloch gasoline-driven chain saw. McCulloch Corp.

Servicing the carburetor To remove the carburetor for cleanup or to service damaged parts, pull the choke knob up and squeeze the throttle trigger in the 11- and 12-level 300 series units. Lift the edge of the air box cover to clear the adjustment screws. Pull the cover out and disconnect the choke rod.

Disconnect the pulse and fuel hoses at the carburetor. Hold the throttle open with your finger, then pull the throttle cable out of the slot with needlenose pliers. Now, remove the two carburetor screws, the carburetor, the air cleaner cover bracket, and the choke.

Eager Beaver 2.1 and MACCAT carburetor removal

To remove the Eager Beaver 2.1 or a MACCAT carburetor, remove the two carburetor fasteners. Remove the air cleaner cover bracket and choke plate. Note the location of the spacer/bushing on which the choke plate pivots. Depress the throttle trigger to release the throttle switch. Remove the air box assembly. Hold the throttle lever at full open and remove the throttle cable from the slot with needlenose pliers.

Remove the pulse and fuel hoses. Notice there is no gasket where the carburetor mounts. The rubber boat is pulled tightly against the carburetor as the mounting fasteners thread into the metal flange behind the air box. Check the carburetor troubleshooting guide in TABLE 4-1 to identify probable carburetor-related problems.

Table 4-1 Troubleshooting McCulloch 300 Series Saws.

	Carburetor	
Start	Won't or hard start (engine cold).	1
	Won't or hard start (engine hot).	2
	Fuel dripping from carburetor.	3
	Engine floods when not running.	4
Idle	Will not idle.	5
	Rich idle (loads up while idling).	6
	Idles with low speed needle closed.	7
	Erratic idle.	8
	"L" needle needs frequent adjustment.	9
Acceleration or deceleration	Will not accelerate.	10
	Engine dies on deceleration.	11
	Poor acceleration.	12
	Slow deceleration.	13
High speed	Will not run at W.O.T.	14
	Poor or low power under load.	15
	Will not 4-cycle under no load at W.O.T.*	16
	"H" needle needs frequent adjustment.	17
	Minor Adjustments	
Low-speed needle.		
High-speed needle.		
Idle-speed screw.		
	Fuel Supply System	
Fuel cap vent (restricted/plugged).		
Fuel filter, line (restricted plugged).		

Table 4-1 Continued.

Fuel Supply System

Fuel line (loose/damaged).
Dirt in fuel passage.

Air Intake and Fuel Pump System

Air filter (restricted).
Carburetor bolts, gaskets (loose/leaking).
Throttle shaft, plate (loose/worn).
Throttle shaft, plate (bent/binding).
Choke shaft, plate (loose/worn/bent).
Pulse passage (leaking/restricted).
Fuel pump diaphragm, gasket (leaking/stiff/misassembled), cover screws (loose).
Inlet screen (restricted/plugged).
Throttle plate screw (loose).
Throttle return spring (defective).
Throttle stop (bent/damaged).

Metering System

Inlet needle (sticking).
Inlet needle leaking (dirty/worn tip/worn seat).
Inlet lever, spring (worn/bent/improperly installed).
Inlet lever (set too high).
Inlet lever (set too low).
Metering disk (worn).
Metering cover vent hole (restricted/plugged).
Metering diaphragm, gasket (leaking/damaged/improperly installed), cover screws (loose).
Welsh plugs (leaking).
Low-speed fuel passages (restricted/plugged).
High-speed fuel passages (restricted/plugged).
Low- or high-speed needle, seat (damaged/worn).
Low- or high-speed tension spring (distorted/weak).
Main nozzle check valve (sticking/blocked).
Main nozzle check valve (leaking).

Note: This guide should only be used when standard engine troubleshooting procedures indicate a problem with the fuel system. First:

- verify fuel condition.
- verify adequate secondary engine compression.
- verify adequate ignition and timing.
- no primary air leaks and must hold adequate primary crankcase compression.
- initial carburetor low speed, high speed and idle adjustment set to manufacturer's recommendations.

*W.O.T.=Wide Open Throttle.

McCulloch Corp.

Servicing a carburetor metering system Inspect the metering side of the carburetor by removing the four metering cover screws and cover. Inspect the diaphragm and gasket for wear, tears, and pliability. Flush the carburetor with clean fuel to remove any dirt or debris.

Remove the metering lever pin retaining screw to release the metering components. Replace the welch plug if a leak is suspected. Gently punch the welch plug, being careful not to damage the casting below. Press in the new welch plug with any device that is of the same dimension. After installation, seal the plug with clear nail polish.

Inspect the rubber tip of the inlet needle valve for swelling, shrinkage, or any other sign of damage. Ensure the metering lever spring is not deformed. Replace any components that are suspect. Reinstall the metering lever system with care. Make sure the spring is seated in the casting and is under the dimple in the metering lever.

Adjust the metering lever so that the back of the lever is flush with the top of the carburetor body. If the lever is not flush, gently bend the lever until the desired setting is achieved (FIG. 4-5).

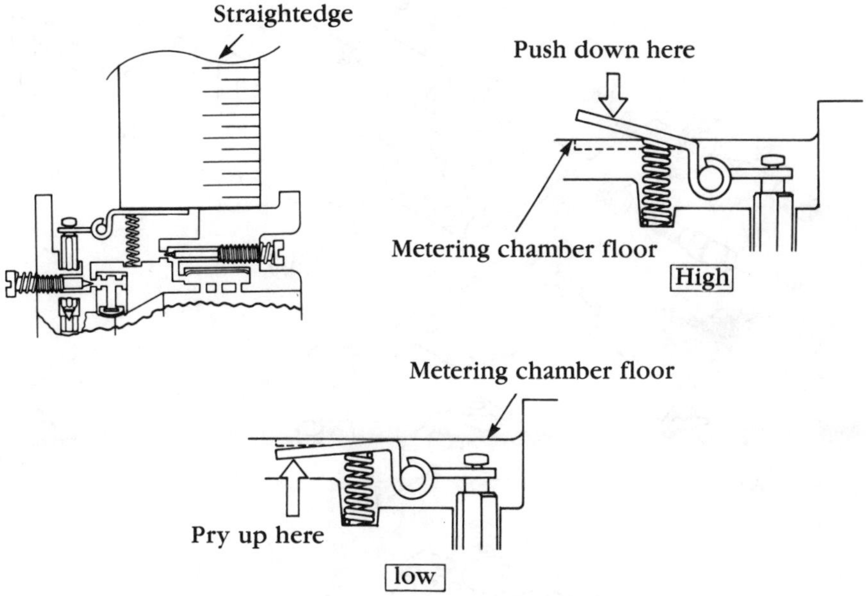

4-5 If the lever is not flush, pry it up until the desired setting is achieved. McCulloch Corp.

The carburetor fuel pump To service the carburetor fuel pump, remove the fuel pump cover screw and cover. Inspect the gasket and diaphragm. Replace if worn, torn, punctured, or out of shape. Make sure the fuel filter screen in the carburetor body is clean.

Remove both the high and low-speed needles and examine each tip and replace if damaged. Replace or install each needle valve carefully. To

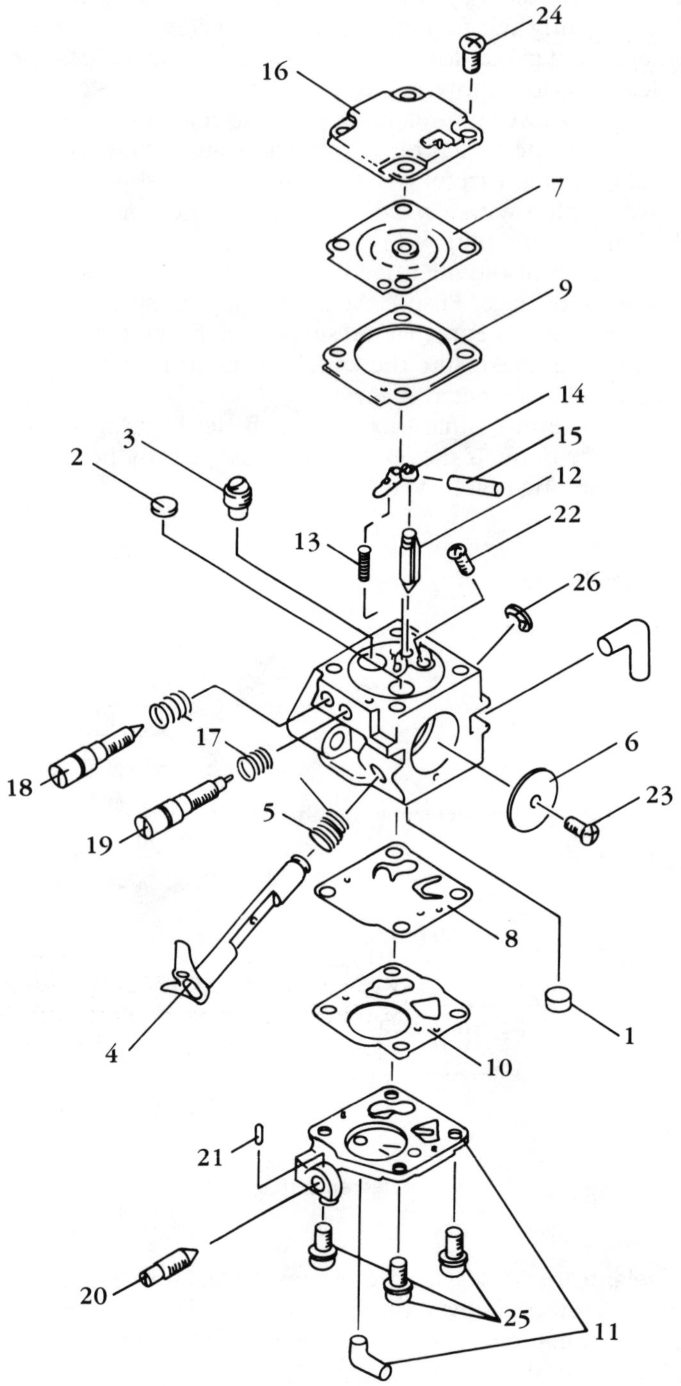

1. Screen, filter
2. Plug, welch
3. Orifice, main fuel
4. Shaft assembly, throttle
5. Spring, throttle return
6. Throttle plate
7. Diaphragm, metering
8. Diaphragm, pump
9. Gasket, metering diaphragm
10. Gasket, pump diaphragm
11. Cover assembly, pump
12. Needle, inlet
13. Spring, lever
14. Lever, inlet needle
15. Pin, lever
16. Cover, diaphragm
17. Spring, needle
18. Screw, main adjust
19. Screw, idle adjust
20. Screw, idle speed
21. Insert, friction
22. Screw, lever pin
23. Screw, plate
24. Screw, diaphragm cover
25. Screw, pump cover
26. Ring, ''E''

4-6 Carburetor parts assembly.
McCulloch Corp.

prevent any damage to the tips or seats, turn the screw in until you feel resistance, then open each needle one full turn. Figure 4-6 is a parts layout for the carburetor.

Carburetor adjustments To adjust the carburetor, first locate the three adjustment controls on the unit (FIGS. 4-7 and 4-8). The HIGH (H) speed mixture needle governs the high speed fuel flow (throttle wide open). The LOW (L) speed mixture needle governs the fuel flow at idle speed and the acceleration from idle to high speed. The IDLE (1) speed screw controls the throttle opening at idle speeds. The idle speed is from 2,700 to 2,900 RPM and the maximum speed is from 10,500 to 11,000 RPM.

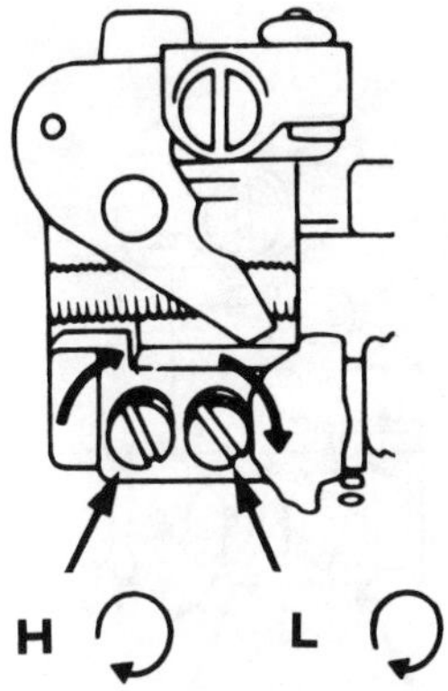

4-7 To adjust the carburetor, close H and L without forcing. McCulloch Corp.

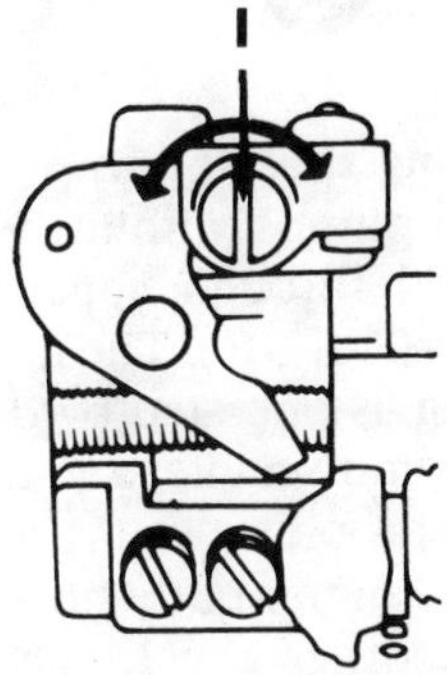

4-8 To keep the chain from moving, adjust the idle speed from 2,700 to 2,900 RPM. McCulloch Corp.

Carefully turn the low and high-speed mixture needle clockwise until resistance is felt, then open (counterclockwise) each needle 1 full turn. Do not turn needles in too tight or you can damage both needle tips and their seats. Start the engine and let it warm up at low speed. If the engine will not idle without stopping, turn the idle speed screw clockwise until engine idles properly. If the saw chain turns on the guide bar while the engine is idling, turn the idle speed screw counterclockwise slowly until the chain stops. Remember that an adjustment of one needle affects the adjustment of the other.

Accelerate the engine several times, adjusting the low-speed needle to obtain a smooth, rapid acceleration without hesitation or falter. The final position of the low-speed needle will usually be about 1 to 1¼ turns open (counterclockwise). If the low-speed needle is out of adjustment, the engine will hesitate or falter when accelerated.

Adjust the high-speed needle for best power under load. The final position of high-speed needle will usually be about 1 to 1¼ turns open (counterclockwise) (FIG. 4-9). Check idle speed again; it might speed again. In this case, adjust it slightly for smooth idle and acceleration. The chain should not move at the correct idle speed.

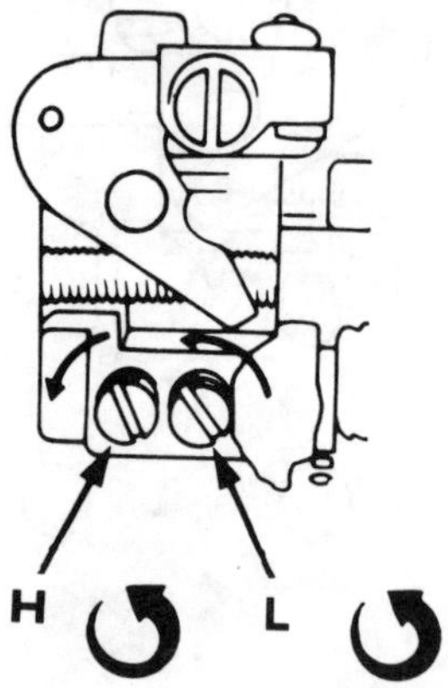

4-9 Open H and L 1 to 1¼ turns on the carburetor adjustment assembly.
McCulloch Corp.

Servicing the oil pump The oil pump incorporates two separate functioning pumps within the same housing. The automatic pump is pulse-operated through a part in the crankcase where the pump housing mounts (FIG. 4-10). The manual pump, located at the top-right of the pump housing, is operated by depressing the manual oiler button. Both pumps use a common inlet and discharge part. The most common cause of oiler system problems is dirt or debris in the oil.

The pump body houses a spring-ball check valve that is not replaceable. Another check valve (floating disk) is serviceable and is located behind the oil inlet part. Both check valves must function for either pump system to work. Early model 300 series saws had an adjustable pump that has since been discontinued.

Cleaning the muffler screen To clean the muffler screen, remove the two deflector shield fasteners to access the muffler mounting fasteners. Remove the muffler bolts and the muffler from the cylinder (FIG. 4-11). Remove the spark arrestor screen and clean or replace it. Use Loctite on muffler bolts and torque from 40–45 inch pounds.

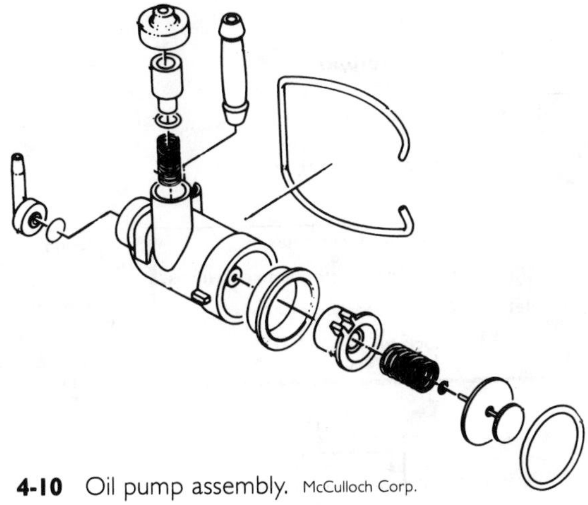

4-10 Oil pump assembly. McCulloch Corp.

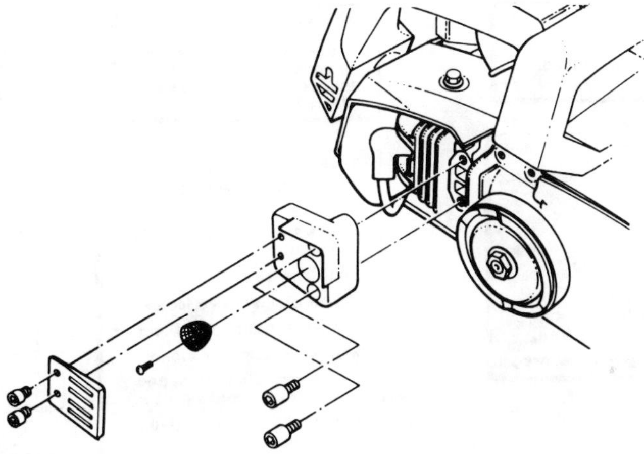

4-11 Remove and clean out the muffler screen from the cylinder. McCulloch Corp.

Check FIG. 4-12 for troubleshooting two-cycle engines. All power head assemblies, carburetor pressure tests, and cylinder pressure tests should be made by professionals with a pressure test meter.

COMPOST TUMBLERS

Compost tumblers that set on a metal rack are perfect for making the right compost mix for the garden or flower bed. Just fill the tumbler with the correct amount of grass, leaves, old weeds, kitchen scraps, etc., and toss them in the tumbler (FIG. 4-13).

Clean the hopper when it is not in use. Lubricate the gear with grease at the handle. If the handle squeaks, apply a few drops of oil on each end.

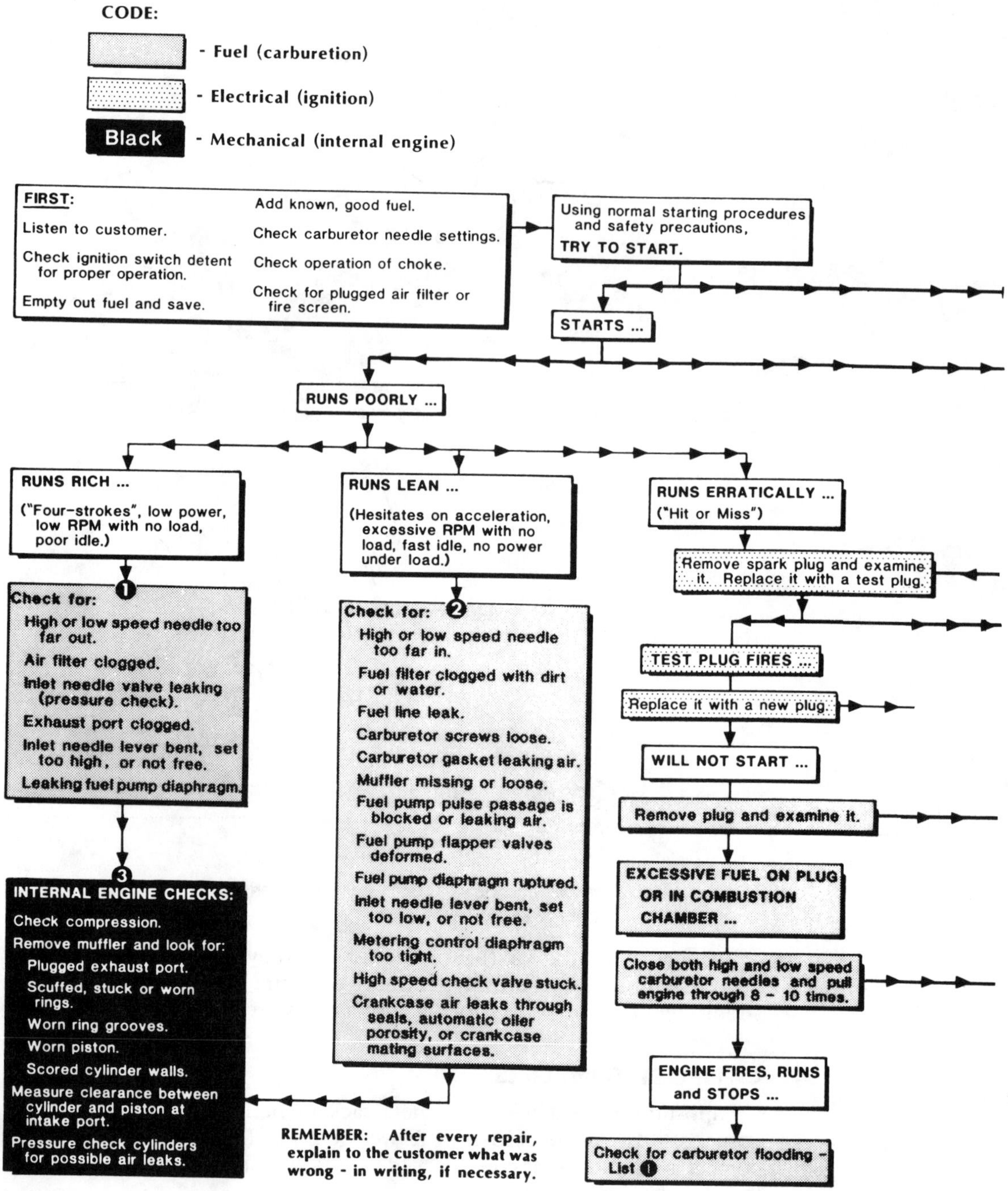

4-12 Troubleshooting two-cycle engines. McCulloch Corp.

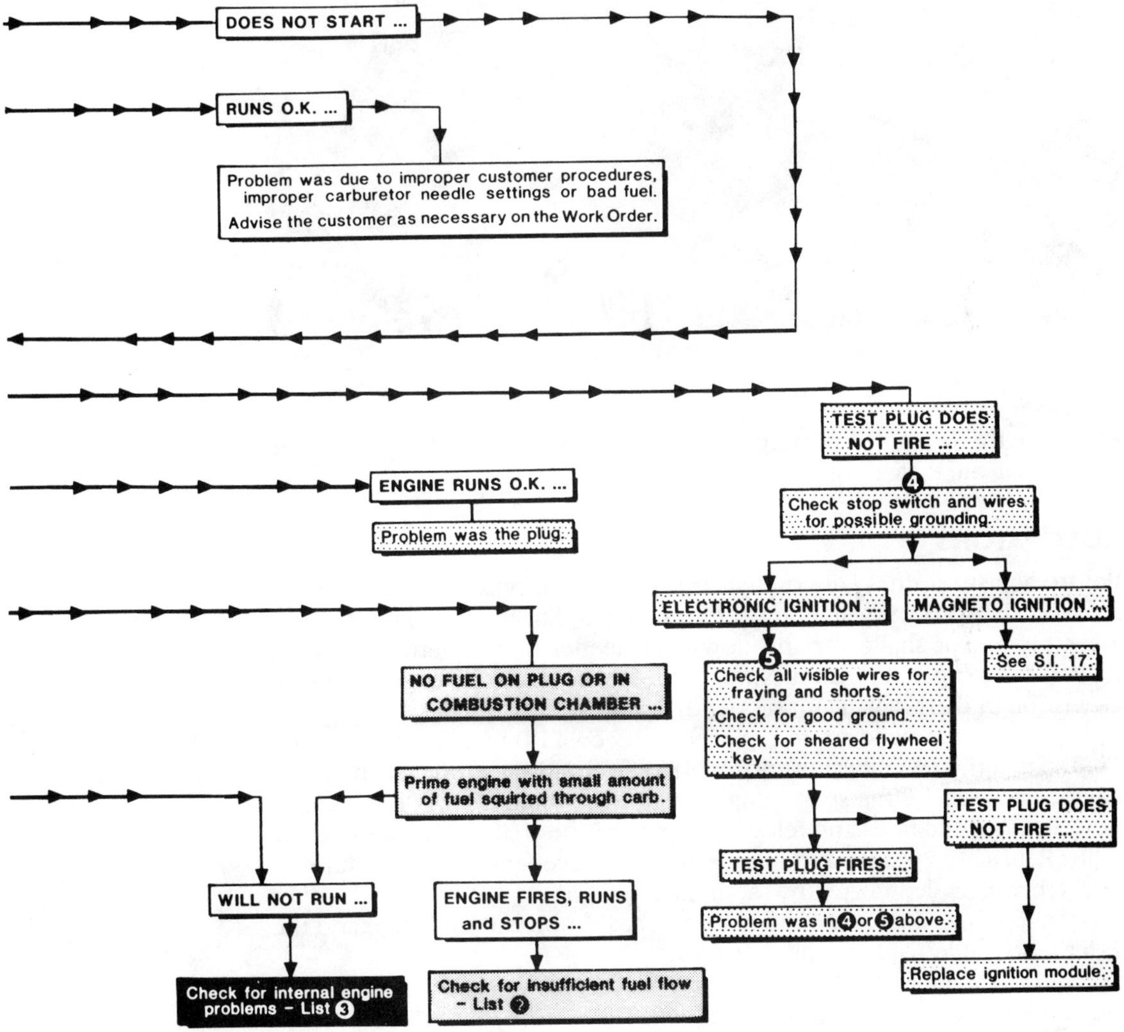
DOES NOT START ...
RUNS O.K. ...
Problem was due to improper customer procedures, improper carburetor needle settings or bad fuel.
Advise the customer as necessary on the Work Order.
TEST PLUG DOES NOT FIRE ...
ENGINE RUNS O.K. ...
Problem was the plug.
4
Check stop switch and wires for possible grounding.
ELECTRONIC IGNITION ...
MAGNETO IGNITION ...
See S.I. 17.
5
Check all visible wires for fraying and shorts.
Check for good ground.
Check for sheared flywheel key.
NO FUEL ON PLUG OR IN COMBUSTION CHAMBER ...
Prime engine with small amount of fuel squirted through carb.
TEST PLUG DOES NOT FIRE ...
TEST PLUG FIRES ...
WILL NOT RUN ...
ENGINE FIRES, RUNS and STOPS ...
Problem was in 4 or 5 above.
Replace ignition module.
Check for internal engine problems – List 3
Check for insufficient fuel flow – List 2

4-13 A compost tumbler can produce compost in just a few weeks.

Lubricate the front rod turning assembly with motor oil. Keep the large round gear track clean of dirt and excess compost.

CULTIVATORS

Before adjusting tines, disconnect the spark plug wire. Loosen (do not remove) the two wing nuts on the tine guard. Strike the wheel bracket assembly up for shallower and down for deeper tine penetration. Now, tighten the wing nuts, making sure that the carriage bolts are seated properly through the bracket. If tine depth is not correct, repeat.

Should tines need to be replaced, replace all four tines at the same time so that they will wear evenly. Work on one side at a time. Turn off the engine and remove the spark plug. Remove the hitch pin clips and clevis pins. Remove the tines and felt cushions from the shaft. Clean and oil the shaft. Replace new tines and felt cushions by reversing the procedure.

When installed correctly, the hubs on the tines will face each other and the letter R stamped on the tines will appear on the right side and the letter L on the left side of the cultivator.

The air filter

Clean and reoil the air filter after every 10 hours of operation. Remove the air filter from the carburetor/air filter cover assembly. Wash it in detergent and water. Rinse the filter thoroughly and allow it to air dry. Apply clean SAE 10W 30 oil to the filter and squeeze to spread the oil.

The carburetor

The engine is squeezed with a diaphragm-type carburetor. A dirty air filter will restrict air flow, so clean it before making any adjustments. A carburetor adjustment might be needed if the following conditions exist:

1. The engine will not idle.
2. The engine hesitates or stalls on acceleration.
3. There is loss of engine power after the air filter and muffler is cleaned.
4. The engine operates in an erratic or fuel-rich condition (smoking).

The diaphragm-type carburetor has idle speed and idle mixture adjustments. The high-speed mixture is preset and high-speed adjustment is impossible. To adjust the carburetor, remove the carburetor filter cover assembly, and locate the adjusting screws underneath the choke lever and air filter base. Adjust the idle speed settings.

For Walbro and Tillotson carburetors, back the idle speed screw out counterclockwise until it does not contact the carburetor throttle lever. Turn the screw in clockwise until it begins to move the throttle lever. Continue turning two full turns.

For Zama carburetors, back the idle screw out counterclockwise until it does not contact the throttle valve located inside the carburetor. Watch the movement of the throttle lever stop. Now, turn the screw clockwise until it just begins to move the throttle lever and continue 1$^1/_2$ turns.

To set the initial idle mixture setting, turn the idle mixture screw clockwise until it is lightly seated, then turn the screw counterclockwise 1$^1/_2$ turns. Start up and warm the engine. Release the throttle trigger and let the engine idle. If the engine stops, turn the idle speed screw clockwise $^1/_8$ turn until the engine idles.

To set the final idle speed and idle mixture settings, adjust the idle speed and mixture for the smoothest engine idle. Adjust the idle mixture screw for the fastest idle, then turn the screw counterclockwise $^1/_8$ turn. Squeeze the throttle trigger, and if the engine falters or hesitates on acceleration, turn the idle mixture counterclockwise $^1/_{16}$ turn at a time until rapid acceleration is achieved. If the idle speed has changed, repeat. Contact a service dealer if adjustments fail to help.

Fuel requirements

Number 2 cycle oil is recommended for cultivators. If another brand of two-cycle oil is used, make sure it is a high-quality oil that is formulated for small, air-cooled engines. Always use clean, fresh, regular-grade, leaded gasoline with an octane rating of 87 or greater. Unleaded regular-grade gasoline is an acceptable alternative, but regular-grade leaded gasoline is preferred. Do not use alcohol-blended fuels, as they tend to absorb moisture.

For proper engine operation, mix a 32:1 fuel/oil ratio when using IDC #2 cycle oil. Put a small amount of fresh gasoline into a clean, 1-gallon fuel can. Add one 4-ounce can of oil. If you will be using oil other than IDC #2 cycle oil, add 6 ounces of oil. Fill the remainder of the fuel can with gasoline. Screw the fuel cap on tightly and shake the can vigorously for at least 30 seconds. Fill the tank only when the cultivator is in a horizontal position.

ELECTRIC EDGERS

Most service problems found with electric edgers are a bad AC plug connection or defective OFF/ON switch and motor brushes. The universal motor rotates the trim blade with a direct shaft. Remove any screws on the motor assembly to get at the brushes and fan assembly (FIG. 4-14). Mark the end bell assembly. Remove screws to remove the end bell of the motor. Pull out the armature and end bearings for lubrication. Check the armature surface while the motor is apart.

4-14 Remove any screws to get at the brushes. Check for worn brushes with excessive firing of armature.

HEDGERS

This section covers two types of hedgers—cordless hedgers and electric hedgers.

Cordless hedge trimmers

Cordless hedge or grass trimmers might operate from a cordless power pack. The cordless hedge trimmer requires no oil or engine maintenance.

The nickel-cadmium power pack is charged up like other chargeable batteries. Nickel-cadmium batteries experience a memory loss when charged too often, reducing the charging and operating time. If the batteries will not charge, check the DC voltage across the charger applied to the batteries.

Metal gear drives and hardened steel blades provide long life. Sharpen the blades on a grinder, large file, or with a Diafold rod. Check, maintain, and lubricate cordless hedge trimmer motors like the cordless weed trimmer.

Electric hedge trimmers

Most electric hedge trimmers have self-lubricating bearings. Lubricate the sleeve bearings with light motor oil after two or three years of operation. Most electric hedge trimmers have a universal AC motor. Remove side screws to check the switch and blade assembly. Check the continuity of the cord, switch, armature, and field coils with the low ohm range of a DMM (FIG. 4-15). The total ohmmeter should read around 24 ohms at the AC plug.

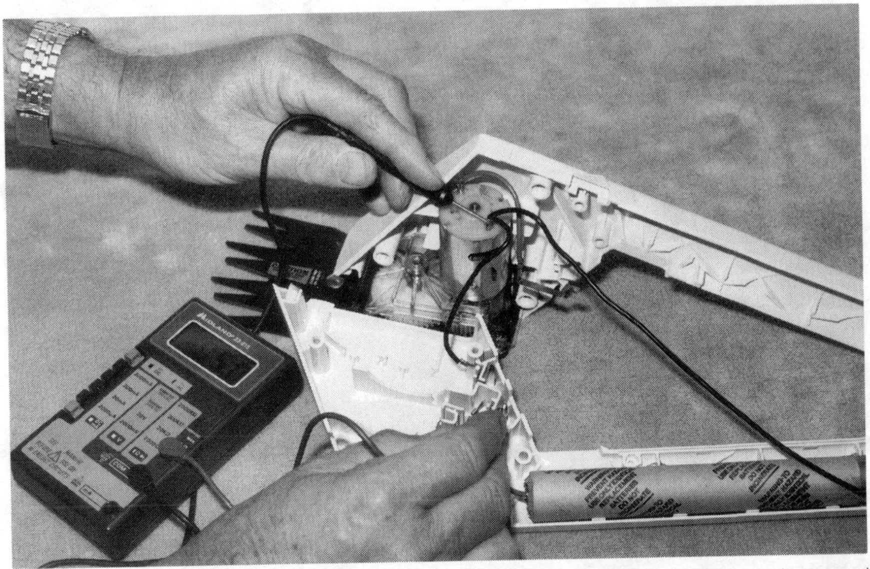

4-15 Check the continuity of motor terminals with a DMM when the battery is normal and there is no motor rotation.

If the blade has any large nicks that prevent normal operation, file or grind them out. Clean off the plastic case and motor assembly with mild soap and cloth. Wipe off blades with an oily cloth.

LEAF BLOWERS

When a leaf blower becomes clogged with dirt, leaves, or grass, turn the unit off and pull out the AC cord. Remove the tubes and carefully reach into the opening and clear out debris. Keep the unit clean with mild detergent and water. Wipe off with a damp cloth.

If the motor fails to operate, suspect a defective cord, plug, or ON/OFF switch. Make sure the whole inlet plastic assembly is in place so that the interlock is closed. Check the continuity of the cord, switches, and motor with an ohmmeter. Connect the ohmmeter leads to the AC cord and push the switch on. The total resistance should be around 8.8 ohms (FIG. 4-16).

4-16 Check the AC cord resistance with the ON/OFF switch turned on for meter continuity (8.8 ohms).

The motor, cord, plug, and switch can be checked individually with the ohmmeter. The resistance across each field coil will measure approximately 4.4 ohms. A dead short should be measured across the interlock and ON/OFF switch. Switch the brushes for worn or hang up with no continuity of the motor assembly.

Round fin disks or impeller blades might wear off at the ends, preventing blower operation (FIG. 4-17). Inspect the blades for wear. Take out the screws to remove the top cover of the leaf blower assembly, and remove the plastic rings. Remove the screws holding the motor assembly to the main plastic body.

Twist off the front inlet assembly by turning counterclockwise. This inlet assembly must be in place to get the motor to operate. A small interlock switch is found under one of the plastic tabs. New blades can be picked up from the manufacturer's dealer or an authorized service dealer if needed.

4-17 Check the plastic impeller for worn or broken ends when heavy air flow is prevented.

LEAF SHREDDERS

The small leaf chipper/shredder operates with an electric motor from 1.8 to 2.2 HP. Before starting up the shredder, check all bolts and cotter pins on the bottom chute door (FIG. 4-18). If the shredder becomes jammed or stalls, remove the AC cord before trying to remove limbs or waste that has stopped the shredder. Do not try to unclog the shredder while the electric motor is operating. Check the overload protector, the AC cord, and the plug when the motor is dead.

WEED AND GRASS TRIMMERS

This section covers cordless trimmers, electric trimmers, gas-powered line trimmers, and gas-powered trimmers.

Cordless trimmers

A new trimmer should be left to charge for about 16 hours. The trimmer will operate for about a half hour before it needs another charge. This is long enough to trim weeds and grass in one setting. After using up the half hour, the batteries will charge back up to full capacity in about two hours (FIG. 4-19).

4-18 Before starting up a shredder, check all bolts and cotter pins on the bottom chute door.

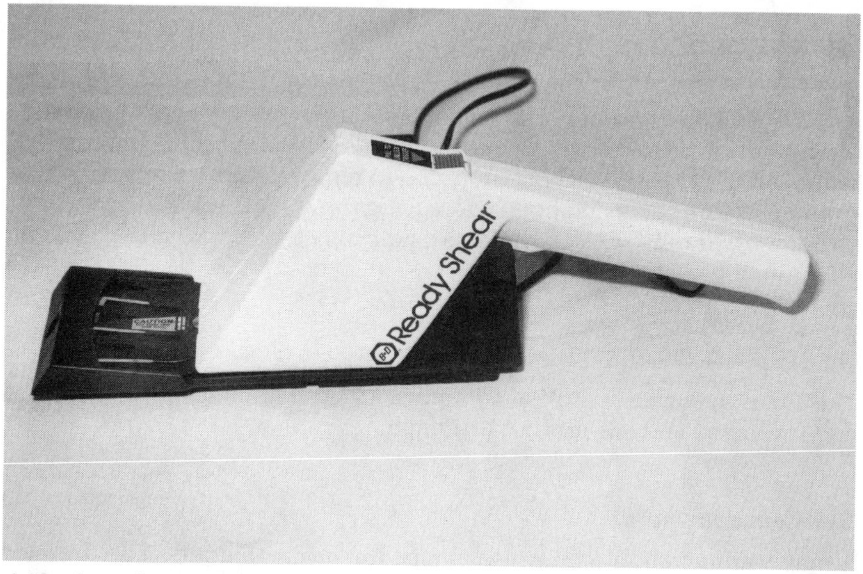

4-19 A cordless grass trimmer in a charging adapter.

Batteries should be charged at around 75 degrees. While charging, the charger might become quite warm. If reduced operating time is noted, it might be due to repeated, partial battery charging and not a defective battery.

Clean up the cordless trimmer with mild soap and damp cloth. Do not use gasoline, turpentine, or paint thinners on the plastic body parts. Keep the housing out of the rain or any other liquid.

Blades Operate the trimmer for a few minutes to clean off all grass and debris, then carefully wash off blades in soapy water. Do not place the motor housing in the water. Dry off and spray the blades with a light oil after each cleanup to prevent rust from forming on the blades.

Check the blades for bent areas, especially if the trimmer is accidentally dropped. If blades are bent out of shape, replace them. Check the housing for cracked or broken areas. Notice if the lock-off switch operates. The blades can be used if a nick or two appears and it does not harm the meshing of teeth.

Replace the blades after a couple of years. Sharpen the blades by clamping in a vise and using a flat file. Sharpen in the same direction on each blade.

Charging the batteries Always operate the trimmer until the unit almost stops operating. Only then, charge the batteries. Nickel-cadmium batteries will experience a memory loss when charged too often, reducing the charging and operating time. If the batteries will not charge, check the DC voltage across the charger applied to the batteries.

If the trimmer becomes noisy, apply a light coat of grease on the gears, even if they are plastic (FIG. 4-20). Light oil squirted in each end of the motor bearing can prevent a noisy motor bearing. Inspect gears for gummed up grass and excess dirt. If debris has collected, drop the motor down and wash out the gear assembly.

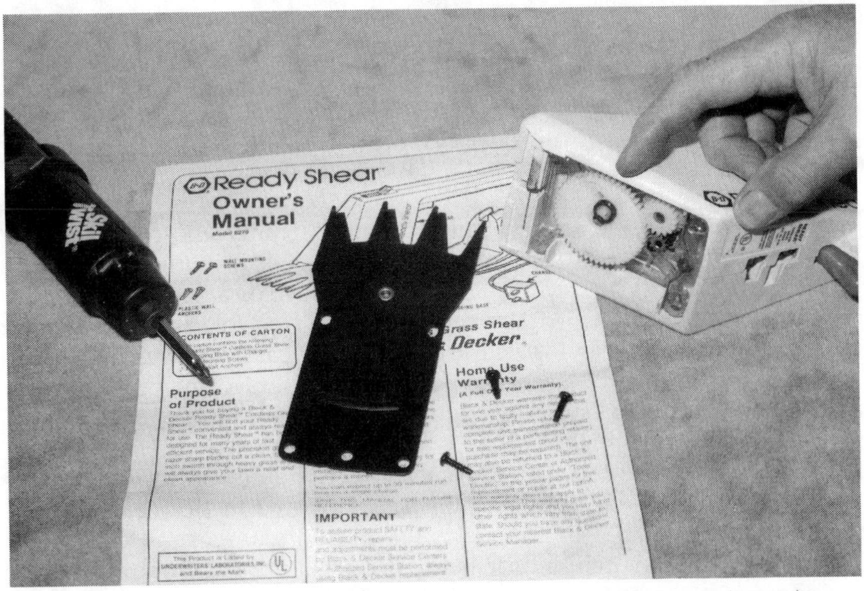

4-20 Remove the screws that hold the cutting blades for cleanup and sharpening.

Check the ON/OFF switch for no operation. Measure the voltage applied to the motor terminals. Check the motor terminals for continuity with the low-ohm scale of a DMM.

Electric trimmers

Electric trimmers come in 8 inches, 10 inches, and 12 inches (FIG. 4-21). Keep cutting head and shield clean. Wipe off after using with a damp cloth or sponge. Remove dirt and weeds from trimmer head assembly.

4-21 The large cutting line rotated by a small AC motor cuts weeds, grass, and light brush.

When dirt and grass forms on the bottom assembly, the removal ring becomes difficult to use. Clean off all dirt and weeds from the ring assembly. Remove the ring by turning clockwise. Remove dirt clogged in slotted areas with a pocketknife. After removal and before replacing, apply light grease or petroleum jelly inside the ring area for easy removal.

It's a lot cheaper to purchase a large spool of replacement nylon cord than to try and repair one. Although regular replacement spools can be slipped in place, you might save a few dollars each year with a large spool. Simply rewind the cord inside the old holder and cut off to the correct length. Thoroughly clean up the inside spool area in detergent before replacing the spool.

To check the switch, motor field, and armature for continuity with the ohmmeter, remove any screws from the bottom guard plate. Remove screws to check the brushes and motor. Use a lubricant or two-cycle engine oil. Make sure gasoline is not more than two months old.

Gasoline-powered line trimmers

Gasoline-powered line trimmers operate the same as the electric line trimmer except it operates with gasoline and oil, and has no dangling AC cords. The gasoline trimmer can get into hard-to-reach places or those out of reach of any AC outlets. Line installation might be the same as the electric unit. On some gasoline-powered trimmers a metal blade is used for cutting.

Adjusting the line Many electric and gasoline line trimmers will release extra line if the head is tapped on the ground or a hard surface. Extra line can be released on a gasoline trimmer by bumping the head on the ground while the engine is at high-trimming speed. Each time the head is bumped, about 1 inch of line is released (FIG. 4-22).

4-22 The head assembly releases about 1 inch when bumped on the ground. Shut off the engine if the line does not release and check the nylon spool.

Sometimes, the line might be cut off close to the line opening and will fall back into the spool area. This means the engine must be shut off before attempting a repair. Some of these spools are difficult to remove, especially after being filled with grass, weeds, and dirt. Remove the spool by holding the outer spool with one hand and rotating the bump knob counterclockwise. Remove the inner spool. Clean up the inside surface.

Wipe out all debris from the head assembly. Check the indexing teeth on the inner and outer-edge of the spool, and replace if cut or damaged.

Usually, when a line gets old, it breaks easily. If the line is old, wind 25 or 30 feet of new trimming line on the spool. Insert one end of the line through the first hole on the inner spool and pull the loose end through the second hole. Wind the line in even and tight layers. If the line is wound backwards, the line will not release. Recheck the direction of winding (FIG. 4-23). Do not fill the spool entirely. You might want to purchase new prewound spools instead of winding your own.

4-23 Check the winding direction on new replacement line because it might not release line when its head is bumped.

Fuel requirements Always use new fuel and oil before mixing. In two-cycle engines, oil must be added to the gasoline in the correct mixture. Follow the manufacturer's recommended grade of oil for small, air-cooled engines. Use clean, fresh regular-grade gasoline. Although regular grade is recommended, leaded gasoline with an octane rating of 87 or greater can be used. Do not use alcohol-blended fuels, as they could damage the engine and fuel system.

For proper two-cycle engine operation, use a 32:1 fuel/oil ratio when using two-cycle motor oil. Using old or improper fuel can damage the engine. Also, improperly mixed fuel can damage the engine and cause difficult starts and erratic operation.

Mix 1 gallon of clean fresh gasoline with 4 ounces of IDC two-cycle oil. Put a small amount of gasoline into a fuel can and pour in a can of IDC two-cycle oil (4 ounces). If another brand is used, pour in 6 ounces of oil, and fill the can up with the remaining gallon of gas. Screw the cap on tightly and shake for one whole minute for a good mixture.

The air filter The air filter in small two-cycle engines should be cleaned after every 10 hours of operation. Remove the air filter from the carburetor/air filter cover assembly (FIG. 4-24). Wash out in detergent and water. Rinse filter thoroughly and dry. Place some 10W 30 motor oil on the filter and squeeze filter so oil filter is covered. Replace filter.

Poulan / Weed Eater.

4-24 Clean up the air filter after 10 hours, and wash out in mild detergent.

The carburetor Follow carefully each manufacturer's carburetor adjustments. This IDC diaphragm-type carburetor might not need any adjustments for several years. Always check and clean the air filter and use a clean, fresh oil-fuel mixture before making carburetor adjustments. A dirty air filter can upset the fuel-air mixture, causing the engine to run improperly.

The IDC gasoline line trimmer engine has idle speed and idle-mixture carburetor adjustments. The high-speed mixture is preset, and no high-speed adjustment is necessary. If the engine will not idle, hesitates or stalls, shows a loss of power, or smokes excessively, it might be necessary to adjust the carburetor.

To adjust the carburetor, stop the engine and remove the carburetor/air filter cover assembly. Locate both adjustment screws (FIG. 4-25). The adjustment screws are located underneath the choke lever and air filter intake. Make initial idle speed settings.

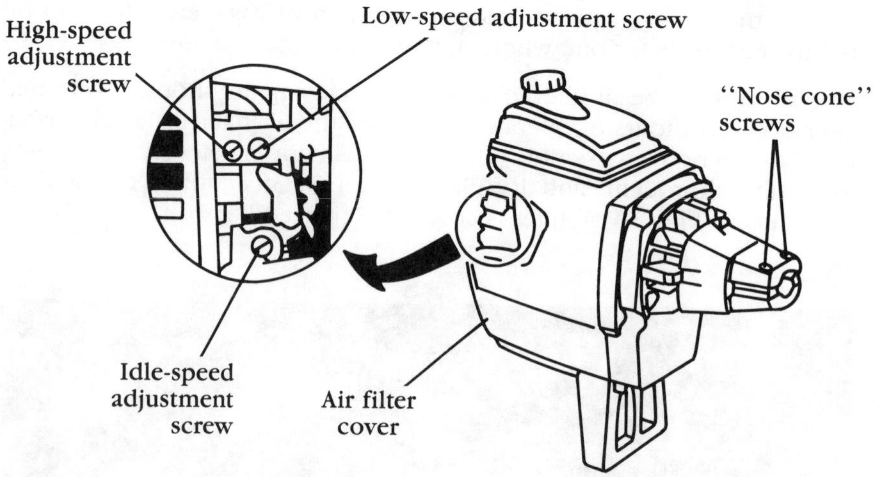

4-25 Make sure the low-speed, high-speed, and idle-speed adjustments are correct for smooth engine operations. Inertia Dynamics Corporation.

For Walbro and Tillotson carburetors, back the idle screw out counterclockwise until it does not contact the carburetor throttle lever. Turn the screw in (clockwise) until it begins to move the throttle lever; continue turning 2 full turns.

For Zama carburetors, back the idle screw out (counterclockwise) until it does not contact the throttle valve. Watch the throttle lever. Now, turn the screw in (clockwise) until it just begins to move the throttle lever, and continue turning 1½ turns.

Turn the initial idle mixture setting with the idle mixture screw clockwise until lightly seated. Rotate the screw counterclockwise 1½ turns, backing the idle screw out.

Start and warm up the engine a few minutes. Release the throttle trigger and let the engine idle. When the engine stops, turn the idle speed screw clockwise ⅛ turn at a time until the engine idles. Adjust both idle speed and mixture for smoothest engine idle. Adjust the idle mixture screw for the fastest idle and then turn screw counterclockwise ⅛ turn. Squeeze the throttle trigger for faster speed. If the engine falters, turn the idle mixture screw counterclockwise 1/16 turn at a time until proper acceleration occurs. Readjust the idle speed screw if the idle speed has changed with the preceding steps. If the engine still does not operate properly, take the unit to an authorized service dealer.

Motor repair If the motor is dead or operates intermittently, suspect a defective switch, broken cord, or worn brushes. Clip the ohmmeter to the AC prongs and check the resistance of the motor circuits. If the resistance is above 15 ohms, suspect a dirty switch or brushes. The normal resistance is around 10 ohms.

Remove the three Phillip screws in the bottom shell and check the switch contacts. Spray the switch contacts with electronic cleaning fluid if the switch is intermittent or appears dirty. Inspect the brushes. If worn, replace. Notice if one of the brushes are hung up. Wash out and clean up the brush holder. Check the cord continuity with an ohmmeter if the grinder operates when the cord is flexed or moved. Notice the three long bottom screws holding the grinder to the top body piece.

Gasoline-powered trimmers

Before operating gasoline-powered trimmers, cutting blades should be sharp and the gas tank full. Tighten any loose or lost nuts and screws before starting the unit. Follow the periodic check and maintenance schedule in TABLE 4-2.

Table 4-2 Maintenance schedule for Solo Weed trimmer.

	Time for check, adjustment, and replacement			
Item	*Before Starting Work*	*Every 20 Hours*	*Every 50 Hours*	*Every 100 Hours*
Check and replenish fuel.	✓			
Check for fuel leakage.	✓			
Check for loose or lost nuts and screws.	✓			
Tighten bolts and nuts.		(First 20 hours)	✓	
Clean fuel filter.	Maximum	✓		
Clean air filter element.		✓[1]		
Clean spark plug and adjust electrodes gap.			✓	
Remove dust and dirt from cylinder fins.			✓	
Remove carbon deposits in exhaust hole.			✓	
Remove carbon deposits on piston head and inside cylinder.			✓	
Remove carbon deposits on piston rings.			✓	
Check the sliding portion of crankshaft, connecting rod, etc.				✓
Clean net of spark arrester, if so equipped.			✓	
Replace fuel tube.	It is recommended to replace every three years.			

[1]When used in dusty environment, every 10 hours.

Solo Inc.

If the engine slowly or erratically returns to idle or idles erratically, adjust the idle speed screw (FIG. 4-26). For low-speed adjustment, turn the low-speed screw slowly clockwise until the speed starts to drop. Turn the low-speed screw counterclockwise until the speed increases. Set the low-speed mixture screw between these two positions.

For high-speed mixture adjustment, allow the engine to idle, then squeeze the throttle trigger fully. Turn the high-speed mixture screw very slowly clockwise until the engine speed is reduced. Now, turn the high-speed control counterclockwise and stop when the engine begins to run roughly. Turn the screw clockwise slowly until the engine runs smoothly.

TDC.

4-26 Before attempting to adjust the carburetor, locate the idler speed and mixture screws.

If the engine does not start, it is probably flooded. Wait a few minutes with the choke in the OFF position, then try again. Lubricate the drive shaft after every 10 hours of operation. Remove the gearbox clamp screw and gearbox from the drive shaft housing. Remove the drive shaft, clean off old grease, then apply new lubricant to the entire surface of the drive shaft. Replace parts in the reverse order (FIG. 4-27).

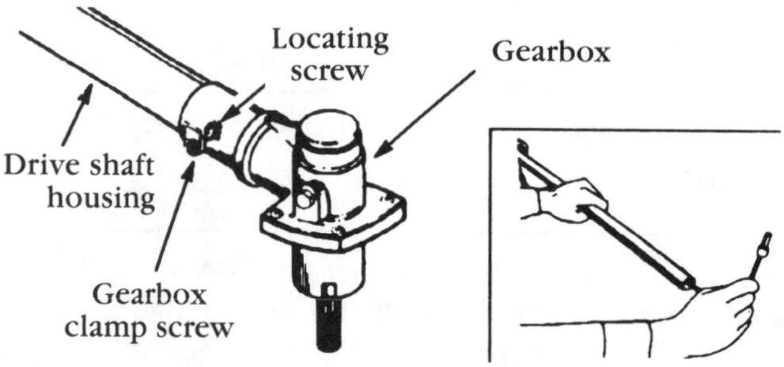

4-27 Remove the drive shaft, lubricate, and replace.

After five tanks of fuel or five hours of operation, charge and clean the air filter. Loosen screws and remove the air filter cover (FIG. 4-28). Wash out in soap and water and squeeze dry. Do not clean the air filter in gasoline.

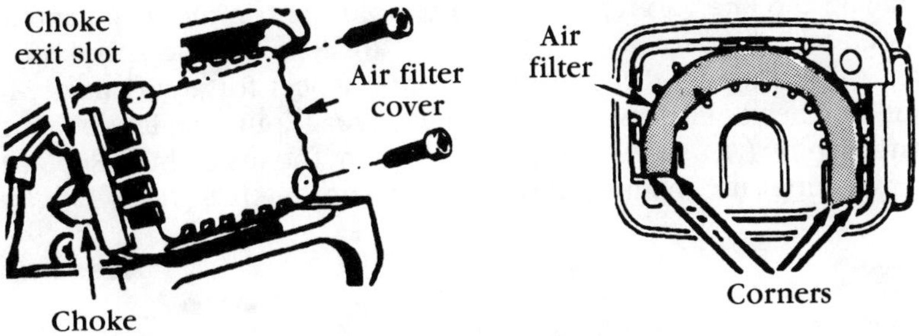

4-28 Remove the two screws and the air filter, then wash out in soap and water. Poulan / Weed Eater.

Recoil starters When the recoil starter assembly will not rotate or it is pulled out and the rope breaks, you will have to remove the recoil assembly and repair. Be careful in handling the spiral spring so as not to be injured. After replacing the rope and making repairs, clean out and check the inside starter case components.

Wind the spiral spring so that its outer diameter is smaller than the inner diameter of the case, and tie the spring with fine wire (FIG. 4-29A). Then, put the spring with its outer end hooked in the case, and remove the wire with a screwdriver. Adjust the inner end of the spring as shown in FIG. 4-29B.

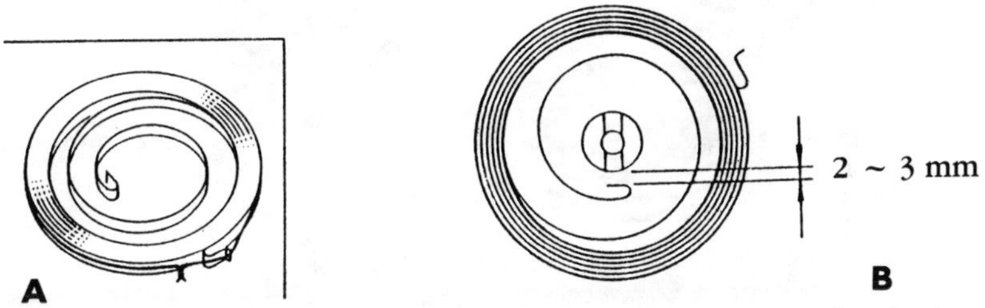

4-29 When replacing a new coil assembly, hook the starter recoil spring in the center of the case. Solo Inc.

Coat the starter shaft with a light grease. Pass the rope through the case and reel, and knot the rope end. Insert the rope end securely into the slot on the reel. Wind the rope $2^1/_2$ rounds onto the reel and insert the rope end into the notch on the outside of the reel. Fit the reel into the starter shaft. Adjust the reel so that it can be hooked securely with the inner end of the spiral spring.

Rotate the reel five turns counterclockwise. Be careful of the reel not coming up from the case. After rotating five turns, hold the reel by the left hand, and draw out the rope through the starter case and return it slowly. Install the washer and tighten screw.

Replacing the line To replace the line, hold the trimmer head and press the lock tab and turn the cover (FIG. 4-30). Remove the spool and the cover. Clean out any dirt and debris, and inspect for any damage. Keep about 6 inches of line outside of the head area. Route the line behind the balancing ping (FIG. 4-31). Pull on the line from the inside hub. Replace the cover, making sure the line is wound between notches (FIG. 4-32).

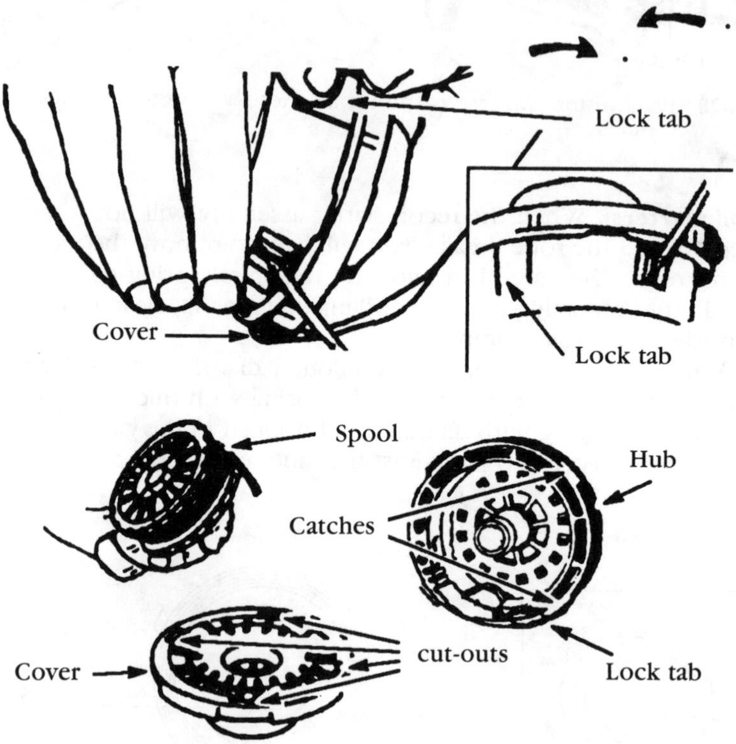

4-30 To check the cutting line, remove and twist the cover off counter-clockwise. Poulan / Weed Eater.

4-31 Leave 6 inches of line outside the head, then rotate the line behind the balancing notch. Poulan / Weed Eater.

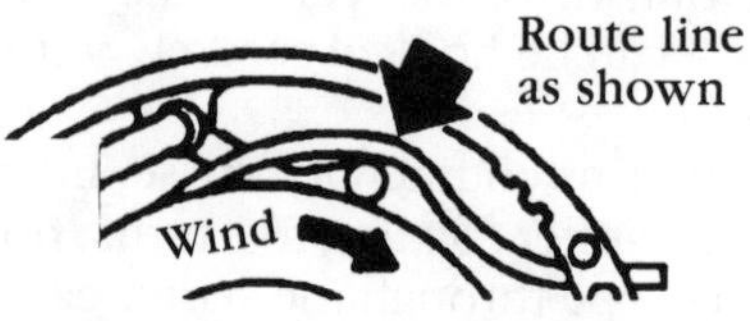

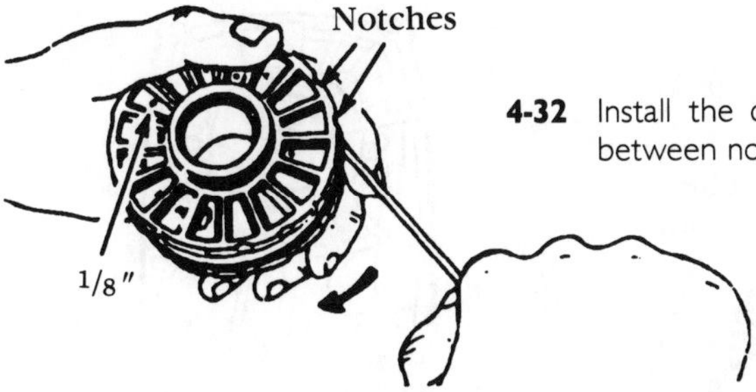

4-32 Install the cord, making sure the line is between notches as shown. Poulan / Weed Eater.

Replacing a broken starter rope Disconnect the spark plug before attempting to repair or replace a broken starter rope and recoil assembly. Remove the screw and nut from the throttle trigger housing. Remove the barrel end and cable from the throttle trigger. Carefully pull the throttle cable out of the foam grip. Loosen screws and remove the shaft housing from the clutch shroud (FIG 4-33). Remove the clutch shroud screws.

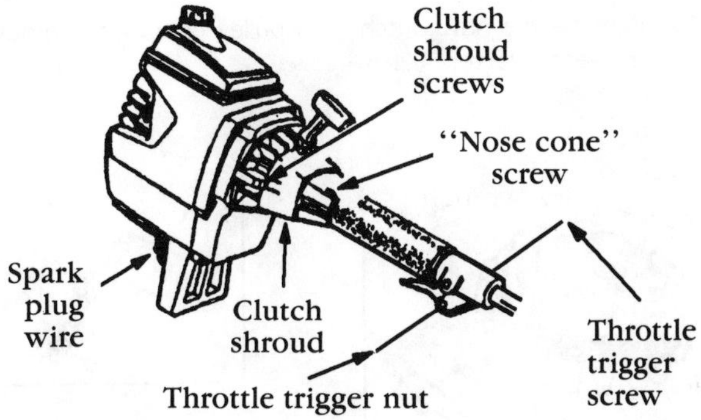

4-33 Remove the clutch shroud, throttle trigger nut, and nose cone to get at the recoil starter assembly. Poulan / Weed Eater.

Separate the clutch shroud from the engine. Slide the clutch off the crankshaft, but do not disengage the clutch. Remove the pulley housing from the engine (FIG. 4-34). Hold the pulley housing and turn the pulley clockwise as far as it will go until the pulley notch is aligned with the housing notch. Replace the rope with a 42-inch-long replacement rope (FIG. 4-35).

Use a match and melt both ends of the nylon rope. Insert one end of the rope through the handle and tie a knot. Insert the other end of the rope through the exit hole. Wrap the rope counterclockwise around the pulley ratchet. Hold the rope taut at the rope exit hole so the pulley will not move. Make sure the spacer is in place. Reverse the procedure to reassemble.

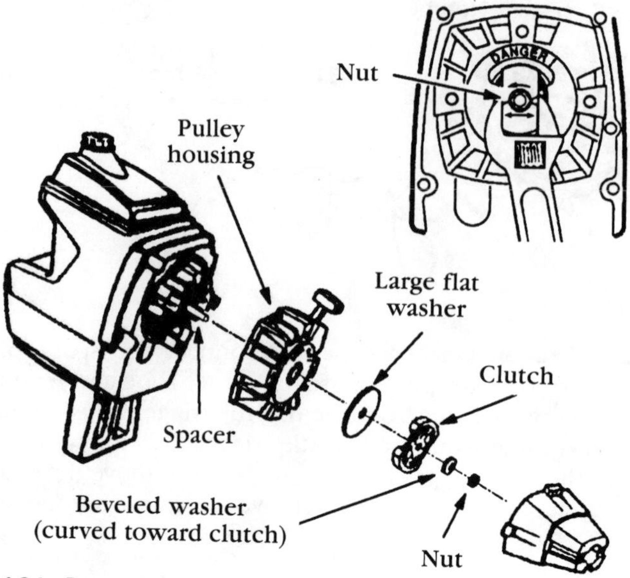

4-34 Remove the nut, clutch, and pulley housing to remove the recoil starter. Poulan / Weed Eater.

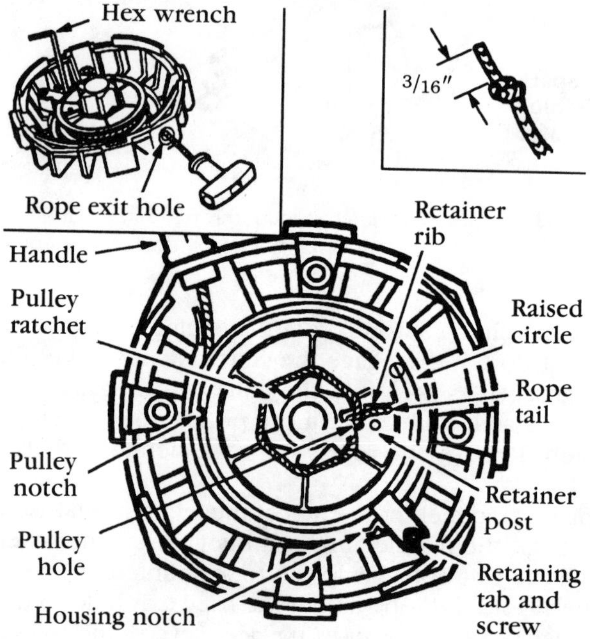

4-35 Wind a 42-inch rope around the pulley and retainer hub of the starter assembly. Poulan / Weed Eater.

Sharpening blades Disconnect spark plugs after engine quits rotating. The weed blade might be reversible. In this case, just turn the blade over when the cutting edge on one side becomes dull. Sharpen the blade when both sides are dull. Make sure the blade is flat before sharpening. If it is not flat, throw away the blade. Sharpen the edge with a small, three-corner or flat file. Touch up both sides when the blade is removed (FIG. 4-36).

4-36 File or grind down brush blade. Poulan / Weed Eater.

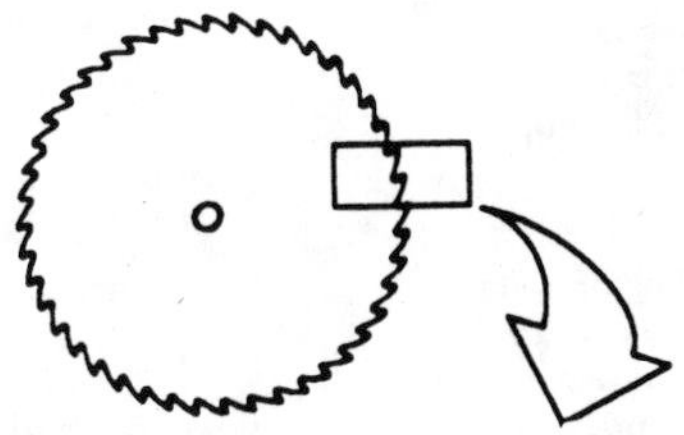

Sharpen the wide edge of the blade with a file. Sharpen only the tip area. File and grind down each area in the same manner so that the blade is balanced (FIG. 4-37). Wear protective gloves when handling brush or weed blades. Always replace a bent, warped, cracked, broken, or damaged blade. Check the troubleshooting chart in TABLE 4-3 for engine, line, and cutting problems.

4-37 File or grind down weed blade. Take off the same amount on each blade for balance. Poulan / Weed Eater.

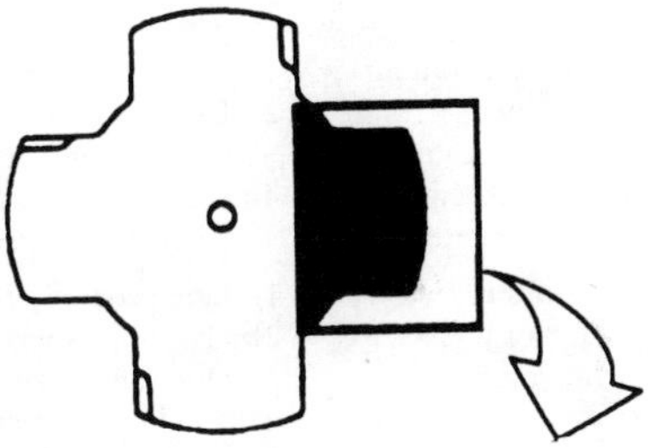

SHARPENING TOOLS

A dull saw blade can cause burned marks, slow feeding, and rough-cut edges. Dull blades are hard on all power equipment. Most tools can be sharpened with a flat file, stones, or a grinder. A grinder is particularly useful for larger surfaces.

Clean up tools after use and wipe off with an oil sock. Keep blades sharp and rust-free with a coat of wax or light oil. Grind down dull edges and finish up on a whetstone for a fine cutting edge.

Choose a Cant Safe back file for sharpening crosscut saws, circular saws, and saws with a 60-degree angle. An 8-inch round with a tapered body file is ideal for sharpening chain saws (FIG. 4-38).

Table 4-3 Troubleshooting engine, line, and cutting.

Symptom	*Cause*	*Remedy*
Engine will not start or will run only for a few seconds after starting.	1. Fuel tank empty. 2. Engine flooded. 3. Spark plug not firing. 4. Fuel not reaching carburetor. 5. Carburetor requires adjustment. 6. None of the above.	1. Fill tank with correct fuel mixture. 2. See "Starting Instructions." 3. Install new plug/check ignition system. 4. Clean fuel filter; inspect fuel line. 5. See "Carburetor Adjustments." 6. Contact your Service Dealer.
Engine will not idle properly.	1. Idle speed set too fast or too slow. 2. Low-speed mixture requires adjustment. 3. None of the above. 4. Throttle trigger screw too tight.	1. See "Carburetor Adjustments." 2. See "Carburetor Adjustments." 3. Contact an authorized service dealer. 4. See the "throttle cable" section.
Engine will not accelerate, lacks power or dies under a load.	1. Air filter dirty. 2. Spark plug fouled. 3. Carburetor requires adjustment. 4. Muffler outlets plugged. 5. None of the above.	1. Clean or replace air filter. 2. Clean or replace spark plug and re-gap. 3. See "Carburetor Adjustments." 4. Contact an authorized service dealer. 5. Contact an authorized service dealer.
Engine smokes excessively.	1. Air filter dirty. 2. Fuel mixture incorrect. 3. High-speed mixture requires adjustment.	1. Clean or replace air filter. 2. Refuel with correct fuel mixture. 3. See "Carburetor Adjustments."
Engine runs hot.	1. Fuel mixture incorrect. 2. High-speed mixture set too low (lean). 3. Spark plug incorrect. 4. None of the above.	1. See "Fueling Your Unit." 2. See "Carburetor Adjustments." 3. Replace with correct plug. 4. Contact an authorized service dealer.
Cutting attachment turns at idle speed.	1. Carburetor requires adjustment. 2. Throttle cable binding. 3. Clutch requires repair.	1. See "Carburetor Adjustments." 2. Contact an authorized service dealer. 3. Contact an authorized service dealer.
Cutting attachment stops under a load or does not turn when engine is accelerated.	1. Drive shaft not engaged. 2. Drive shaft broken. 3. Carburetor requires adjustment. 4. Clutch requires repair.	1. See the "Assembly," "Drive Shaft Housing." 2. Contact an authorized service dealer. 3. See "Carburetor Adjustments." 4. Contact an authorized service dealer.
Line does not advance or breaks while cutting.	1. Line properly routed in head. 2. Line improperly wound onto spool. 3. Line size incorrect. 4. Too little line outside head. 5. Dirt accumulated on cover cut-outs.	1. Remove cover. Check line routing. 2. Rewind line tightly and evenly. 3. Use only .080" line. 4. Remove cover. Pull 4" of line to outside. 5. Clean cover cut-outs.
Line welds on spool.	1. Line size incorrect. 2. Incorrect spool. 3. Crowding line against material being cut. 4. Cutting at higher speed than necessary.	1. Use only .080" line. 2. Use proper spool 3. Cut with tip of line. 4. Reduce cutting speed.
Line releases continuously.	1. Line improperly routed in head.	1. Remove cover. Check line routing.
Line use is excessive	1. Line improperly routed in head. 2. Line size incorrect. 3. Cutting at high speed around hard objects. 4. Crowding line against material being cut.	1. Remove cover. Check line routing. 2. Use only .080" line. 3. Reduce speed around hard objects. 4. Cut with tip of line.
Line pulls back	1. Too little line outside of head.	1. Remove cover. Pull 4" of line to outside.

Note: Many of these instructions under Remedy refers to the owner's manual.

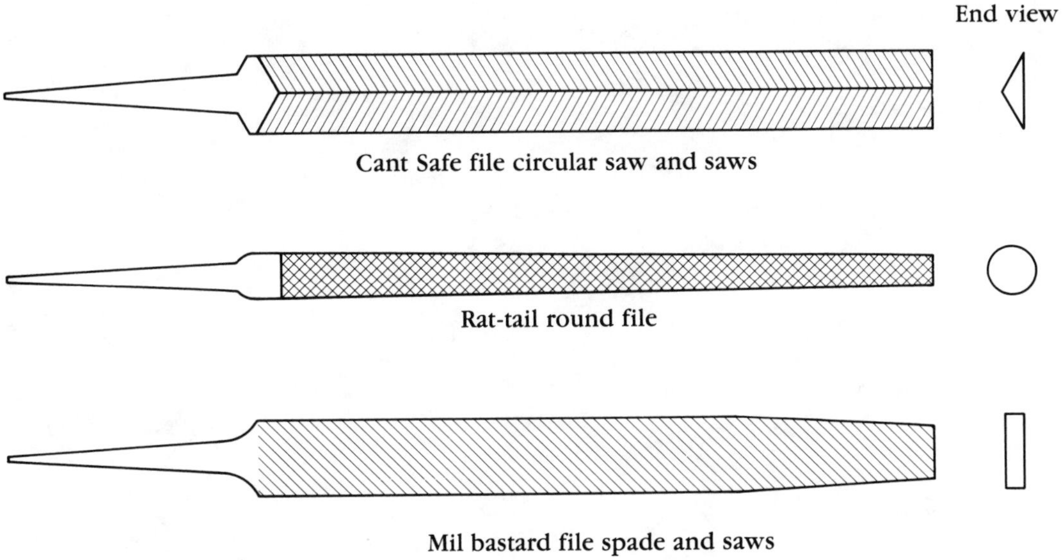

4-38 Three different inexpensive files can be used for sharpening saws.

Chapter 5

Servicing medium power garden and lawn equipment

Medium garden and lawn equipment would include large chipper/shredders, snowblowers, and lawn mowers. Power lawn and garden equipment is quite expensive, but it can last a lifetime if it is properly maintained and repaired. Proper lubrication, a few minutes of inspection before and after using, checking for loose components, and proper storage is all that is required. For specific information on servicing engines, see Part 2.

Power garden equipment can be dangerous if not operated properly. Always shut off the power equipment before removing clogged or jammed objects. Do not attempt any repairs until the unit is shut off. Avoid sharp tongs and blades by wearing a pair of gloves for safety. Do not attempt to maintain or repair any equipment until you have first read chapter 1 on safety. Always remove the spark plug or spark plug wire (if so equipped) from power equipment before attempting any service work.

PERIODIC INSPECTION

All power tools and garden/lawn equipment should have an annual check up and regular maintenance. The engine oil in a new mower, shredder, or tiller should be changed after the first five hours of operation. After that, change the oil every 25 hours of operation. The engine air filter should be checked every 25 hours. The spark plug should be inspected once a year along with regular annual maintenance. Periodically tighten mounting bolts on both engine and equipment, tiller blades, shredder, and mower blades.

Check small portable power tools for excessive firing at the brushes. If brushes are worn down, drip oil down on the armature. Check the commutator for excessive dust. Inspect the AC cord for broken or bent prongs. Make sure that the grounding prong is still intact.

Periodic cleanup helps keep power tools running longer. Brush out all dirt and dust from the motor housing of power tools then suck it up with a shop vacuum. Wash the plastic housing of power tools with soap and water. Scrape off all old chipped paint. Scrub and clean off all rust areas. A touch up with spray paint prevents rust and can make a power tool look like new again.

Just about any lawn, garden, or power tool will rust if left in a damp basement, garage, or outdoors. The way to protect valuable equipment is by keeping them clean, lubricated and maintained.

LAWN MOWERS

Before operating any power lawn mower, check for loose nuts and bolts. Check the engine oil level and gas level. If you are unsure of the proper fuel or oil mixture you should be using for the climate and temperature you are operating the equipment in, check the owner's manual or read chapter 2 on general lubrication and fuel requirements. Remember, never attempt any service work on a lawn mower or tip the lawn mower over without first removing the spark plug.

It is important to keep the mower clean after each use and before it is put in storage (FIG. 5-1). Do not attempt to clean or store the unit until it has cooled off. Never store the mower with fuel in the tank. Fuel left sitting for a period of time develops a film that can clog fuel lines and hamper the operation of the unit. Remove the spark plug wire before tipping the motor and cleaning and checking the blade.

5-1 Clean up underneath the blade after each use.

The spark plug

Always remove the spark plug with the correct tool and inspect the tip of the spark plug. If the tip is gray, ignition is normal. Replace the plug if it is excessively white and corroded, the points are burned, or it's cracked. Set the spark plug gap according to the manufacturers operations manual.

An improper carburetor setting or a damaged fuel diaphragm or line can cause a plug to overheat and turn white. An improper fuel mixture in a two-cycle engine can also cause overheated spark plugs. If the plug is dark and wet, suspect an overfilled oil level, worn rings, clogged air filter, or improper idle adjustment. Often, replacing the suspected spark plug solves engine starting and running problems.

Air filters

Remove and inspect oil filters for excessive dirt. Always check the oil filter each time the oil is changed. Replace dry element air cleaners if they are dirty or damaged. Remove oil foam filters, wash out with cleaning fluid, and dip foam in clean oil. Metallic mesh air cleaners can be cleaned with a solvent, dipped in engine oil, and replaced. Polyurethane air filters can be washed in detergent and water. Dry polyurethane elements thoroughly and apply a light coat of motor oil on the face of the element.

The carburetor

Clean up around the carburetor and gas line. If the mower has a sediment bowl, remove it and dump any debris. Inspect the carburetor for dirt when the top air filter is removed. Don't mess with the carburetor adjustments unless it is not running properly. Follow the manufacturers engine carburetor settings (see Part 2).

Fuel tank

Inspect the fuel tank for grimy material at the bottom of the tank. Remove the gas line to the carburetor and wash out the tank with a solvent or carburetor cleaner or lacquer thinner. While the line is disconnected, blow out the line from the tank to the gas line. If the gas tank has been drained every fall before storage or STAY-BUILT has been added to the tank, very little deposits should be found in the gas tank. Reassemble and tighten up all connections at the tank and carburetor.

Minor repairs

Most lawn mower breakdowns are related to the engine and moving parts. Part 2 provides more detailed instructions for engine maintenance and repairs. How to keep the mower operating, repairing blade problems, lubricating wheels, adjusting lever controls, and repairing loose components are covered in this chapter. How to adjust the cutting height, the drive clutch control, sprocket, and belt drive systems are also given.

Throttle control repairs The throttle control controls the engine speed and is located on the handle of most mowers. Often, after several years, the control might not shut off the motor or increase the speed. Check for slippage in the control itself or where it connects on the throttle lever. Inspect for a loose cable clamp screw, letting the outside shield move with the internal wire. Readjust the speed and tighten the screw so when the lever is down, it will shut off the engine (FIG. 5-2).

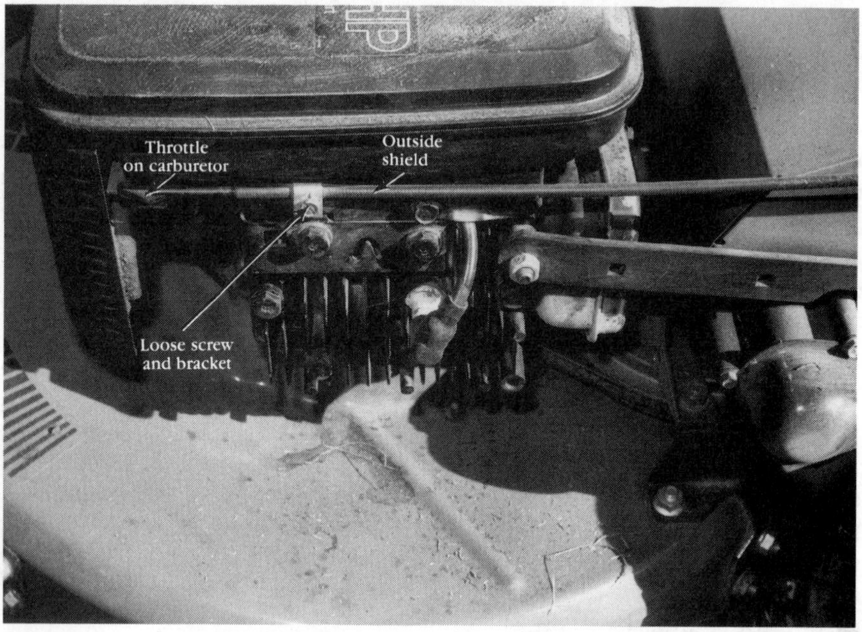

5-2 When the engine will not shut off or you can't adjust for the correct speed, check for a loose metal screw holding the throttle wire.

Engine runs—no forward motion If the engine runs but there is no forward motion, suspect a defective drive clutch control assembly, improper drive adjustment, or excessive grass and weeds in the clutch assembly. Remove the cover to get at the clutch, drive pulley, or wheel drive shaft assembly (FIGS. 5-3 and 5-4). Clean out any dirt, mud, or grass from the assembly. Inspect the drive belt for slippage, breakage, or an enlarged belt or chain. Lubricate drive wheel and pulley bearings with a light oil. Check the rear wheel gear assembly for dry or broken parts.

No forward speed adjustment If there is no forward speed adjustment, inspect the speed adjustment rod that sets the forward pulley speed. Notice if the rod is out of the speed lever. Check for a missing cotter pin (FIG. 5-5). If the lever seems stuck, remove the lock nut from the top plate and move the lever by hand. Grease the large pivot bearing. In the Ariens mower in FIG. 5-6, the sliding bar indicates the forward speed.

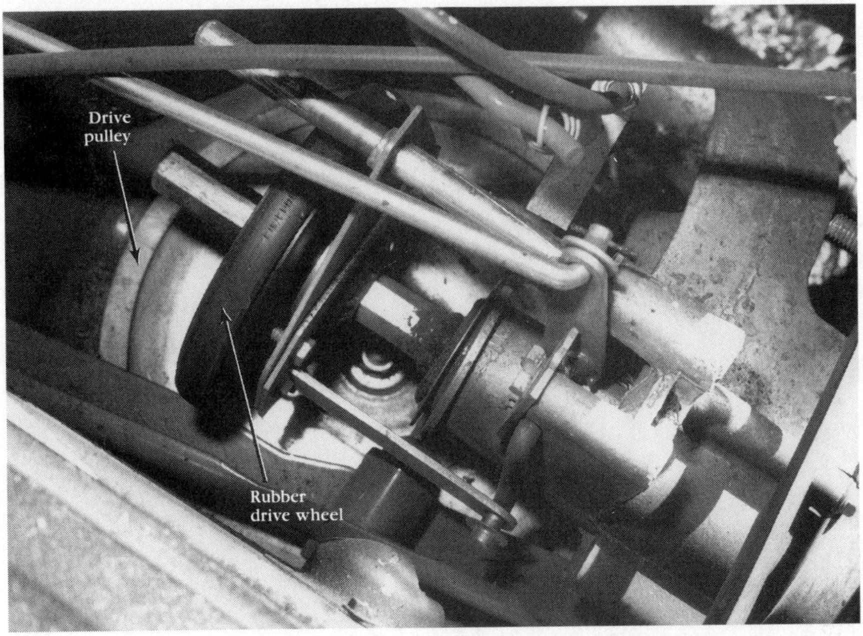

5-3 Excess grass and weeds in the large rotating clutch can prevent a unit from moving.

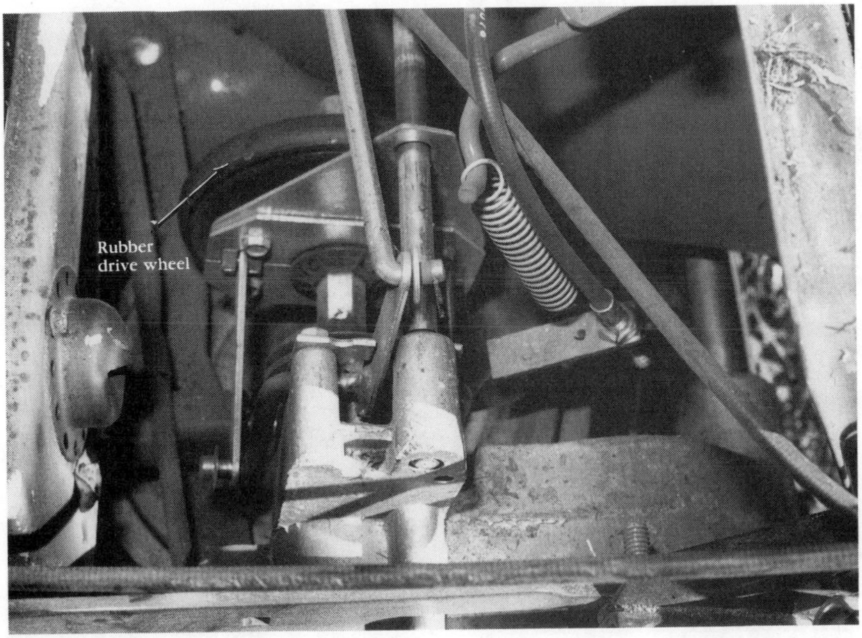

5-4 For no forward motion, remove the back cover to check the rear shifting gears or rubber wheel.

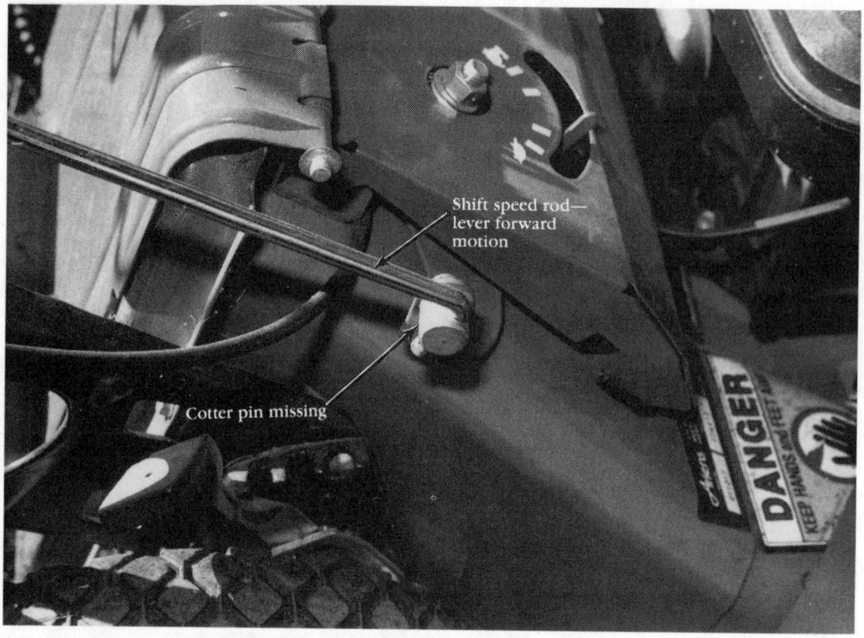

5-5 Notice the cotter pin is missing on this speed forward lever. The speed can't be varied if the rod slips out.

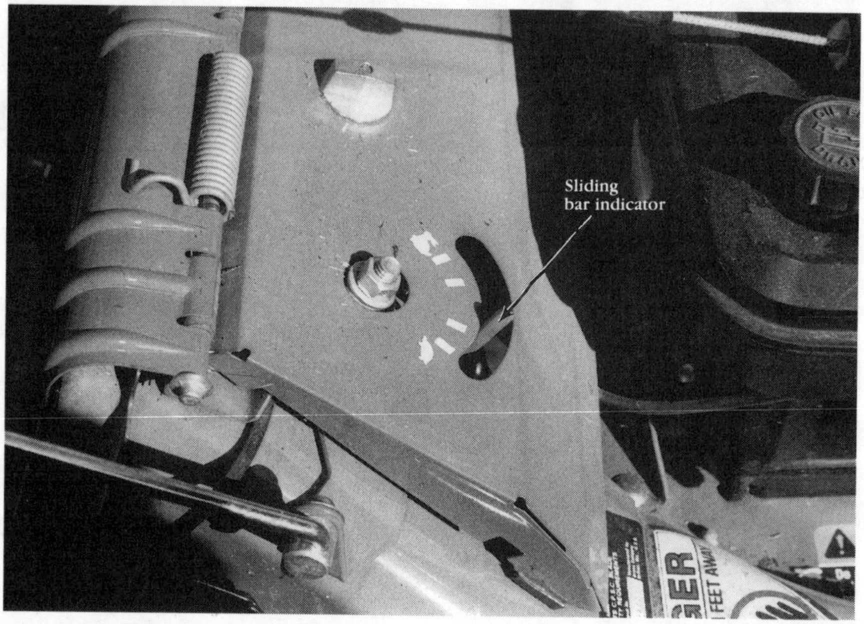

5-6 The sliding bar indicates the forward speed in this Ariens self-propelled lawn mower.

Lock bar does not pull downward When the safety bar is pulled upward and held in place to keep the engine and mower operating, a heavy spring pulls down the bar to shut off all engine and mower action. If the spring slips out or the spring end is broken, the safety bar will not pull down and stay in the OFF position. Inspect the lever for bent areas, a missing spring, or a broken lever.

Improper front wheel adjustment If the front wheels will not raise the wheel and lock into position, suspect a loose bolt or nut. Check for a loose assembly. Some of these bolts are so tightly fitted between the wheel and lock assembly, a single end wrench is needed to tighten up the assembly. Temporarily tie the adjustment arm with a stiff wire to finish the mowing job. Then, either remove the entire assembly and repair, or hunt up the required wrench.

Poor rear wheel adjustment The adjusting plate and thumb lever at each wheel position allows the cutting height to be adjusted. Each adjusting plate has 5 or 6 slots. The height is changed when the thumb lever is moved from one slot to the next. Check the adjustment lever when the rear wheel jumps out of the selected height position. Suspect a loose lever nut or bolt (FIG. 5-7).

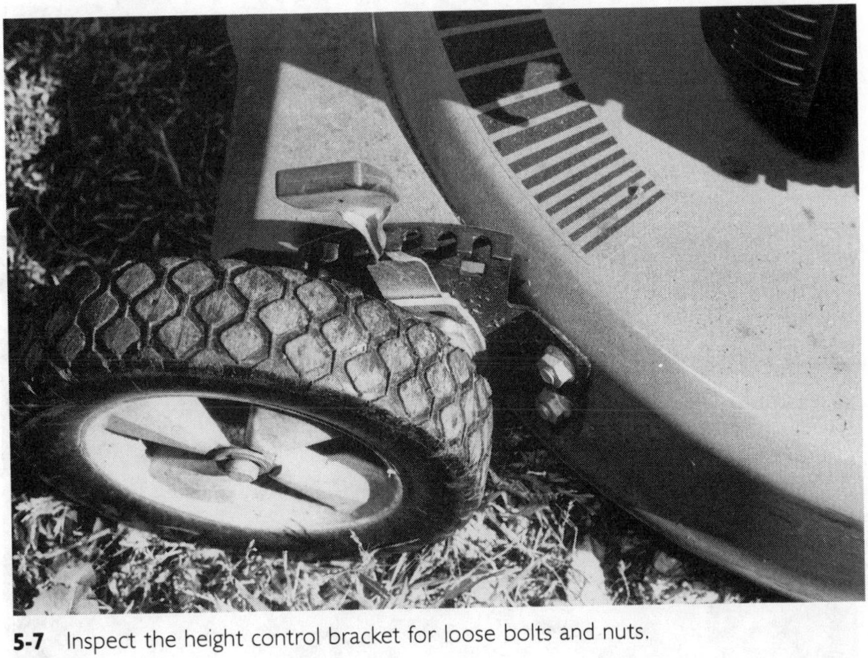

5-7 Inspect the height control bracket for loose bolts and nuts.

Poor blade cutting Improper cutting or tearing of the grass indicates a very dull mower blade. Suspect a dull blade when mower pulls down when making small lawn cuts. The blades of grass might turn while after several days of cutting. Remove the spark plug wire and inspect the mower blade (FIG. 5-8). Remove the center bolt holding the blade to the engine shaft. Some mower blades are attached with two hex nuts and washers with another center bolt. These bolts should be inspected periodically for correct tightness. Use the correct wrench or socket to prevent bolt head damage. Sharpen and balance the blade on a grinder or with a file (FIG. 5-9). Always sharpen the mower blade at the start of the mowing season or just before fall storage.

5-8 Remove the spark plug wire before removing the lawn mower blade.

5-9 Stick a screwdriver blade through the hole in the blade to see if it is balanced. Grind out all large dents and nicks on both sides.

Sharpening mower blades

Before beginning to mow grass in the spring, check the mower blade for sharpness. Inspect the blade each month for deep nicks or dull edges (FIG. 5-10). Reel-type mowers should be inspected annually. If the blade is dull, take it to a professional or do it yourself. If you have a good flat file or grinder, you are in business (FIG. 5-11).

5-10 Take out any nicks on the edge of the mower blade.

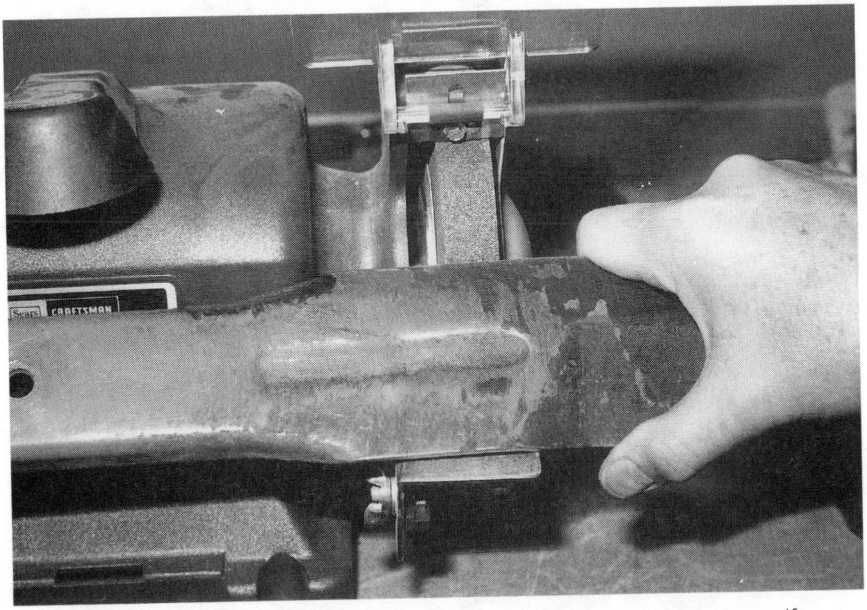

5-11 Either take the dull blade to a professional or sharpen the blade yourself.

Before replacing the mower blade, clean out all excess dirt and debris from around and above the mower blade (FIG. 5-12). Matted grass and excessive dirt seems to stick to the underside of mowers. Scrape off residue with a putty knife. Brush off dirt with a large old paint brush. Binding twine, rope, and soft wire can find its way around mower blades. Make sure the blade bolt or nut is tight before turning the mower over. Always remove the spark plug wire before turning the mower over. Tape it off to the side. It's best to remove the blade so that motor will not start up when removing the old blade. When removing and replacing the mower blade, wear a pair of gloves for protection.

5-12 Clean matted grass and dirt above the mower blade. Make sure the spark plug wire or plug is removed.

First, remove the blade nut, placing it somewhere where it will not get lost. The nut tightens as the blade rotates, so remove the nut in the opposite direction of blade rotation. Select the correct socket wrench to remove the bolt holding the blade shaft (FIG. 5-13). Do not use a pair of pliers. You can easily skin up a few knuckles and damage the unit.

If you will be doing your own sharpening, touch up the mower blade with a bench grinder. Small nicks can be ground out with a bench grinder. Be careful to take off the same amount on both sides so that the blade is balanced. An improperly balanced blade can cause excessive vibration and damage to the power mower. The blade balance can be checked by placing a screwdriver blade through the mounting hole. If the blade is balanced, it is level.

5-13 Remove and replace the mower blade after removing the spark plug wire with the correct socket wrench.

Be careful not to apply too much pressure with a bench grinder. Make an even cut along the front of the blade. Be careful not to overheat the blade and burn the cutting edge. If black spots or rough edges appear, the metal edge is overheating. Dip the blade end into a pail of water to keep it cool between cuts. Do not ruin the temper of the metal cutting edge. It's best to make a light angle cut several times than making one large cut that might overheat the blade.

Usually, a small flat file can quickly touch up blades with a little even pressure. Place the blade in a vise so it's easily filed. Do not round off the cutting edge. Make a sharp edge towards the top edge of the mower blade. If the blade is extremely worn, replace it with the exact part number or one that is made for your mower. After the blade is sharpened and balanced, check for bent areas. The blade should be bent exactly the same at both ends. If the blade is bent or badly nicked, install a new blade.

SHREDDERS/CHIPPERS

Shredders/chippers dispose of waste material and turn yard waste into rich compost for the garden and lawn. Small shredders process leaves and light garden waste while larger machines have a chipper element that pulverizes limbs, prunings, and brush material. Smaller machines might operate from a power line and bigger units from large HP engines (FIG. 5-14).

The chipper might have hardened steel blades or knives on one side of a flywheel to eat up small limbs. Most blades can be removed and

5-14 A 5 HP Briggs & Stratton engine powers this portable chipper/shredder.

sharpened. Always remove the spark plug wire or pull the AC cord before adjusting or working on a shredder. If the shredder becomes jammed, shut off the engine and remove the spark plug wire.

The air filter

Like the tiller, shredder/chipper air cleaners should be checked after every 15 to 25 hours of use. Clean and wipe up dirt and dust around the air cleaner assembly, carburetor, and gas tank. Remove the air cleaner from the carburetor and wash it out. Wash out the foam cleaner in detergent and water. Dry thoroughly and dip in light oil. Notice the center screw hole inside the throat of the carburetor for the air cleaner mounting screw. Carburetor adjustment screws are found underneath the air cleaner on this 5 HP shredder engine.

The muffler

Remove the muffler just before storage time and clean off with a steel wire brush. Inspect the metal area for cracks or split metal seams. Often, the opening end piece of the exhaust (tail pipe) goes to pieces after several seasons. Small holes and cracks can be temporarily filled with auto muffler repair kits. If the muffler is damaged, replace it.

Loose bolts and shields

Most shredder/chipper machines make a lot of noise and vibrate excessively. This vibration can loosen nuts and bolts, shields, and covers.

Check for loose bolts and shields after shredding a lot of material. Inspect the shredding screen assembly. Before leaving the field, remove the shredding screen and clean out. Wipe off all loose dust that might cling to the sides of the shredder.

If the machine makes any unusual noise or vibrating, stop the engine, disconnect the spark plug wire from the spark plug, and allow the engine to cool before inspecting for damage. Check for loose parts, bolts, rods, and broken hammers or spacers. Visually examine the rotor for possible defects.

Lubrication

Lubricate the shredder/chipper side rotor bearing before operating and after every 10 hours of operation with a multipurpose grease. The belt-side bearing on the Mighty Mac Shredder is self-lubricating and requires no greasing. Check the bearing collar set screws regularly to be sure they are tight. If loose, reset them with EV-grade Loctite or equivalent.

If the hard steel hammer becomes dull or round on the cutting or leading edge, it can be reversed. Remove the belt guard. Remove the round cover plate to access the hammer rods. Each rod is held in place by a grooved pin. Use extreme care to reinstall the spacers in exactly the same order.

When the steel chipping knife needs replacing or sharpening, rotate the chipper disc until the three countersunk screws holding the blade are behind the access panel. Apply EV-grade Loctite on the threads so the knives don't come loose.

When sharpening the blade, be careful to maintain the correct level and a straight cutting edge. Check the clearance between the knife and the wear plate when installing a knife. This clearance or gap should be minimum 3/64 inch, maximum 1/16 inch (FIG. 5-15). To adjust the clearance,

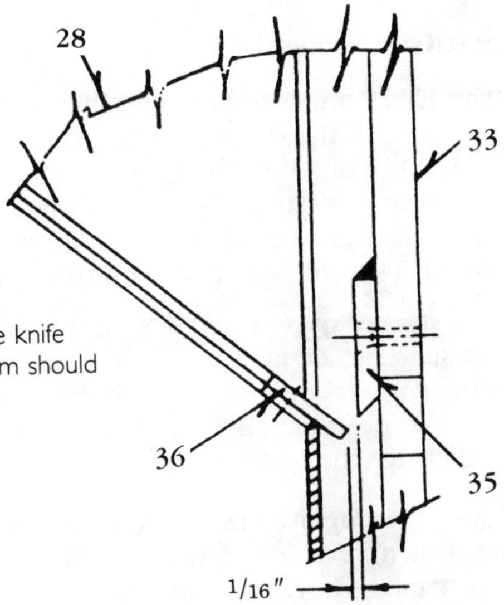

5-15 Check the clearance between the knife and wear plate (36). The minimum should be 3/64 of an inch. MacKissic Inc.

loosen the three, 1/4-inch flat head bolts located on the outside of the chipper wear plate next to the chipper side plate. Move the wear plate in or out as necessary and tighten the 1/4-inch nuts securely.

If the gap between the wear plate and knife is excessive, the unit will vibrate when chipping and the blade will appear dull.

If the chipper must be disassembled for repairs, the chipping disc must be installed in its exact position on the shaft (FIG. 5-16). Notice the 5/16-inch distance between the snap ring and the flywheel.

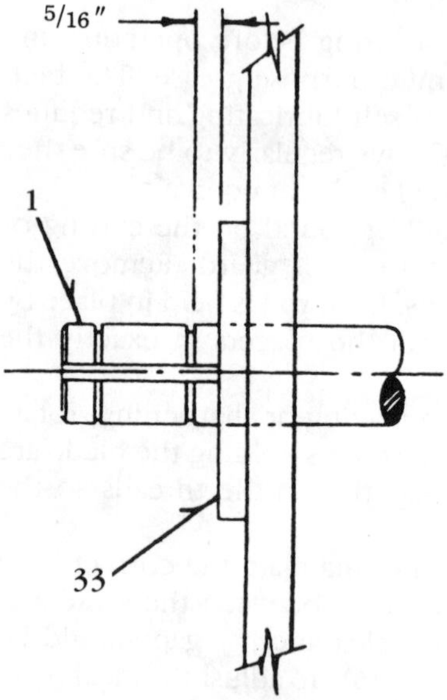

5-16 The distance should be no more than 5/16 inch between the knife and the flywheel. MacKissic Inc.

MacKissic model 12PE7 and 12PTE shredder

The 12PE7 and 12PT5 model shredder/chipper can be started with a battery or with the recoil rope starter. The battery can be charged overnight with a 12-volt, 4- to 6-amp trickle charger. Let the engine run 45 minutes to charge the battery. Add electrolytic to the 12-volt battery or have an auto service center charge the battery. Figure 5-17 shows the parts layout for a 12P-5 and 8-HP unit with the parts list (FIG. 5-18).

The starter system Make sure the battery is fully charged. Do not allow the starter to crank for long periods of time. Recheck the starting wiring if the engine won't turn over. If the battery is not charged, place the key in the RUN position, choke and pull the recoil starter rope to start the engine and charge the battery.

The centrifugal clutch The centrifugal 3/4-inch clutch is permanently lubricated. If the drum wobbles excessively, replace the bushing. Replace any damaged screws. Always replace the shoes and springs in pairs.

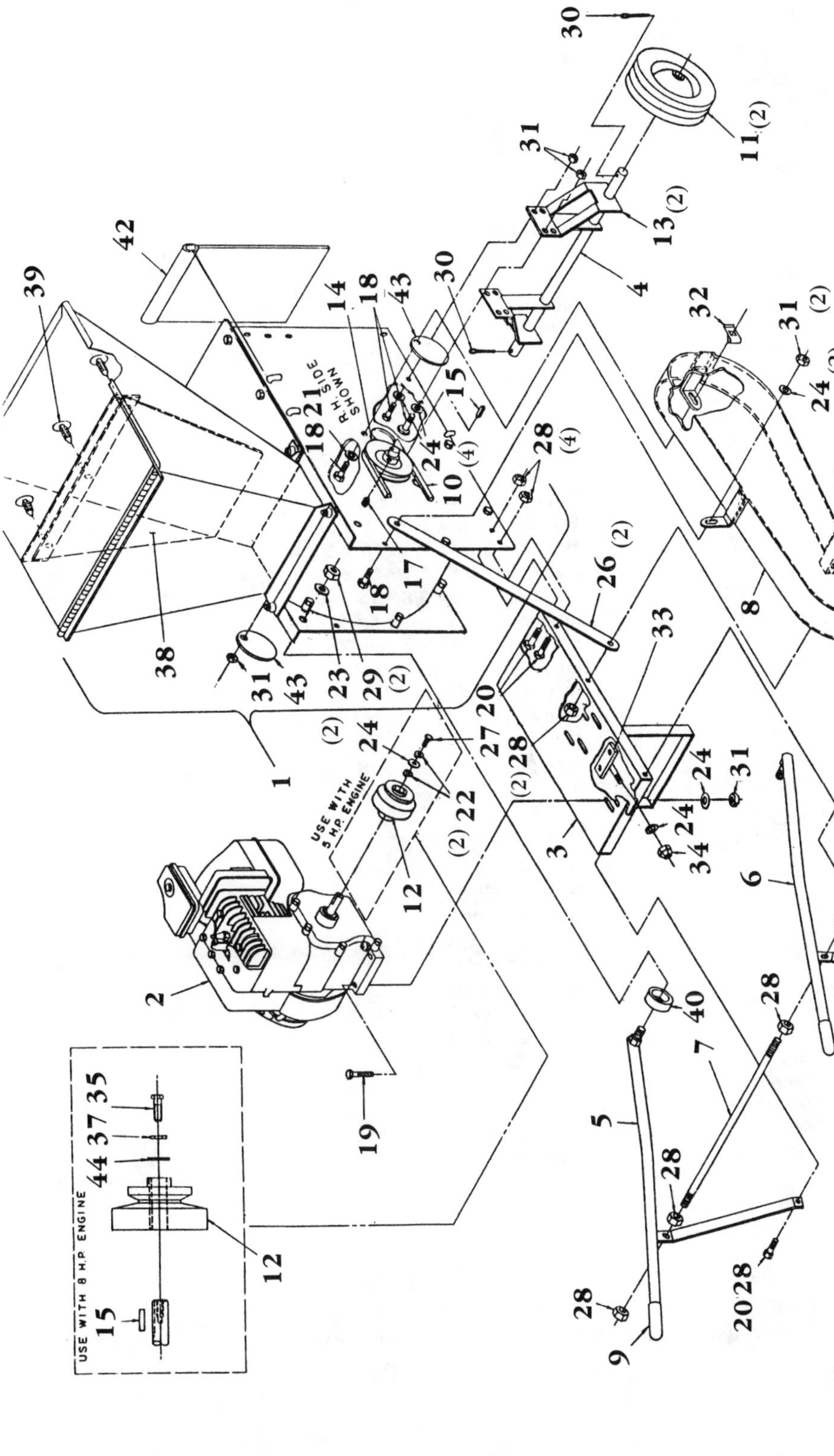

5-17 Parts layout of 12P shredder/chipper. MacKissic Inc.

Item No.	Part No.	Description	Quantity 12P5	Quantity 12P8
1	900-0094	Basic Shredder-Chipper	1	1
2	030-0075	8 H.P. Engine	0	1
	508-0017	5 H.P. Engine	1	0
3	908-0038	Engine Base	1	1
4	908-0048	Axle, Rear	1	1
5	908-0036	Handle, Left	1	1
6	908-0037	Handle, Right	1	1
7	908-0006	Handle Tie Rod	1	1
8	900-0102	Belt Guard	1	1
9	500-0041	Grip	2	2
10	030-0145	Belt	1	0
	030-0144	Belt	0	1
11	703-0012	Wheel	2	2
12	030-0110	Clutch 3/4" Bore	1	0
	030-0077	Clutch 1" Bore	0	1
13	908-0060	Axle Bracket	2	2
14	030-0127	Rotor Pulley	1	1
15	500-0031	Shaft Key - 1/4 x 1/4 x 1	1	2
17	080-0053	Set Screw 5/16-18 x 5/16	1	1
18	090-0066	Hex Cap Screw 5/16-18 x 3/4	8	8
19	090-0071	Hex Cap Screw 5/16-18 x 1 3/4	4	0
	090-0072	Hex Cap Screw 5/16-18 x 2	0	4
20	090-0098	Hex Cap Screw 3/8-16 x 3/4	6	6
21	090-0224	Internal Lock Washer 5/16	8	8
22	090-0392	5/16" Split Lock Washer Pltd.	2	0
23	090-0220	Internal Lock Washer 5/8	2	2
24	090-0233	Flat Washer 5/16	12	11
25	090-0234	Flat Washer 3/8	2	2
26	908-0008	Brace	2	2
27	090-0408	5/16-24 x 3/4" Hex Head Cap Screw GR5 Pltd.	1	0
28	090-0042	3/8-16 Grip-Co Lock Nut	12	12
29	090-0210	Hex Nut 5/8	2	2
30	090-0247	Cotter Pin 1/8 x 1 1/4	2	2
31	090-0048	Grip-Co Lock Nut 5/16-18	11	11
32	090-0438	5/16-18 J-Nut, Plain	1	1
33	500-0057	Belt Tensioner	1	1
34	090-0032	Flex Lock Nut 5/16	1	1
35	090-0152	Hex Cap Screw 7/16-20 x 3/4	0	1
36	090-0010	Hex Head Cap Screw 3/8-16 x 1	2	2
37	090-0226	Internal Lock Washer 7/16	0	1
38	900-0073	Hopper Flex-Guard	1	1
39	800-0026	Push Button	3	3
40	900-0103	Handle Spacer	0	1
42	900-0010	Baffle Plate	1	1
43	900-0040	Cover Plate	1	1
44	090-0244	Flatwasher 7/16	0	1

5-18 Parts list for 12P 5 and 8 HP shredder/chipper. MacKissic Inc.

Whenever shoes are changed, replace both the springs. Remove and replace each component as it comes off the shaft (FIG. 5-19).

If the 314-inch clutch assembly has the same symptoms, replace the same parts. To reassemble, be sure to position the shoes correctly on the

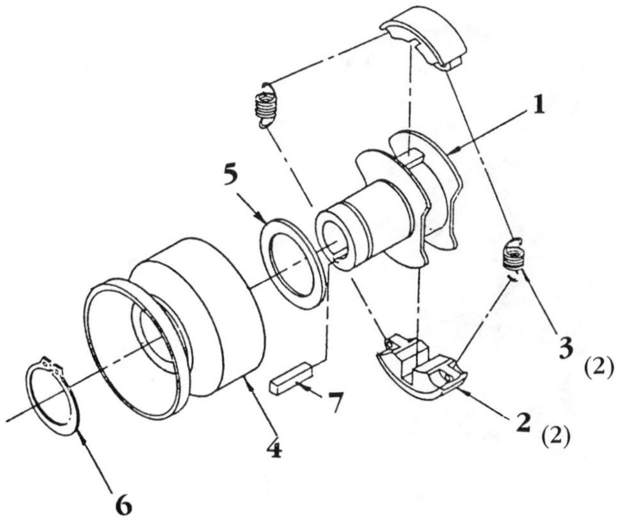

Key No.	Part No.	Description	Quantity
1	030-0158	Hub assembly	1
2	030-0159	Shoe	2
3	030-0156	Spring	2
4	030-0157	Drum assembly	1
5	030-0082	Washer	1
6	030-0083	Retaining ring	1
7	100-0018	Shaft key	1

5-19 Clutch parts and layout for 3/4-inch bore 3 and 5 HP engines.
MacKissic Inc.

hub for required rotation. Place one end of each spring over a shoe pin, then stretch the spring to the clear pin on the other shoe. Replace the fiber washer on the hub shaft. Reassemble the drum to the hub and secure the retaining spring. Locate the key in the keyway of the hub. Slide the clutch onto the crankshaft, then install the spacers or washer. Tighten set screws or cap screws.

Crary Bear Cat chipper/shredder

Tighten all bolts on the Crary Bear Cat shredder/chipper to 20 feet pound torque. As with other shredders/chippers, the Bear Cat is prone to heavy vibration. Inspect the shredder/chipper before each use to ensure that all bolts, nuts, and screws are tight (FIG. 5-20).

The cutting blade Sharpen the cutting blade before mowing each spring. Unscrew screw 1 for model 520 or the two screws for model 720. Sharpen knife edges and balance the blade. Keep the rotary-mower lubricated. Periodically check the oil level through vent plug F, and fill up using SAE 90 oil.

Crary Co.

5-20 The crazy Bear Cat chipper/shredder.

Maintenance

Pull the spark plug wire before servicing or unclogging the chipper/shredder. Check engine oil recommended by the engine manufacturer. Keep chipper knives sharp. It is recommended that chipper knives be sharpened every 5 to 15 hours of chipper operation.

To remove chipping knives for sharpening, remove the discharge screen. Remove the 5/16-inch retaining bolt and pull the screen outward. Rotate the rotor so that the bolt holding the chipping knife is most accessible. Remove the two 5/16-inch bolts holding the knife and the knife itself. Repeat for the second knife.

Regrind the angled edge of the chipping knife to 45 degrees (FIG. 5-21). Grind down on a bench grinder or have a professional do it. Be careful not to let the blade get too hot and change color. Use short grinding times and cool the knife in water as it overheats. Replace the blades and tighten to 20 ft lbs. Replace the discharge screen.

The shredder knife sections can be reversed if they become dull. Remove the rotor from the assembly. Remove the lower belt guard. Slip the drive belt off the pulley. Loosen the set screws on the rotor pulley hub. Remove the bearing lock collar, and loosen the set screw. Using a hammer and punch, slightly tap the collar so that it rotates and releases from the bearing. Repeat for the front bearing.

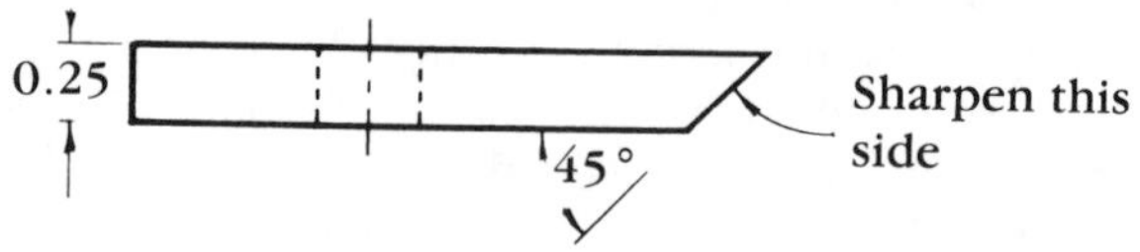

5-21 Sharpen knives at a 45-degree angle.
Crary Co.

Remove the eight nylock nuts that hold the front cover/chipper chute on and remove the cover. Pull the rotor assembly out of the housing. Working one shaft at a time, remove the bolt and nut from the shaft. Push the knife shaft out of the rotor assembly and remove the knife spacers (FIG. 5-22). Keep track of how many spacers and in what order they are removed. Reverse the knife sections and reassemble to the shafts using the second hole in the section. Reinstall the rotor by reversing. Reinstall the drive belt and tighten the engine mounting bolts.

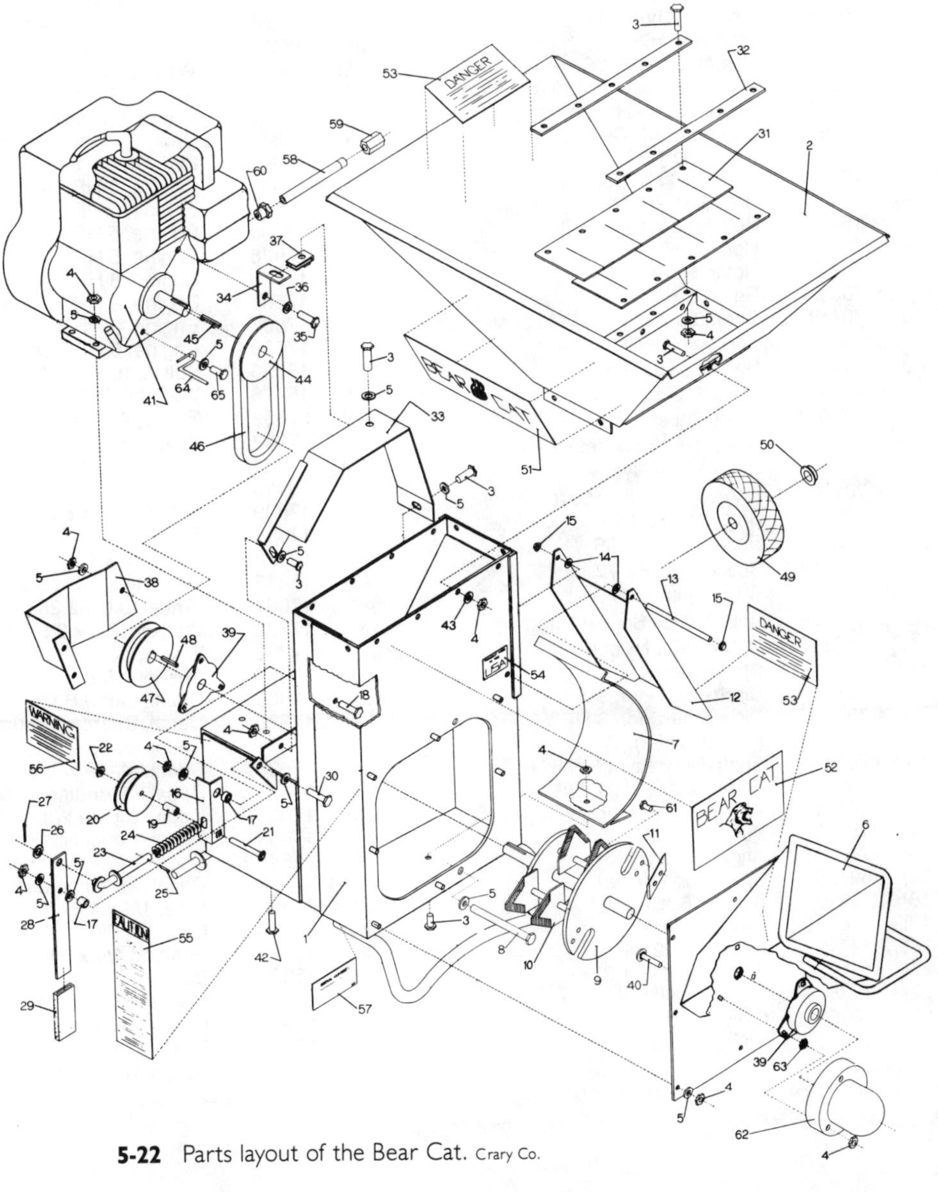

5-22 Parts layout of the Bear Cat. Crary Co.

No.	Part No.	Description	Qty.
1)	70196	Shredder Frame, 3HP	1
	70197	Shredder Frame, 5HP	1
	70198	Shredder Frame, 8HP	1
		(Includes #55 & 56)	
2)	70191	Hopper, 3 HP	1
	70192	Hopper, 5 HP	1
	70193	Hopper, 8 HP	1
		(Includes #53)	
3)	15003	Bolt, 5/16 x 3/4	26
4)	15356	Nut, 5/16 Nylock	47
5)	15416	Washer, 5/16 SAE Flat	25
6)	70190	Chipper Chute, 3 HP	1
	70189	Chipper Chute, 5 & 8 HP	1
		(Includes #53)	
7)	70095	Screen 3 & 5 HP Coarse	1
	(SN 3-3500 & Under, SN 5-4450 & Under)		
	70310	Screen 3 & 5 HP Coarse ,	1
	70097	Screen, 8 HP Coarse	1
	(SN 8-4175 & Under)		
	70301	Screen, 8 HP Coarse	1
8)	15407	Bolt, 5/16 x 7-1/2 (5 HP)	2
	15408	Bolt, 5/16 x 10 (8 HP)	2
9)	70044	Rotor, 3 HP	1
	70277	Rotor, 5 HP	1
	70062	Rotor, 8 HP	1
10)	70119	Shredder Kit, 3 & 5 HP consists of:	1
	70047	Shredder Section*	16
	70115	Spacer, .75 x 1.55	4
	70114	Spacer, .75 x 2.45	4
	70031	Shaft, knife	4
	17898	Bolt, #10-24 Socket Head	4
	15397	Nut, #10-24 Nylock	4
	70120	Shredder Kit, 8 HP consists of:	1
	70047	Shredder Section*	24
	70115	Spacer, .75 x 1.55	8
	70116	Spacer, .75 x 2.77	4
	70064	Shaft, knife	4
	17898	Bolt, #10-24 Socket Head	4
	15397	Nut, #10-24 Nylock	4
11)	70121	Chipper Knives (Set of 2)	1
12)	70194	Discharge Door, 3 & 5 HP	1
	70195	Discharge Door, 8 HP	1
		(Includes #53)	
13)	70087	Shaft, Door Pivot 3 & 5 HP	1
	70088	Shaft, Door Pivot 8 HP	1
14)	15409	Washer, 5/16 Nylon Flat	2
15)	15411	Pushnut, 5/16	2
16)	70038	Angle, Clutch Pivot	1
17)	69126	Spacer, Idler Pivot	2
18)	15219	Bolt, 5/16 X 1	1
19)	70046	Spacer,Idler	1
20)	17740	Pulley, 3-1/2 Idler	1
21)	15102	Bolt, 3/8 x 2-3/4 CRG	1
22)	15388	Nut, 3/8 Nylock	1
23)	70068	Clutch Rod	1
24)	17833	Spring, Clutch	1

No.	Part No.	Description	Qty.
25)	15354	Roll Pin, 5/32 x 3/4	1
26)	15097	Washer, 1/2 SAE Flat	1
27)	15375	Cotter Pin, 1/8 x 1	1
28)	70040	Arm, Clutch Engagment	1
29)	17524	Grip, Clutch Arm	1
30)	15436	Bolt, 5/16 x 1-1/4	1
31)	70070	Guard, Shedder Inlet 3 & 5 HP	2
	70071	Guard, Shedder Inlet 8 HP	2
32)	70069	Strip, Guard Retaining	2
33)	70078	Belt Guard, Upper	1
34)	70082	Angle, 3 HP Guard Support	1
	70254	Angle, 5 HP Guard Support	1
	70256	Angle, 8 HP Guard Support	1
35)	15413	Bolt, 1/2 x 3/4 NF	1
36)	15097	Washer, 1/2 SAE Flat	1
37)	15402	Nut, 5/16 Tinnerman	1
38)	70083	Guard, Lower Belt	1
39)	17831	Bearing, 1 inch flushmount	2
40)	15301	Bolt, 5/16 x 1 CRG	6
41)	17864	Engine, 3 HP B&S	1
	17825	Engine, 5 HP B&S	1
	17860	Engine, 5 HP B&S I/C	1
	17928	Engine, 5 HP Honda	1
	17826	Engine, 8 HP B&S	1
	17861	Engine, 8 HP B&S I/C	1
	17862	Engine, 8 HP B&S Elec. Start	1
	17930	Engine, 8 HP Honda	1
42)	15250	Bolt. 5/16 x 1-3/4	4
43)	15416	Washer, 5/16 Flat	12
44)	17959	Pulley, 4 x 3/4 B (3 & 5 HP)	1
	17958	Pulley, 4 x 1 B (8 HP)	1
45)	15434	Key, 3/16 x 1-1/2 Sq. (3 & 5 HP)	1
	15418	Key, 1/4 x 1-1/2 Sq. (8 HP)	1
46)	17829	Belt, 5L27 (3 & 5 HP)	1
	17830	Belt, 5L29 (8 HP)	1
47)	17828	Pulley, 4 x 1 B	1
48)	15418	Key, 1/4 x 1 1/2 Sq.	1
49)	17867	Wheel, 8.0 x 2.25 (3 HP)	2
	17832	Wheel, 10.5 x 3.5 turf (5 & 8 HP)	2
	17892	Wheel, 10.5 x 3.5 (I/C)	2
50)	15406	Pushnut, 5/8	2
51)	17835	Decal, Large Bearcat	2
52)	17836	Decal, Bearcat Picture	1
53)	17837	Decal, Danger	3
54)	17838	Decal, Made in USA	1
55)	17846	Decal, Operating Instructions	1
56)	17851	Decal, Clutch Warning	1
57)	17868	Decal, Serial Number 3 HP	1
	17847	Decal, Serial Number 5 HP	1
	17852	Decal, Serial number 8 HP	1
58)	17497	Pipe, 1/4 x 4	1
59)	17496	Cap, 1/4 Pipe	1
60)	17865	Bushing 1/4 x 3/8 NPT (8 HP)	1
61)	15300	Bolt, 5/16 x 5/8	4
62)	17981	Cap, rotor shaft end	1
63)	15178	Nut, 5/16 centerlock	3
64)	17794	Belt guide	1
65)	15381	Bolt, 5/16 x 3/4 UNF	1

*Replacing an odd number of sections on a rotor may cause imbalance and vibration. If sections are worn, replace a complete set to maintain rotor balance.

5-23 Parts list for the Bear Cat shredder/chipper. Crary Co.

Cleaning a plugged rotor To clean out a plugged rotor, stop the engine, disengage the rotor clutch, and allow the machine to stop. Remove the spark plug wire. Remove the 5/16-inch bolt holding the discharge screen in place. Pull the screen out of the machine.

Clean the debris out of the shredding rotor. Turn the rotor by hand to see if it is free to rotate, then replace the screen. Replace the spark plug wire and restart the engine.

Cleaning the discharge screen Optional screens with different holes can be used with the chipper/shredder. Stop the engine. Remove the spark plug wire. Remove the 5/16-inch bolt and pull out the screen. Clean out any trash or debris from the screen area. Change the screen hole size and replace the screen. Tighten the bolt to 20 ft lbs.

The complete chipper/shredder parts layout is shown in FIG. 5-22 and the parts list in FIG. 5-23. The electric start and parts list (FIG. 5-24). Check the troubleshooting chart in TABLE 5-1 for possible malfunctions.

Lubrication

Use only high-quality, detergent products of API service classification SF to lubricate the crankcase. For warm weather, use SAE 30. Also, SAE 10W 40 can be used in warm weather. For temperatures below 32 degrees, use 10W 40 or 10W 30 weight oil. For extreme cold temperatures, use SAE 5W 30 or 5W 20 oil.

Check the oil level at each use. Change the oil after the first 5 hours of operation and each season thereafter. Make sure the unit is level when checking with a dipstick. Always run the engine to get it warm before changing the oil. Shut down and remove the drain plug.

The gearbox requires SAE 80/90 or SAE 90 EP (extreme-pressure) gear oil. Do not fill oil above the full mark. Check the dipstick after every 50 hours of operation. Twist the dipstick around so the flat side is toward the center of the transmission gearbox.

SNOWBLOWERS

Large snowblowers are equipped with 5 to 10 HP engines to move heavy snow over a wide area (FIG. 5-25). Larger HP engines are found on the big snowblowers. The horizontal-driven engine drives the augur and blowing of snow through a belt-driven pulley, and a worn gear drives the front-end cutting blades. Chains are added to the rear wheels for greater traction on snow and ice (FIG. 5-26).

Before pulling the snowblower out of the garage or shed, fill the gas tank and check the oil level. Wipe excessive dirt from around the gas cap before filling. Check the oil dipstick or remove the cap to check the oil level, depending upon what type of engine you have. Keep the oil level on the line, and do not overfill. If too much oil is added, the engine will sometimes smoke. Choke the engine before pulling the rope.

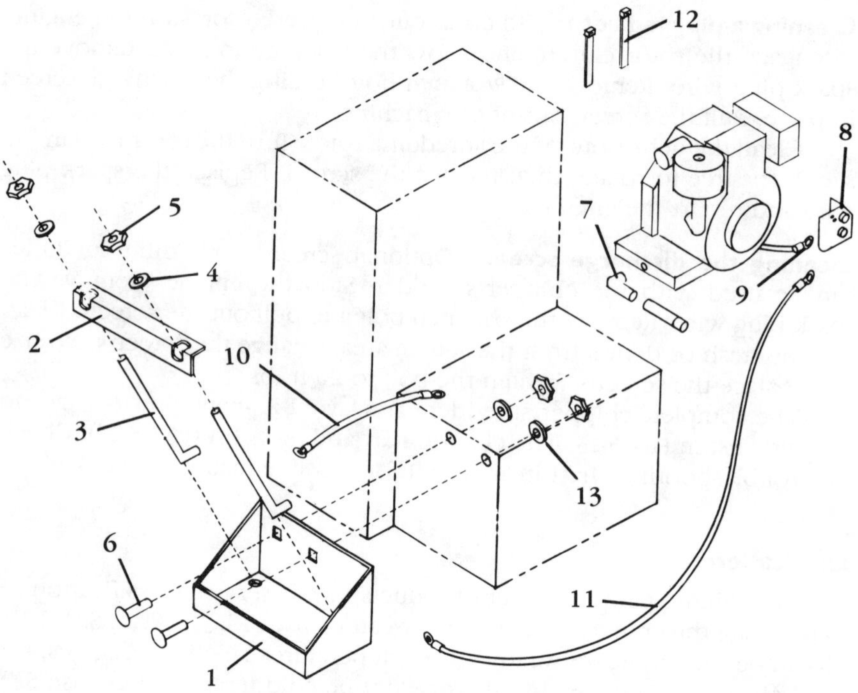

No.	Part No.	Description	Qty.
1)	70141	Battery box	1
2)	70144	Angle, battery hold down	1
3)	15419	Bolt, 5/16×8-3/4 L	2
4)	15250	Washer, 5/16 flat	2
5)	15356	Nut, 5/16 nylock	4
6)	15301	Bolt, 5/16×1 carr.	2
7)	17771	Elbow, 1/4 NPT street	1
8)	17863	Panel, started control	1
9)	17890	Terminal, 3/8 ring	1
10)	17889	Cable, battery negative	1
11)	17888	Cable, battery positive	1
12)	17320	Tie, nylon cable	2
13)	15416	Washer, 5/16 SAE flat	2

5-24 Bear Cat electric start layout and parts list. Crary Co.

Before and after blowing snow, inspect the levers, rods, and nuts and bolts for loose parts (FIG. 5-27). Because large snowblowers vibrate a lot, little parts often become loose and fall off into the snow. In the Briggs & Stratton engine shown in FIG. 5-28, a speed control knob vibrated off. Some of these special parts are difficult to obtain.

Table 5-1 Bear Cat Troubleshooting chart.

Problem	*Probable Cause*	*Remedy*
Engine will not start.	1. Improper settings.	1. Use proper manual setting.
	2. Lack of fuel.	2. Fill fuel tank.
	3. Internal problems.	3. Check spark plug and engine firing.
Engine or rotor stalls.	1. Obstructed discharge.	1. Use branch or object to clear discharge.
	2. Plugged rotor.	2. Clear rotor.
Hard to feed chipper or power needed to chip.	1. Obstructed discharge.	1. Use similar object or branch to clear discharge.
	2. Dull chipper knives.	2. Sharpen knives.
	3. Improper knife clearance.	3. Adjust clearance.
Shredder requires excess power or stalls.	1. Obstructed discharged.	1. Use branch or similar object to clear.
	2. Plugged rotor.	2. Clear rotor.
	3. Green material will not discharge.	3. Alternate feed dry material or install coarse discharge.
Engine stalls or belt squeaks when engaging clutch.	1. Too fast engagement.	1. Lift chipper lever more slowly.
	2. Plugged rotor.	2. Clear rotor.
Material from chipper wraps around rotor.	1. Stringing green material bypasses chipper knife.	1. Rotate branch or material when feeding to cut completely.
	2. Improper knife clearance.	2. Adjust clearance.

Crary Co.

5-25 This Montgomery Wards 7 1/2 HP snowblower can move a lot of snow.

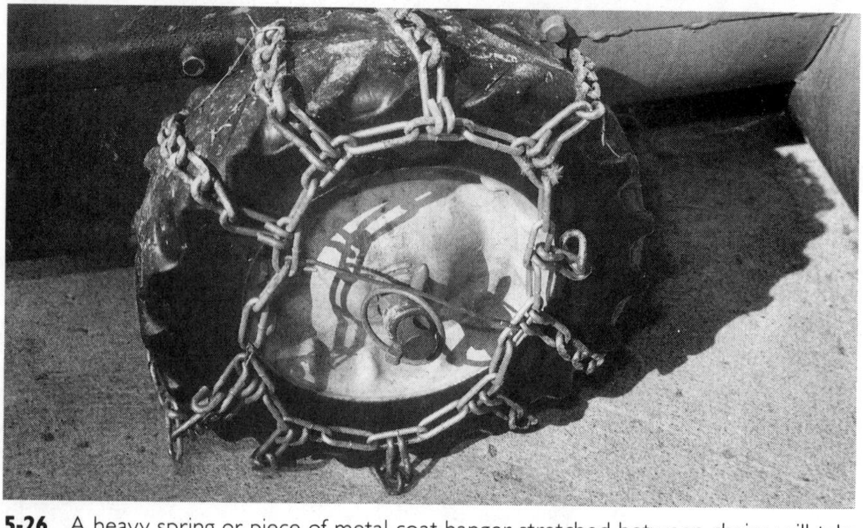

5-26 A heavy spring or piece of metal coat hanger stretched between chains will take up the slack.

Some of these special parts are difficult to obtain.

The following section covers basic snowblower troubleshooting. For information on servicing and troubleshooting motors, see Part 2. Always pull the spark plug wire before beginning any work on a snowblower. Never try to dislodge packed snow in the bonnet or chute with the engine running. Keep away from the rotating blades, and shut the engine down should twine or other debris become tangled in the unit.

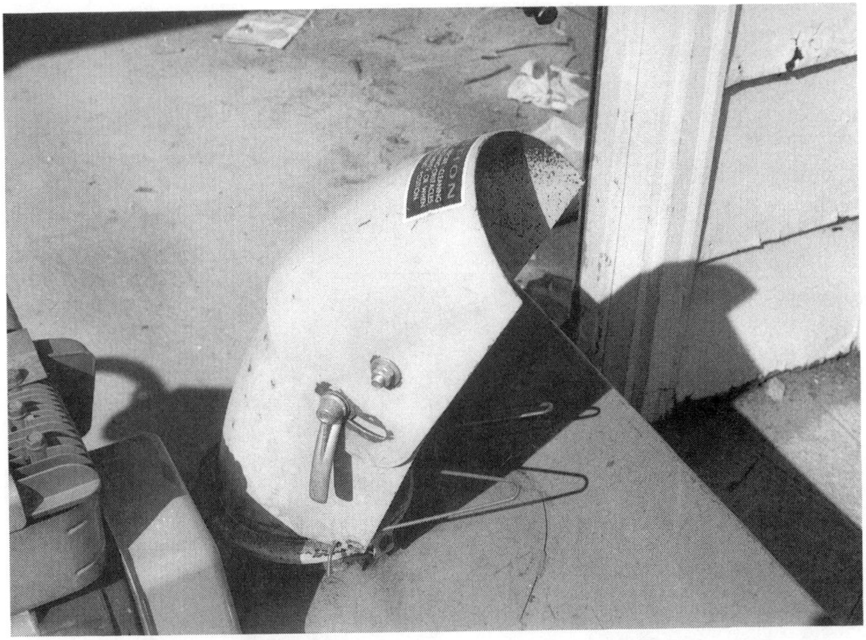

5-27 Check all wing nuts, brackets, and bolts on the snow chute of the blower.

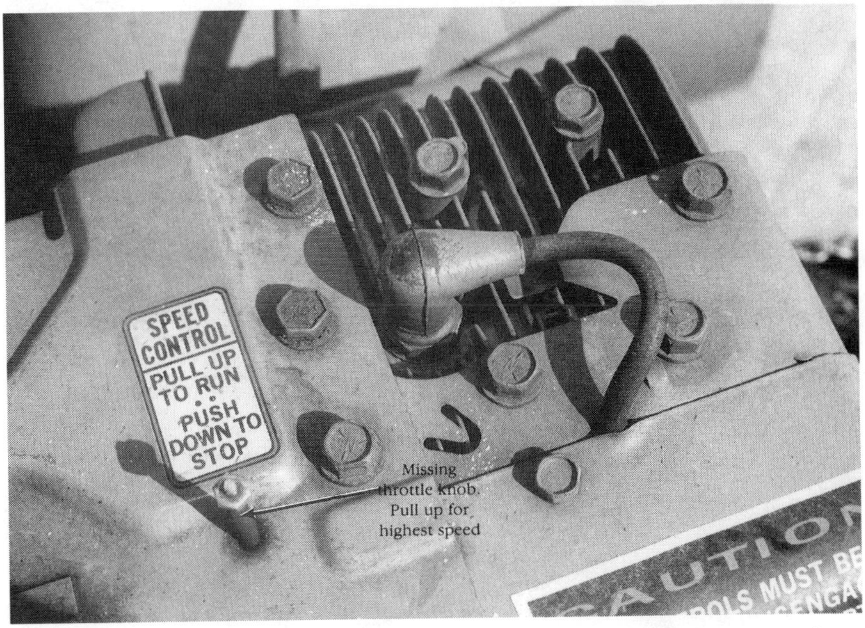

5-28 This speed control knob vibrated off and became lost during snow removal.

The starter rope

Larger snowblowers often require a great deal of strength to start the engine, but if properly tuned up, they should start with one or two turns. Sometimes, the starting rope pulls off at the handle or breaks at the end of rotation (FIG. 5-29). In this case, remove the outside cover and inspect the rope, coil spring, dogs, and gear assembly. Replace any broken rope or recoil spring.

5-29 Remove the recoil starter assembly when the rope breaks or will not pull the rope back into the assembly.

Won't shift in gear

If the snowblower won't shift into gear, let the snowblower run for at least 10 minutes before attempting to move any snow. This allows the engine and gear shifting mechanism to warm up. When the temperature is below zero, the grease is heavy and it's difficult to shift gears. If the snowblower still won't shift into gear after this time, check for loose or broken gear levers. Finally, put a drop of oil on each moving joint and tighten each bolt and nut, so they will not become loose and vibrate off into the snow.

Chute will not rotate

If the chute will not rotate, check the long rotate rod for a lost cotter pin or bolt. Inspect around the chute for excessive ice or snow. If the chute is difficult to turn, squirt oil down into the chute area. If a cotter pin is not available, temporarily slip a small nail through the angle joint and rod, and bend the nail over so it will not come out (FIG. 5-30).

5-30 If the chute will not easily rotate, inspect all the brackets on the snow chute assembly.

Snow chute jammed

If the snow chute becomes jammed, inspect all rods and knuckles that rotate the chute 180 degrees. Remove the bolts holding the chute or bonnet. Inspect the gear for broken teeth or binding assembly. Clean and wash out the lower gear track. Lubricate the gear assembly and replace. Replace any broken parts.

Noisy revolving blades

If revolving blades become excessively noisy, suspect dry bearings if the noise is chattering sounds heard in the front end of the snowblower. To isolate rotating blades, lift up the gear assembly to disengage the revolving blades. If the noise stops, the front end needs attention. Remove the end bearing assembly and inspect for dry bearings. Wipe off old grease and apply light automotive grease. Recheck each end bearing.

Remove the square cap from a worm gear assembly and inspect for dry worm gear. Lubricate the gearbox and around each end of the blade assembly (FIG. 5-31). Now, work the grease and oil in by engaging and rotating the blade assembly. If the revolving assembly is properly lubricated, there is rarely any problems.

5-31 Lubricate the gearbox assembly with 90 gearbox grease. Check the bottom cap for the correct fill.

TILLERS

Tillers are rotating machines that can quickly turn over the soil in a garden plot or work compost or spent garden produce right into the ground (FIG. 5-32). Tillers come in a front revolving—tine and rear—tine models. Revolving blades are dangerous, so always keep feet and hands away from revolving blades or tines.

5-32 The front-end tiller makes quick work of cultivating the garden or flower bed.

Front-tine tillers usually have a horizontal drive engine with drive belts while rear-type tillers have speed transmissions and large-diameter front tires. The revolving tines of the front-drive tiller are placed into action with a gear lever that engages drive belts along side the horizontal engine. Often, the front-end tiller must go over the chewed up soil several times to work up the ground enough for normal garden planting.

Excessive dirt should be cleaned off the tiller each time it's used (FIG. 5-33). Brush off excess dirt with a large paint brush or whisk broom. Oily dirt usually clings around the motor filler cap and gas tank. Do not fill with gasoline or fuel until all dirt is brushed away. Wipe around the fuel tank cap before filling with gasoline.

5-33 Clean off all excess dirt with a brush or small broom after tilling.

Check the tiller over completely for loose bolts, nuts, or missing cotter pins. Because tillers vibrate excessively, loose parts can be a problem (FIGS. 5-34 and 5-35). Tighten any loose nuts. Inspect all shields and levers for loose components, and make sure all levers and rods are firmly adjusted.

The air filter

Clean or replace the engine air filter after every 15 to 25 hours of use. Air cleaners must be cleaned up more often than in any other engine. Remove the top screw or bolt holding the cleaner assembly in position (FIG. 5-36). Only one center bolt is removed on this 5 HP Briggs & Stratton tiller engine (FIG. 5-37).

5-34 Check for loose bolts and cotter pins before and after tilling.

5-35 Check all the arms, handle, and body bolts and nuts before and after using the tiller.

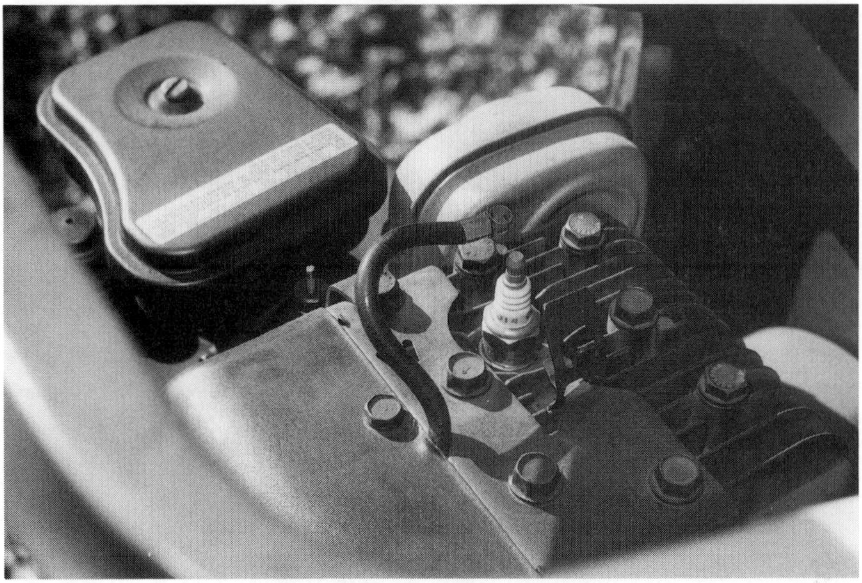

5-36 To remove the air cleaner assembly, remove the center bolt, screw, or wing nut.

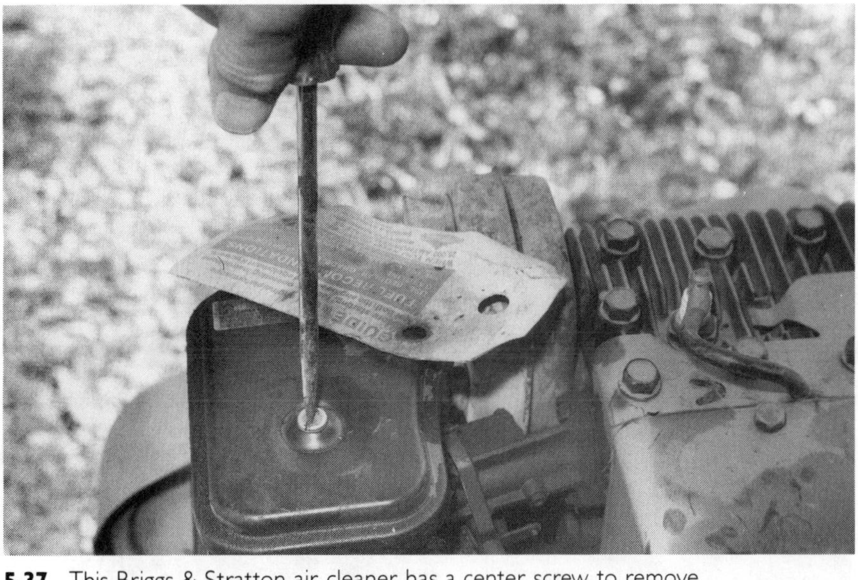

5-37 This Briggs & Stratton air cleaner has a center screw to remove.

The foam-type cleaner comes in three sections, top and bottom plate and foam filter. Remove the foam filter and wash out in soapy water, dry thoroughly. Dip the foam in light motor oil, squeeze out surplus, and replace between covers. Notice how dirty the intake side of the filter in FIG. 5-38 is. Sometimes, it is the top side of carburetor.

5-38 When foam cleaners are clogged with dirt, wash in detergent and water.

The belt

If the tiller tines will not revolve or the tiller moved forward with proper levers thrown, suspect a broken or loose belt. Remove the shield covering the drive belt gear assembly (FIG. 5-39). Two bolts are at the top and two at the bottom front-edge of the metal shield.

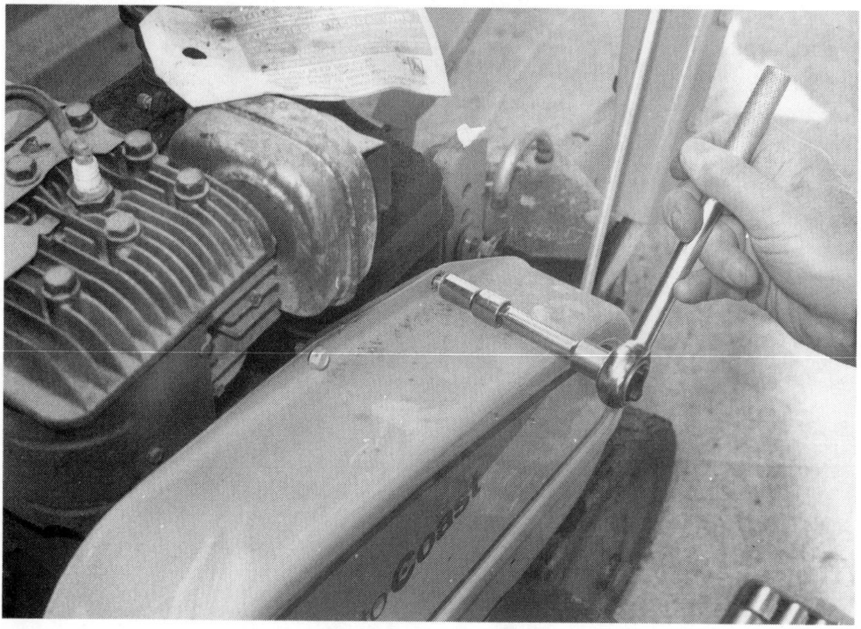

5-39 Check the drive belts for slippage by removing the bolts holding the belt shields.

Check the belts for cracked, worn, or slick areas. Make sure the tension stop is not bent out of place. Inspect the belt pulleys for oil or grease (FIG. 5-40). Clean up belts and wipe away all debris.

5-40 Inspect the belt for excessive dirt, grease, or cracked areas.

Tines

Before attempting to clean up or repair bent tines, remove the spark plug wires. Tip the tiller backwards on the handlebars to get at the revolving tines. Clean off tines each time you have finished tilling for the day. Use a putty knife, hardwood paddle, or steel brush to remove excess dirt. To sharpen tines, remove the tines assembly.

Wheels

Remove rear wheels to clean and lubricate. Only one large bolt is removed on front-line tillers. Wash out the wheel bearing with solvent and apply light grease on the bolt axle (FIG. 5-41). Clean off all dirt and wash with hose and water. Most front-end tillers have solid rear tires. Before tilling in the spring, check the tire pressure on large tillers.

The Mainline Rotary VMC90 tiller

The Mainline Rotary VMC90 tiller is manufactured in Italy with several different attachments. Besides a rotary tiller, the VMC90 operates with gasoline or diesel fuel and has attachments for a sickle bar, rotary mower, and snowblower (FIG. 5-42).

5-41 Remove the cotter pin or large C washer to remove the wheels. Clean off any old grease and oil and apply light grease to the wheel axle.

5-42 The Mainline Rotary Tiller. Mainline of North America.

Adjusting the cutting height The cutter bar can be adapted to different soil conditions as well as for the nature of the grass to be mowed. To set the cutter bar for middle or low cut (FIG. 5-43):

1. Unloose screw G.
2. Raise or lower bar shoe V.
3. Tighten screw G again.

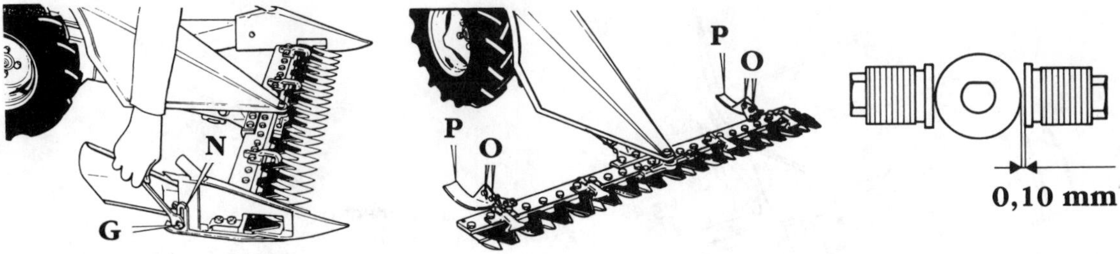

5-43 Cutting height adjustment of sickle bar cutter. Mainline of North America.

To adjust a double knife cutter bar:

1. Unloose O nuts.
2. Raise or lower bar shoe P.
3. Tighten O nuts again.

To adjust the cutting height of the rotary mower, remove the fixing pin and arrange different spaces. For the minimum cutting height, use the spacers on the top end of front wheel pin. For higher cutting height, use the spacers at the bottom of the front wheel pin.

The transmission After the first 10 working hours, grease all transmission greasing points. After the first 50 working hours, change the transmission oil with the engine warm. First remove the RH wheel away from hub V. Let the oil drain out of plug E. Refill with new oil through dipstick hole Z. Tighten the screws fixing the rotary hood and the tines.

Periodic maintenance After the first 100 hours of operation, check the transmission oil level with the engine cold and level. The oil level should range between the minimum and maximum notches on dipstick F. Check if screws fixing the rotary hood and the tines are tightened. After the first 300 hours, check the following:

Clutch. The clutch control level has to make an idle stroke of about 5 to 6 mm before disengaging the clutch. If the idle stroke is insufficient (clutch slippage) or excessive (defective disengagement), adjust it with adjuster T after loosening jam nut U (FIG. 5-44).

Throttle Lever. To adjust engine minimum or PM, loosen nut M and act on adjuster L (FIG. 5-45). It is also possible to recover any idle stroke of the throttle lever with this adjustment.

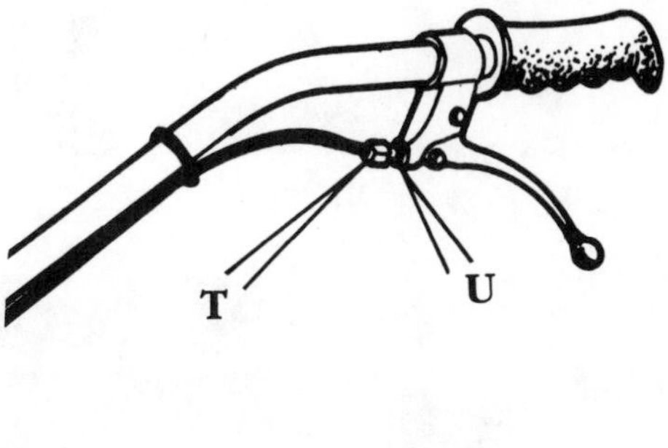

5-44 Check the adjustment of the handlebars. Mainline of North America.

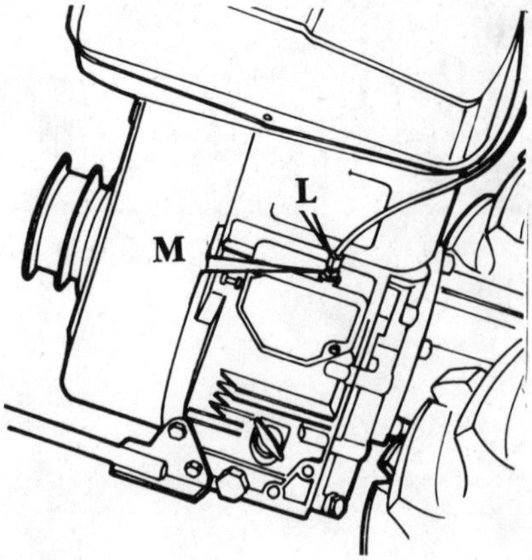

5-45 Throttle lever adjustment of the VMC90 Mainline tractor/cultivator. Mainline of North America.

Knife Holder. The clearance between the knife and knife-holder should not be excessive. If it is, loosen fixing screws 4 and tighten head screw 5 until you obtain a good knife motion (FIG. 5-46).

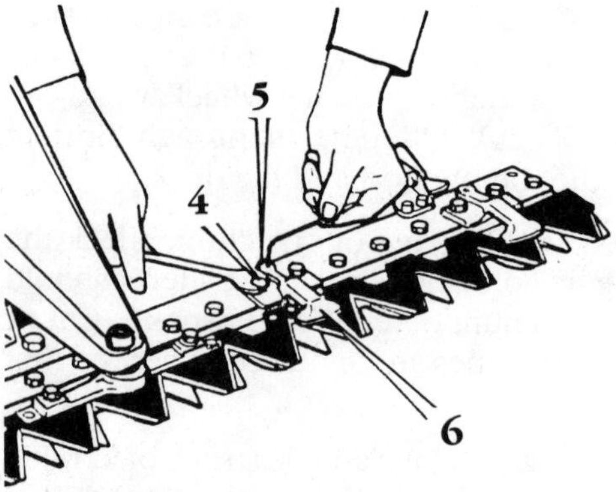

5-46 Adjustment of the knife holder on the sickle bar mower. Mainline of North America.

Chapter 6

Large power mowing and weed-cutting equipment

This chapter covers large power mowing and weed-cutting equipment—weed cutters, riding mowers, and rear mowers. Always use caution when operating large power equipment. Children and pets should not be in the area when any of these machines are in use. Make sure you know how to operate each power unit. Go over the operator's manual several times. Stay alert at all times. If you have not read chapter 1 on safety, do so now before beginning this chapter. Never remove a mower blade or tip a motor over without first disconnecting the spark plug.

Most lawn mower breakdowns are related to the engine and moving parts. Part 2 provides more detailed instructions for engine maintenance and repairs by engine type. How to keep the mower operating, blade problems, wheel lubrication, lever controls, and loose components are covered in this chapter. How to adjust the cutting height, the drive clutch control, sprocket, and belt drive systems are also given.

POWER WEED CUTTERS

Although the lawn mower cuts its share of weeds, power weed cutters do it quick and easy, especially in large areas. Some of these commercial weed cutters will cut brush up to $1^{1}/_{2}$ inch in diameter, while the regular cutter bar does a better job of cutting field overgrowth and light brush up to $^{3}/_{4}$ inch in diameter. The first section covers the Kinco Mountain Goat cutter but many of these specifics will apply to other cutters as well. Always read the owner's manual that came with your own cutter. Should your unit require more extensive service, Part 2 covers engine specifics in detail by engine type.

Kinco Mountain Goat cutters

The Kinco Mountain Goat is a self-propelled mower. A regular and commercial cutting bar is interchangeable on models. The KMG438C has a Briggs & Stratton 4 HP engine with a 38-inch commercial guarded cutter bar and the KMG438K has the same engine with a regular 38-inch guardless cutter bar (FIG. 6-1). An industrial commercial Briggs & Stratton 5 HP IC engine with a regular guardless cutter bar is found on the KMG538C model. The KMG538R has a Briggs & Stratton 5 HP IC engine with a 38-inch regular, guardless cutting bar, and the KMG542K model has the same size engine with a 42-inch regular guardless bar.

Kinco Inc.

6-1 The Kinco Mountain Goat II power weed cutter operates with a Briggs & Stratton engine.

Figure 6-2 is a parts layout. The tools you will need to do the service, maintenance, and repairs in this section, can most likely be found around the workshop or garage. The following components are the most likely ones to wear and become damaged. Lubricate these components regularly for maximum service.

Wheel clutch lockouts When the control rods are adjusted properly, they are centered in the operating slot. When the wheel clutch lockout is engaged, the wheels should move freely. If the rods are not in the centered position, adjust them by removing the cotter pins and washers in the ends of the control rods and screwing rods in or out of the wheel idler arm pivot. Notice this adjustment does not control the wheel belt tension.

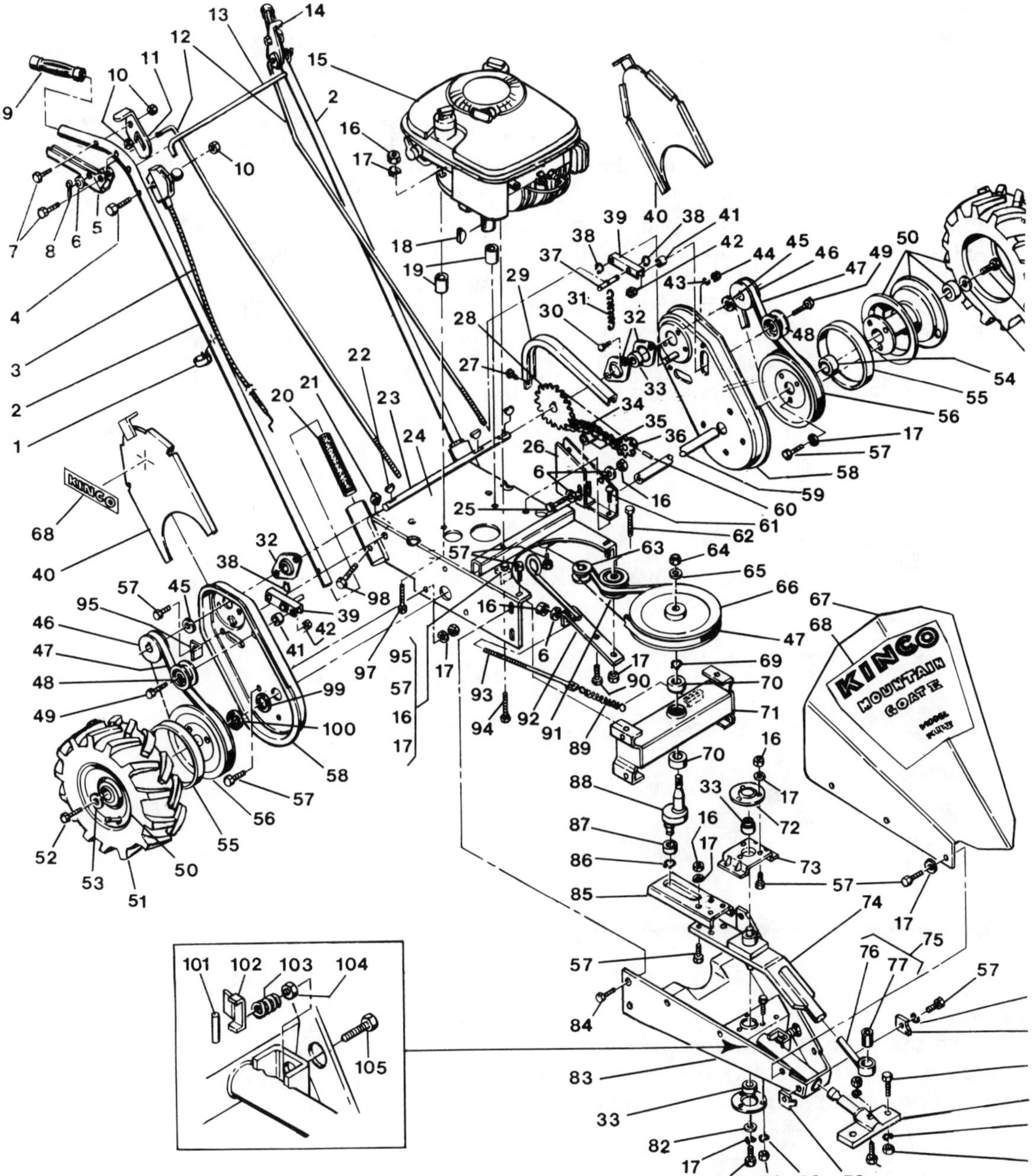

6-2 Parts layout of the Kinco power weed cutter. Kinco Inc.

Adjusting wheel belt tension Normally, belt tension is sufficient to allow good wheel tracking when the tension spring is in position. A second spring position hole is provided in the engine deck if the spring becomes weakened or the belt has stretched.

Checking bolts The back and forth movement of cutting blades in all sickle bars creates vibration that aids the cutting action, shaking off loose brush from the bar and helping to feed its way into weeds and brush. This vibration does, however, sometimes loosen bolts in the machine.

Periodically check the tightness of all bolts and nuts. Keep the 7/16-inch adjustment screw tight (FIG. 6-3). The correct tightness will allow the cutter bar to rotate freely (float) without having any in or out movement of the attachment mounting bracket in the front housing pivot tube. Make sure the two 3/8-inch nuts and center bolt that holds the mounting bracket to the cutter bar are tight (refer to numbers 42 and 79 of FIG. 6-2).

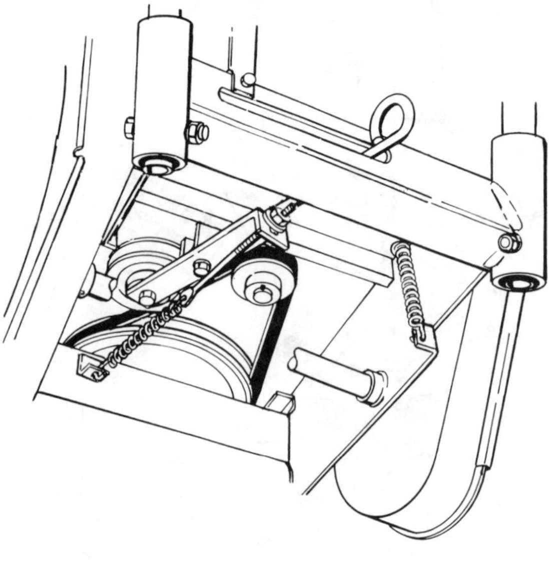

6-3 Keep the 7/16-inch adjustment nut tightened so the cutter bar can operate freely. Kinco Inc.

Adjusting the knife clutch idler Belt tension for the cutter bar drive is set at the factory. If increased idler pulley (1) tension is necessary (usually due to spring fatigue or belt stretch), tighten the nut on the spring adjustment rod (2). (Refer to FIG. 6-2).

Chain maintenance Remove the #10 pan-head screw (27) and slide off the chain cover (29). Loosen and pry up the chain idler (34) so that there is a slight deflection of chain on the drive side. Tighten the nut and screw in the adjustment slot. A good time to check chain tightness is when oiling.

Adjusting knife and wear plate (commercial bar) Keeping blades sharp and properly adjusted allows the mower to cut easier and with less power.

Test the tightness of the knife bar (switch to knives) by moving back and forth (FIG. 6-4). Maximum play should be 1/32 of an inch. Play can be taken up by loosening the jam nuts on the plow bolts and sliding the wear plates forward until the knife bar is snug against the guard surface. Then, back-off wear plates slightly and tighten jam and plow nuts securely.

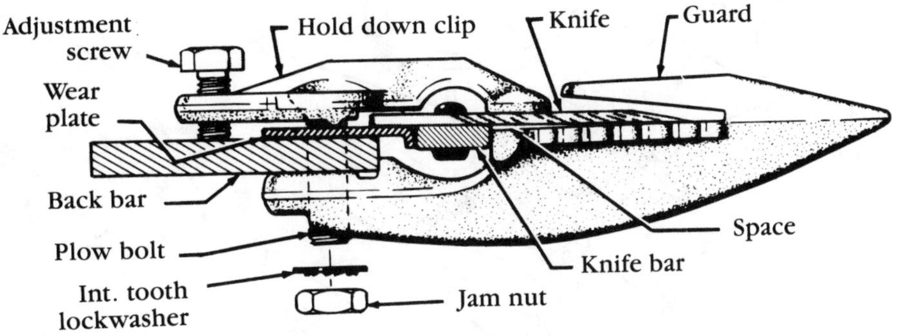

6-4 Commercial bar adjustment of the knife and wear plate. Kinco Inc.

Little or no space between ledger plates and bottom surface indicates a worn out plate. Knives should be free to move in guards with slight tension. Tighten knife tension by turning the adjustment screw clockwise.

Adjusting knife and wear plate (regular bar) Loosen the locking nuts in the hold-down clip. Slide the clip in the slot until there is slight tension against the wear plate. The knife bar and knives should be free to slide on the ledger plate. It's important to oil the cutter bar after every 4 to 6 hours of use. Tighten knife tension by turning the adjustment screw clockwise.

Cutter bars The entire commercial cutter bar knife and knife bar assembly can be removed with four specially threaded machine screws and bolts. The tension bolts in the hold-down clips must be loosened and two top screws and internal tooth-lock washers removed from the top of knife head. The head must then be removed before the knife assembly can be slid out the end of the cutter bar in the regular cutter bar assembly.

Inspecting parts A hammering noise or different operating sound might indicate worn parts. Shut down the engine before checking for worn components. Reach under the front housing (1) and grasp the eccentric channel 2 and move it side to side (FIG. 6-5). If there is noticeable play, a worn eccentric bearing (3) or channel needs replacing.

Check for excessive tube wear in the eccentric arm welchment (4), pitman assembly shaft (5), and knife head. Remove the fender (7) and V belt (8) and check for looseness. Rotate the drive mechanism by hand and observe the play between parts. Worn and loose parts create chattering sounds and are an indication of early failure.

Check radial eccentric bearings (3), bearing (9), and eccentric arm pivot bearings (12) for loose bearings. Tighten all bolts and check again

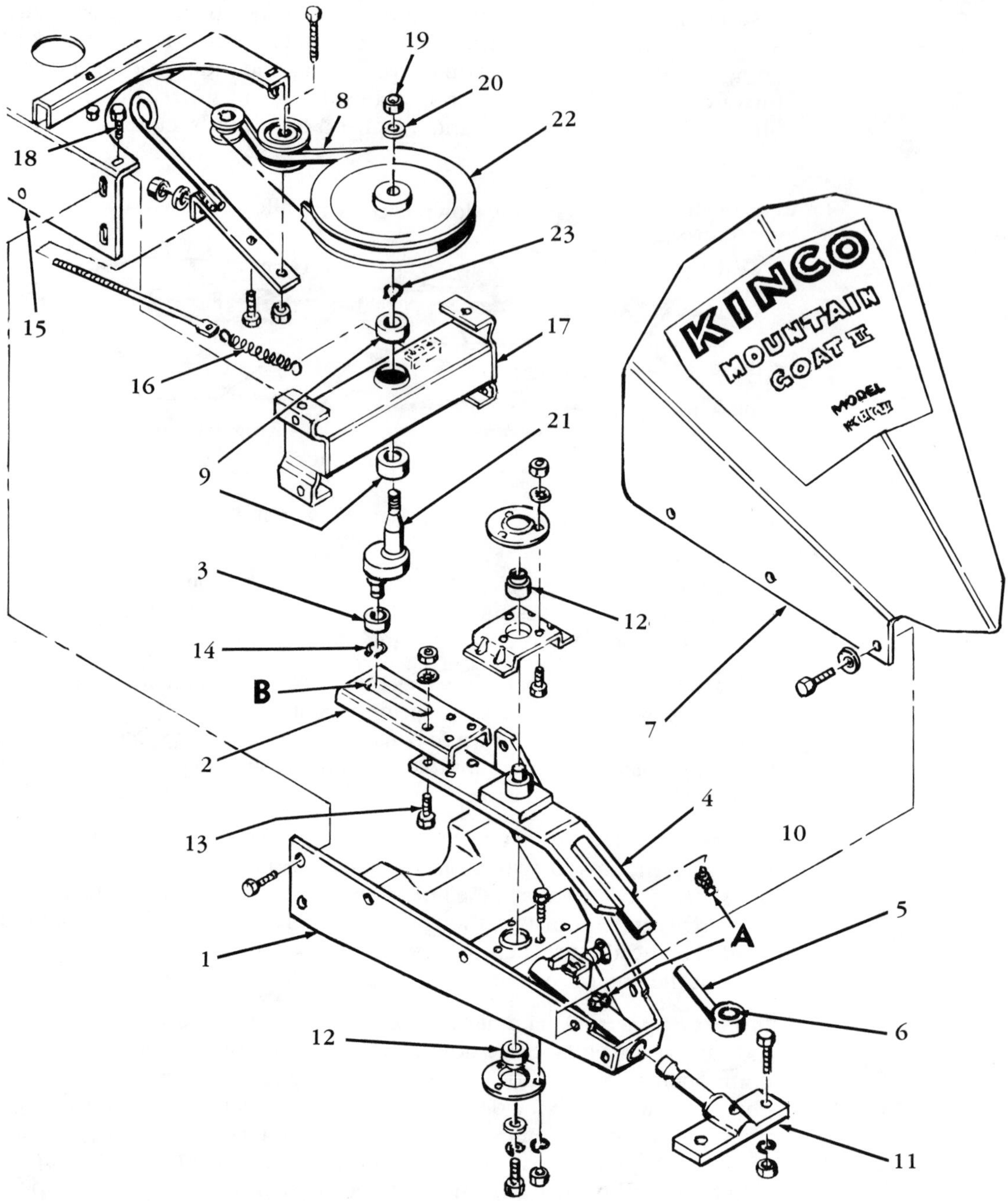

6-5 Check bearings 3, 4, 5, 8, 9, and 12 for excessive wear. Kinco Inc.

before replacing bearings. After an extended period of time, check lock screw adjustment (10) and the attachment mounting bracket (11). If play is detected, with no further adjustment, replace parts.

The wheel belt drive Replace the wheel drive belts (1) if they become frayed, broken, or stretched to a point where the idler pulley can no longer control tension. (FIG. 6-6). To service:

1. Remove the wheel belt guard cover (3) by pulling the handle up and sliding off the belt guard (4).
2. Move the wheel clutch on the handlebar to the *out* position. Slip the drive belt off the idler pulley (2) and countershaft pulley (10).
3. Remove the 7/16- × -3/4-inch hardened hex-head cap screw (5) and flat 7/16-inch washer (6) from the wheel axle.
4. Slide the wheel assembly off the axle (7).
5. Replace the belt and reassemble. Be careful not to remove machinery bushing (8) and spring washer (9), which stay on the axle. Clean up parts and reoil.

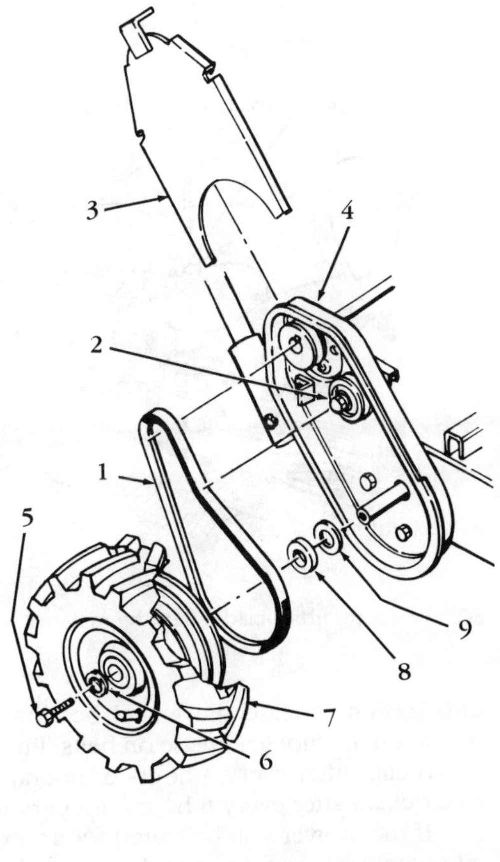

6-6 Removing or replacing a broken or frayed wheel belt. Kinco Inc.

The knife assembly First, determine if sharpening is necessary. If knife sections are dull, contain nicks, or are missing pieces, either sharpen or replace. Special grinding tools are available commercially. Wear gloves when handling knives and wear safety goggles or a full face mask when removing and replacing knives.

If the knives are to be sharpened by hand with a hand file, clamp the knife assembly in a vise so that the knife points are facing away from you. Push the file away from you while maintaining the same cutting angle as the original sharpened edge. File or grind the top (angled) surface of the blade. Do not touch the bottom side of blade.

Rest the knife assembly in a vise so that the knife bar is supported by the vise jaws and held tightly. Strike the top of the knife section to be removed with a hard blow. This action will shear most heads. Remove the rest of the rivets with a flat punch. Rivets can also be removed by knocking off heads with a sharp cold chisel.

Replace knife sections with a special rivet-support tool available from Kinco (FIG. 6-7). When replacing, make sure the beveled cutting edge of knives is facing away from the knife bar and the beveled holes in the knife bar are facing away from the knife section (A).

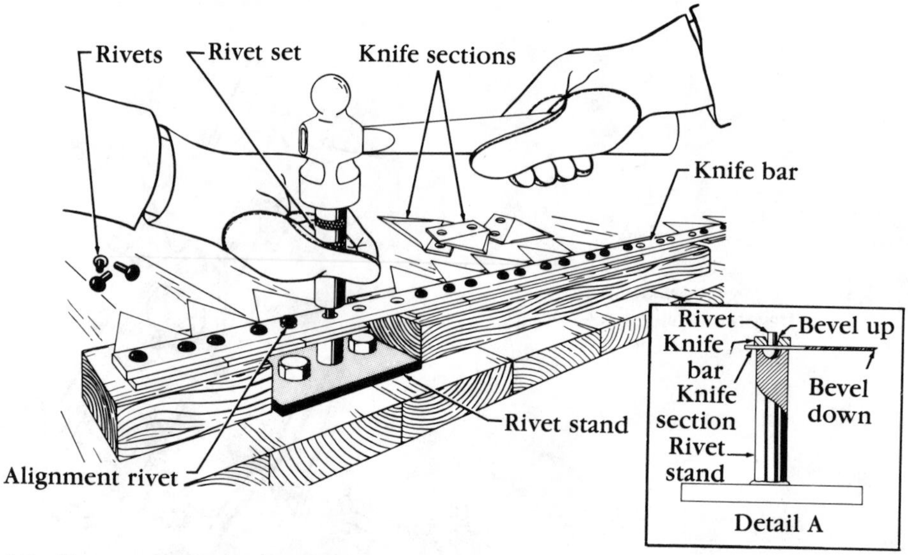

6-7 Rivets or cutting blades must be replaced with a special Kinco rivet tool.

Lubrication Grease the wheel bearings lightly after every 8 hours of operation. Do not get grease on belts. Put a drop or two of oil under hold-down clips after every 3 hours of operation. Oil lightly the engine drive roller chain after every 8 hours of operation.

If the mower will be stored for an extended time, put a light film of oil on knives to prevent rust. Lubricate the attachment mounting brackets and pitman assembly pivot shafts with one or two shots of grease after every 8 hours.

Wipe the oil groove of the eccentric channel and apply grease every 8 hours. Follow engine recommendations of lubrication by the engine manufacturer.

REAR-END MOWERS

A careful operator is the best insurance against accidents. Read the instruction manual thoroughly. Know how to operate the machine and the tractor it is attached to.

Adjusting the cutting height

Place the mower and tractor on a level surface. Be sure the tractor engine is off and the PTO is disconnected before making any adjustments. Avoid very low-cutting heights to prevent blades from striking the ground, which can damage the mower and drive (FIG. 6-8).

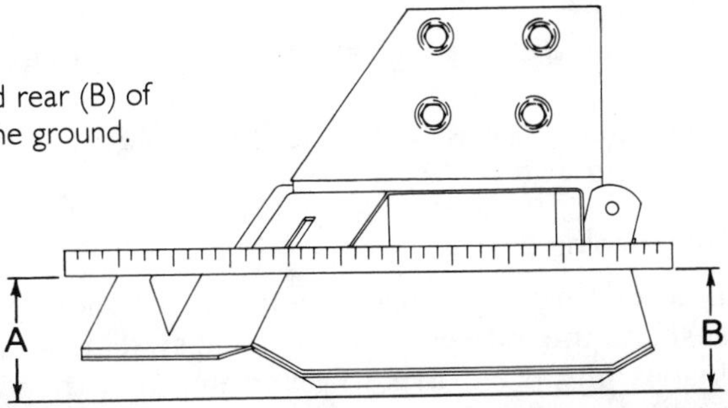

6-8 Adjust the front (A) and rear (B) of the mower level with the ground.
Woods Inc.

Level the mower from side to side and adjust using three-point arm leveling device. Best mowing results when the front is level with the rear or slightly lower than the rear. To raise the front of the mower, shorten the check chains. To raise the rear of the mower, move the caster adjustment brackets rearward.

Lubrication

Use an SAE multipurpose-type grease for all locations. Be sure to clean the fittings thoroughly before using a grease gun. Use SAE 90 gear lube in the gearbox. Daily lubrication of the PTO slip joint is necessary. Keep fingers out of the slot (2) to prevent injury (FIG. 6-9).

Servicing belts

One of the major causes of belt failures is improper belt installation. Check pulley shafts and bearing wear before installing a new belt. Check the pulley for cleanliness and that it spins freely and doesn't wobble.

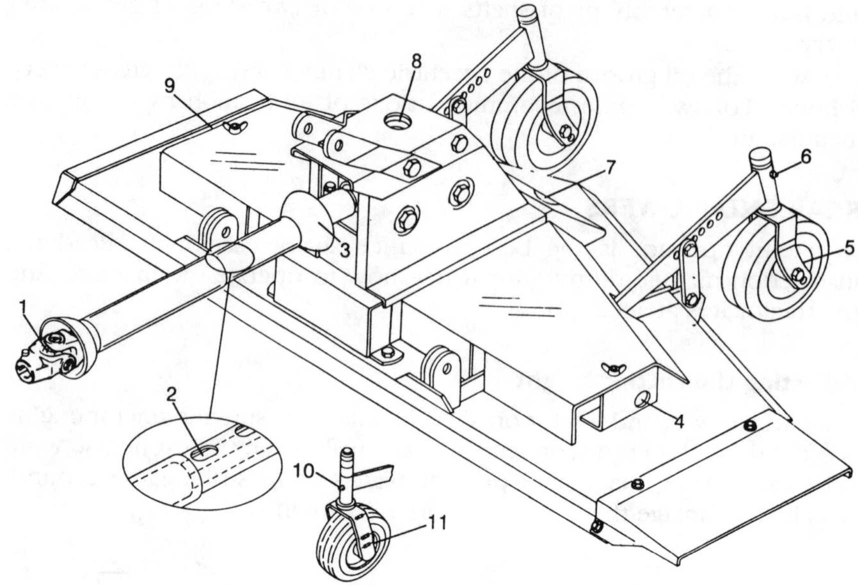

6-9 Lubrication points on the Woods RM500 mower. Woods Inc.

Clean out grooves with a nontoxic degreasing agent, commercial detergent, and water.

Sharpening blades

Before sharpening blades, remove the mower from the tractor. Do not suspend the mower on a hydraulic system. Wear gloves to handle mower blades. Inspect blades to determine that they are mounted tight and in good condition. Replace any blade that is bent, excessively nicked, worn, or has other damage. Small nicks can be ground out while sharpening.

Install the blade wrench over the spindle bolts to prevent the spindle from rotating while removing the blade bolts (FIG. 6-10). Remove the bolt, which has a left-hand thread (7); cup washers (6); flat washer (5); and blade (4). Reverse reinstall the sharpened blade. Replace flat blade washers if they are burned or show signs of blade slippage. Always sharpen both cutting edges of each blade at the same time to maintain balance and do not sharpen the back side of the blade. Do not sharpen to a razor edge, leave 1/32- to 1/16-inch blunt edge.

Servicing the spindle

Special tools are needed for spindle repair. You can save time and money by installing a new spindle, however. Remove the complete spindle assembly, and lubricate the new cups with light oil. Make sure all parts of the spindle assembly fit perfectly. Apply a thin coat of Permatex to the shaft area where sleeve with seat. Insert the spindle assembly through the bottom of the mower and install four mounting bolts. Position grease fittings toward lubrication access areas.

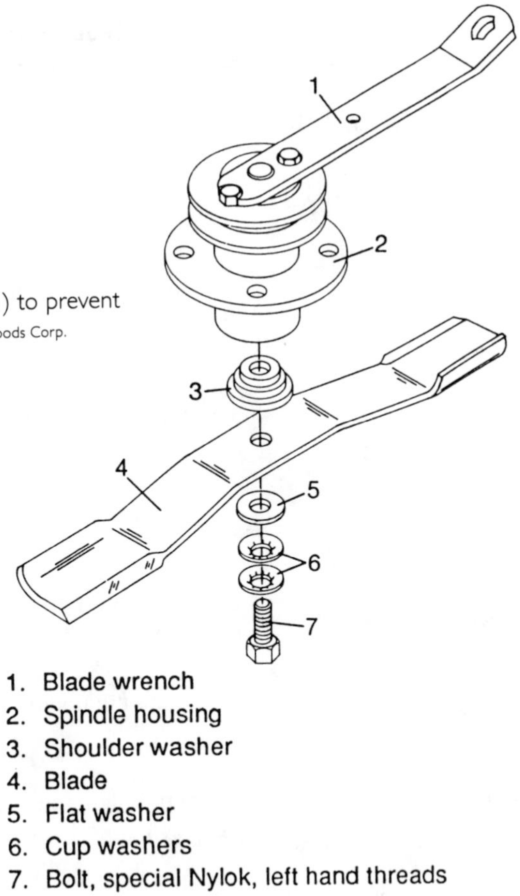

6-10 Apply the blade wrench (1) to prevent the pulley from slipping. Woods Corp.

Maintaining the gearbox

Always keep the gearbox half full of SAE 90 gearbox lube. Bearing failure is indicated by noise and excessive side play and end play in the gear shafts. Leakage might occur at the top cover, vertical or horizontal seals, and the square O ring between the front housing and the gearbox. Repair the gearbox with Permatex sealant.

Servicing the universal joint

A noisy and popping universal joint indicates repair is needed. Remove and replace parts that are needed. TABLE 6-1 is a troubleshooting chart of possible belt trouble.

Servicing other components

The horizontal seal installation, drive pulley assembly, and universal joint repairs should be made by a professional machinist.

Table 6-1 Troubleshooting belt conditions.

Problem	*Possible Cause*	*Solution*
Belt slippage.	Mower overloading; material too tall or heavy.	Reduce tractor ground speed but maintain full PTO RPM. Cut material twice; one high pass and then mow at desired height. Cut a partial swath.
	Oil on belt from overlubrication.	Be careful not to overlubricate. Clean lubricant from belt and pulleys with clean rag. Replace oil-soaked belt.
	Belt hung up or rubbing.	Check belt for free travel in pulleys and belt guides. Check under mower and around blade spindle shafts for wire, rags, or other foreign material. Clean all material from under mower.
Frayed edges on cover.	Belt misaligned or belt rubbing guide.	Realign belt or guide. Be sure belt doesn't rub any other part while running.
	Pulley misalignment.	Inspect to ensure belt is running in center of backside idler. Shim idler as necessary to align.
Belt rollover.	Pulley misalignment.	Realign.
	Damaged belt.	Replace belt.*
	Foreign object in pulley grooves.	Inspect all pulley grooves for rust, paint, or weld spots and remove.
	Worn pulley groove.	Replace pulley.
Damaged belt.	Rollover, high-shock loads or installation damage.	Replace belt.*
Belt breakage.	High-shock loads.	Avoid abusive mowing. Avoid hitting the ground or large obstructions.
	Belt cam off drive.	Check drive alignment for foreign material in grooves. Ensure proper tension. Avoid hitting solid objects or ground.

*Check belt for damage by laying it flat on floor. If belt does not lie flat (has humps or twists), which indicates broken or stretched cords, it must be replaced.

Woods Corp.

BCS 700 POWER UNIT

BCS 715, 725, and 745 power units are similar in many respects. Model 715 is the smallest and 745 the largest. Model 725 has five gears forward and two reverse, with speed selection aided by a Hi/Lo gear-reducer lever device (FIG. 6-11). Model 725 operates as a rear tine tiller, cutter bar mower, power sweeper, rotary mower, snow thrower, sprayer, 36-inch dozer/scraper, and a chipper/shredder. Swinging the control column around from the PTO end of the unit to the engine end converts it for front-mount attachments. The Model 725 is equipped with a Kohler 8 HP engine or a 10 HP BCS engine.

BCS Inc.

6-11 The BCS 725 Tiller Power Unit.

BCS A220 and AL 330 engines

Remove and discard the thimble-shaped clear plastic cover from the oil breather tube located to the left of the carburetor. Remove the crankcase oil filter plug (or dipstick) and check that the oil is at the proper level.

Remove the pipe plug on top of the attachment gear housing of the tiller, rotary mowers, snow throwers, and power sweepers. If the oil level is more than 2 inches below the filter hole, fill to the top with SAE 80/90 or SAE 90 EP gear oil. Maintain at the nearly full level.

Cleaning the air filter

The dry element air filters used on the BCS and Kohler can be removed and cleaned. Optional commercial-type pre-cleaner elements are available to fit these air cleaners. Pre-cleaners are recommended particularly when using the power sweeper, dozer blade, or tiller in dry, dusty conditions.

Open the air cleaner and check the air filter at regular intervals, Check often under very dusty conditions. A clogged filter raises engine temperature. Dry elements can be cleaned by tapping gently against a flat surface, but it is far better to replace a dirty filter. Pre-cleaners can be cleaned with soap and water or mineral spirits. Dry thoroughly. Soak the cleaned and dried pre-cleaner in clean engine oil. Squeeze out oil before reinstalling.

Maintenance

Change oil, filters, etc., and clean cylinder fins and crankcase breather as before. Clean up the machine daily after use. Hose down everything but the engine. Avoid cracking the engine, let it cool down.

After the first 10 operating hours, tighten nuts and bolts, check tire pressure, and check clutch cable after every 50 hours. To adjust, hold the cable nut to keep it from turning and tighten or loosen the clutch cable adjusting screw as required (FIG. 6-12).

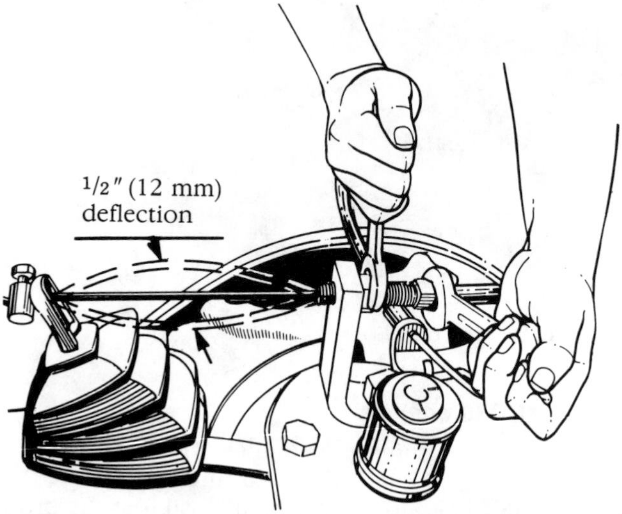

6-12 Adjust the clutch cable on 725 engines as shown. BCS Inc.

Occasionally, clean any dirt and old grease from the PTO connections of all equipment and pack with clean bearing grease (FIG. 6-13). Every season, lubricate the control cable with light oil. Lubricate the hinge on the hood with light oil. Do not use mineral oil. Clean parts thoroughly and apply grease to the control indexing rod or lever, column fork, column support, or pivot post.

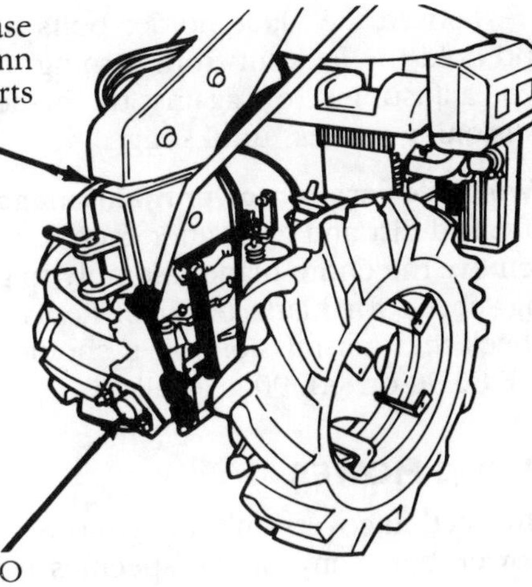

6-13 The areas to grease on the PTO. BCS Inc.

Coupling attachment to PTO

For a direct coupling attachment, remove the locknuts and washers from the tractor PTO studs. Align the tractor PTO with the connecting flange of the attachment. Always bring the tractor to the attachments. If necessary, use props to level the attachment. Slide the PTO studs into the attachment flange and secure with the washers and locknut.

For quick hitch attachment, the hitch consists of male and female parts held together by a captive, T-handled pin. Pull and turn this pin sideways to separate the parts. Remove the two nuts from the PTO studs and two bolts and nuts from the quick hitch. Line up the holes and attach both parts. Install and tighten up nuts. Fit the attachment into the PTO part. Twist the pin so it drops down into locking position. To uncouple, pull the pin.

Mower bar maintenance

Wash down and oil parts after each use. After every four operating hours, pump lithium-based grease into the blade control mechanism through the two grease fittings. Remove dull blades and sharpen on a grinder. Remove the two bolts and the blade coupling. Slide out the blade.

When play between the wear strip and blade becomes excessive, loosen the wear strip clamps and push the wear strip closer to the blade with a screwdriver tip to adjust. Tighten the clamp bolts securely.

Because the sickle bar has no adjusting areas, loosen the blade holder bolts, and support the assembly on a firm surface. Slide a screwdriver shank under the neck of the blade with light hammer strokes. Tighten the bolts and check the blade tension.

Loosen the blade holder bolts and increase the tension by turning the blade holder adjusting screw clockwise on the mulching bar. Tighten the bolts and check the tension. Repeat until snug.

Loosen the blade holder bolts of the combination bar, then loosen and hold the locknut from turning. Use a wrench to turn the jack-post-type adjusting screw against the blade holder. Check the tension. Repeat tensioning process until snug.

Two-blade rotary mower maintenance Clean the underside of the deck of caked dirt and grass after each use. Check blades for knicks and wear. Remove the entire blade assembly to grind down each blade. After grinding, check for blade balance. Replace cracked or bent blades at once. Check the transmission oil; it should be to $^1/_2$ inch of the top. Fill with SAE 80/90 or SAE 90 gear oil.

RIDING MOWER

This section covers one riding mower in particular, the John Deere Riding Mower, but many of the specifics here will also apply to other riding mowers.

Leveling the mower

Park the riding mower on a hard, level surface. Put the PTO lever fully rearward. Put the shift lever at N. Stop the engine and lock the park brake. Wait for all moving parts to stop. Remove the key. Check the tire pressure. Front tires should be 14 psi and rear tires 10 psi. Put the mower at the $2^1/_2$-inch cutting height.

Leveling mower side to side To level the mower side to side, turn the blade or blades sideways. Lift the mower chute and measure from the right blade tip to the floor (dimension A). You can use a leveling gauge or short ruler to level the blade. Measure the left blade tip for dimension (A). Dimension (A) must equal more than $^1/_8$ inch on both sides of the mower (FIG. 6-14). To adjust, loosen three nuts (A), turn the leveling cam (B) with a $^{15}/_{16}$-inch socket to raise or lower the left side of the mower, as needed (FIG. 6-15). Check mower blade tips for the dimension shown in the first measurement. Tighten up nuts.

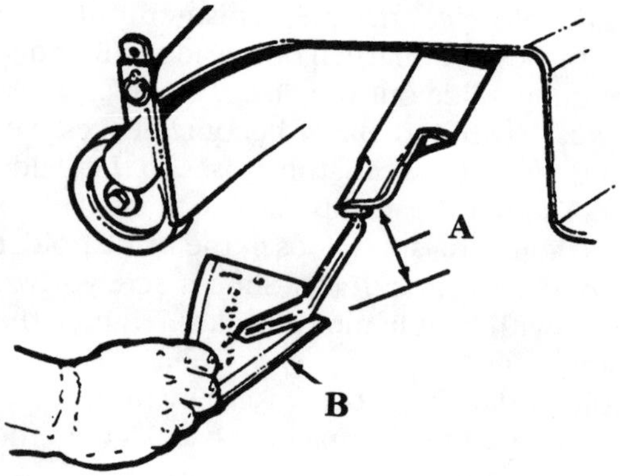

6-14 Dimension (A) must be $^1/_8$ of an inch on both sides of the mower.

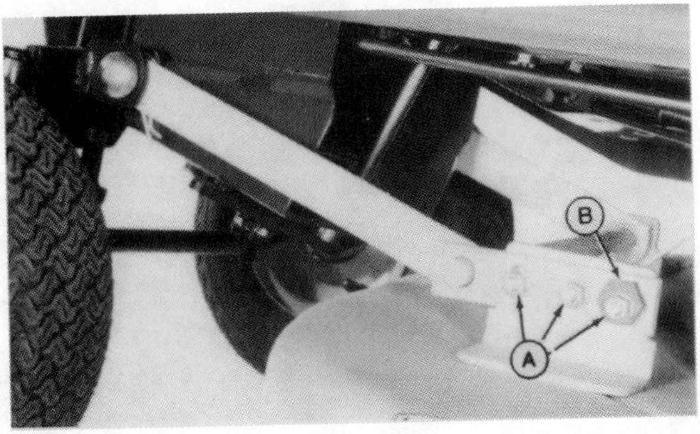

6-15 With a 15/16-inch socket wrench, raise or lower the left side as needed. Reproduced by permission of Deere & Company. C19XX Deere & Co. All rights reserved.

Leveling mower front to rear To level the mower from the front to the rear, turn the blade(s) so it points straight ahead. Measure from the front blade tip to the floor (dimension A). Use a leveling gauge (B) or short ruler to level the blade. Measure from the rear blade tip to the floor (FIG. 6-16). Dimension (A) on the rear blade tip should be equal or no more than 1/4

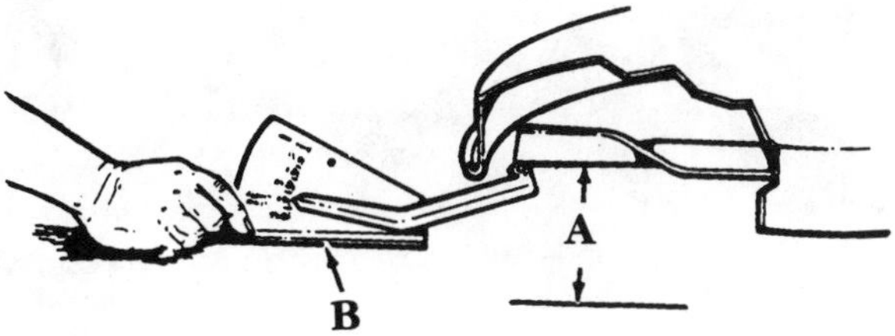

6-16 Use a leveling gauge or short ruler to level the front and rear of the mower. Reproduced by permission of Deere & Company. C19XX Deere & Co. All rights reserved.

inch than dimension (A) on the front blade tip. To adjust, lift the seat, and loosen the three nuts (A). Turn the leveling cam (B) with 1 1/8-inch socket to raise or lower the rear of the mower as needed. Tighten nuts (A) (FIG. 6-17).

After mowing

After mowing, clean the top of the mower deck (A), engine compartment, and bagger support bracket with a brush or compressed air. Clean under the mower deck with water from a garden hose and lower the mower to the ground (FIG. 6-18).

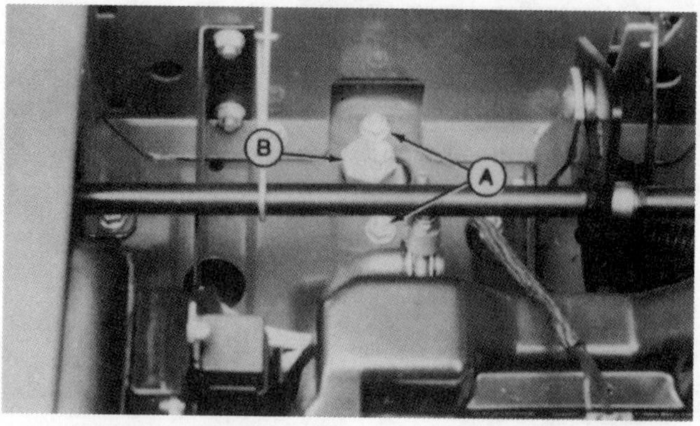

6-17 Loosen the three nuts and turn the leveling cam to raise or lower the rear of the mower. Reproduced by permission of Deere & Company. C19XX Deere & Co. All rights reserved.

6-18 Clean up under the mower with a garden hose. Reproduced by permission of Deere & Company. C19XX Deere & Co. All rights reserved.

Fuels and lubricants

The RX75 riding mower holds 1 gallon of gasoline. Fill with unleaded gasoline. Regular leaded gasoline can be used if it has an anti-knock index of 87 or higher. Avoid switching from unleaded to regular gasoline to prevent engine damage. Fill the fuel tank each time it is used. Fill fuel tank only to the bottom of the filler neck.

Engine oil/lubricants Use only premium-quality engine oils that meet the performance requirements of API Service Classification SD, SE, SE/CC, or SF. In warm weather, use SAE 30 oil. In cold weather, use SAE 5W 20 oil. Quality engine oils are blended, so additives are neither required nor recommended.

General purpose grease John Deere Multipurpose grease is recommended. If other greases are used, they must be SAE Multipurpose grease or SAE Multipurpose grease containing 3 to 5 percent molybdenum disulfide. At temperatures below −22 degrees, use arctic grease such as those meeting military specifications MIL-G10924C.

Lubricate axle spindles after every 10 hours of use (FIG. 6-19). Lubricate each axle spindle (A) with one or two shots of John Deere Multipurpose grease after every 10 hours of use. Wipe off excess grease from around the sleeve and lower part of the spindle. Always use a service schedule to check the many different parts to be oiled or lubricated (TABLE 6-2).

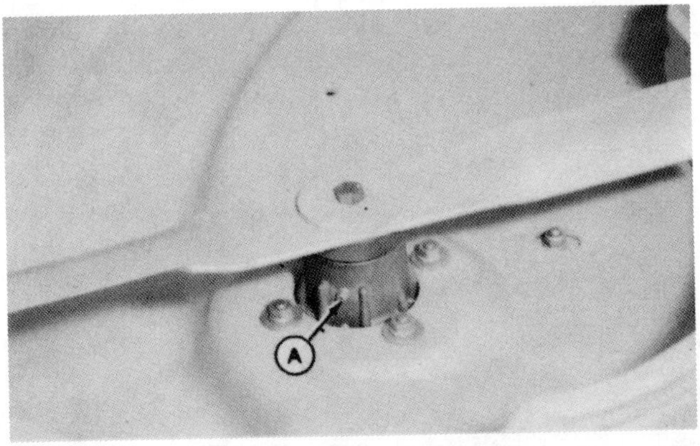

6-19 Lubricate axle spindles after every 10 hours of use. Reproduced by permission of Deere & Company. C19XX Deere & Co. All rights reserved.

Table 6-2 SX75 service schedule.

	Time Intervals					
Check	*Before Each Use*	*5 Hours*	*10 Hours*	*25 Hours*	*50 Hours*	*Annual*
Engine oil level.	✓					
Clean engine blower screen.	✓					
Lubricate front axle spindles.			✓			
Tire inflation.			✓			
Mower Spindles.			✓			
Clean air cleaner.				✓		
Drive belts.				✓		
Battery electrolyte level.				✓		
Change engine oil.		✓*			✓	
Spark plug.						✓
Change fuel filter.						✓
Change optional oil filter (RX95 and SX95).		✓*				✓

*Important: To help prevent engine damage, change engine oil (and optional filter) after first 5 hours of use.

Changing the engine oil Change engine oil after every 50 hours. Park the mower on a level surface and lock the park brake. Run the engine approximately 2 minutes to warm the oil. Stop the engine and remove the key (FIG. 6-20). Be careful not to burn hands on hot oil or engine parts.

Install a drain hose on the drain valve. Turn the knob counterclockwise to open the drain valve. Drain oil into a pan or container. Close the drain valve after all the oil is drained (FIG. 6-21). Lift the engine shroud on SX75 and SX95 mowers. Remove the engine dipstick (A). The oil capacity of RX75 is 2¼ pints and SX95 model is 3 pints. Pour oil into the dipstick fill tube (FIG. 6-22). Reinstall the dipstick. Leave the dipstick cap unthreaded for the correct oil level reading. Remove the dipstick and check the oil level. Add oil if necessary. Install and tighten dipstick.

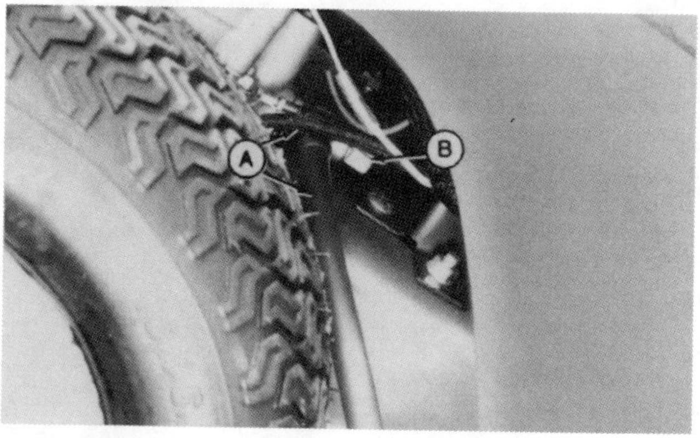

6-20 Check the engine oil after every 50 hours. Check it each time the mower is used. Reproduced by permission of Deere & Company. C19XX Deere & Co. All rights reserved.

6-21 Pour oil into the dipstick fill tube. Reproduced by permission of Deere & Company. C19XX Deere & Co. All rights reserved.

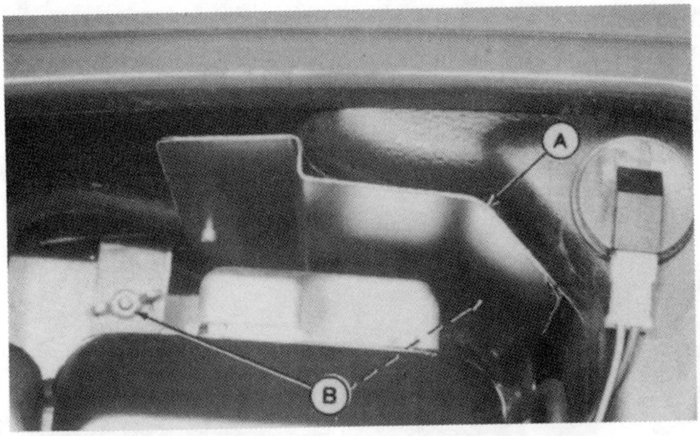

6-22 Remove the heat shield to check the spark plugs. Reproduced by permission of Deere & Company. C19XX Deere & Co. All rights reserved.

Changing engine oil filter Change oil and filter after every 100 hours of use or annually, whichever comes first. Turn the oil filter (A) counter-clockwise and remove it. Apply a film of clean oil on the new filter's seal. Install the new filter by turning until the seal contacts the mounting surface. Then, turn by hand 1/2 turn more.

Run the engine at slow speed for 2 minutes. Check for any leaks around the filter. Stop the engine and check the oil level. Add oil only to the full mark on the dipstick. Install and tighten dipstick.

Changing the fuel filter Check the fuel filter annually. Make sure the engine is stopped and cooled down. Turn the fuel shutoff knob (A) so that the points on the knob are facing away from the carburetor to the closed position (FIG. 6-23). Remove the fuel filter from the fuel lines. Replace the fuel filter from the fuel lines. Replace the fuel filter with an original one when possible. Install fuel lines on the fuel filter. Fasten with clamps. Turn

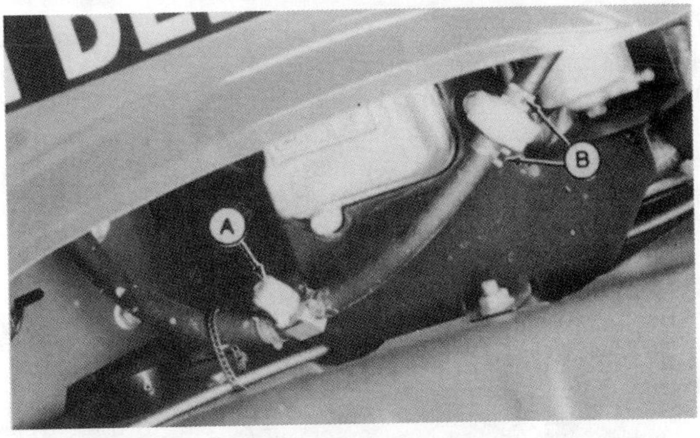

6-23 Change the fuel filter each year. Reproduced by permission of Deere & Company. C19XX Deere & Co. All rights reserved.

the shutoff valve so that the points on the knob are facing the carburetor to the open position (FIG. 6-24).

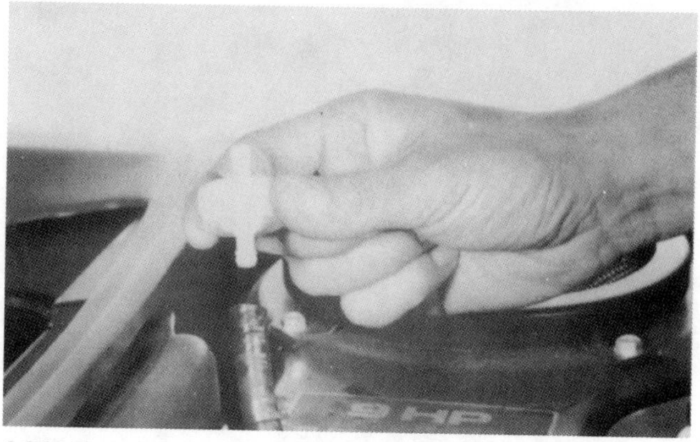

6-24 Turn the shutoff valve so that the points on the knob are facing the carburetor to the open position. Reproduced by permission of Deere & Company. C19XX Deere & Co. All rights reserved.

Cleaning the blower screen

Before cleaning the blower screen, make sure the engine is cool. A plugged mower screen can cause engine damage. On SX75 and SX95 models, lift the engine shroud. Clean out the blower screen.

Checking the tires

Check the tires with an accurate air gauge, and inflate the front tire to 14 psi and rear tires to 10 psi if necessary. Inspect the tires for damage.

Cleaning the air cleaner

Clean up the air cleaner after every 25 hours. Clean or replace the air cleaner elements more often under extremely dry and dusty conditions (FIG. 6-25). Remove the knob and cover. Remove the air cleaner. Remove the pre-cleaner from the air cleaner. Wash the pre-cleaner with detergent and water. Put approximately 1 ounce of clean engine oil on the pre-cleaner, then squeeze to distribute evenly.

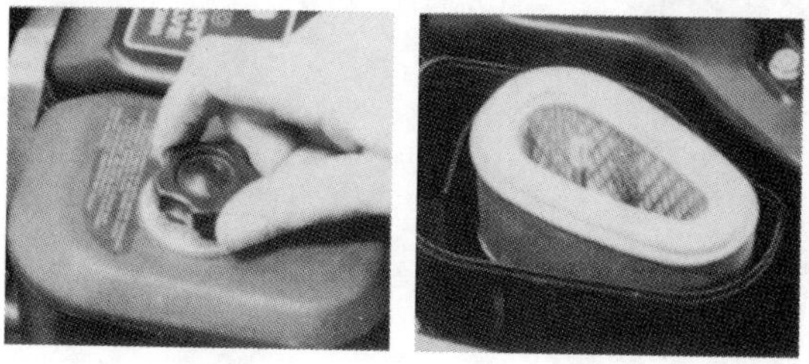

6-25 Check the air cleaner after every 25 hours of use. Reproduced by permission of Deere & Company. C19XX Deere & Co. All rights reserved.

To prevent engine damage, do not use compressed air to clean the air cleaner. If the air cleaner is very dirty or oily, replace it (FIG. 6-26). Tap the air cleaner lightly.

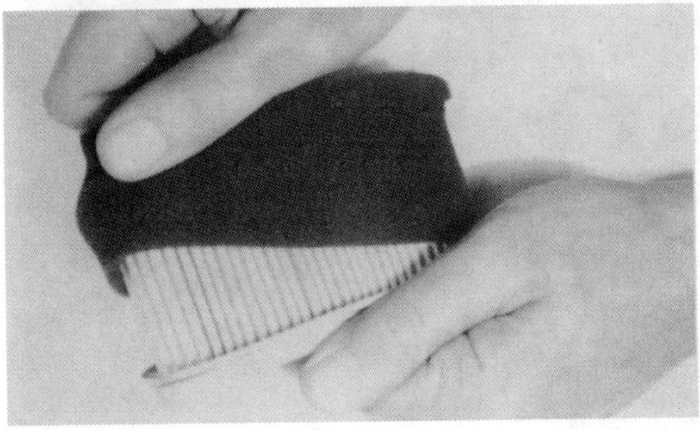

6-26 Replace the air cleaner if it is dirty, oily, or worn. Reproduced by permission of Deere & Company. C19XX Deere & Co. All rights reserved.

Checking belts

Lower the mowing deck to its lowest setting (1). Remove the cap screws (A) and shield on SX95 models. Check belts for wear and damage (FIG. 6-27). Check the guide belt adjustment. Clean under the deck and drive belt area with water pressure from a garden hose.

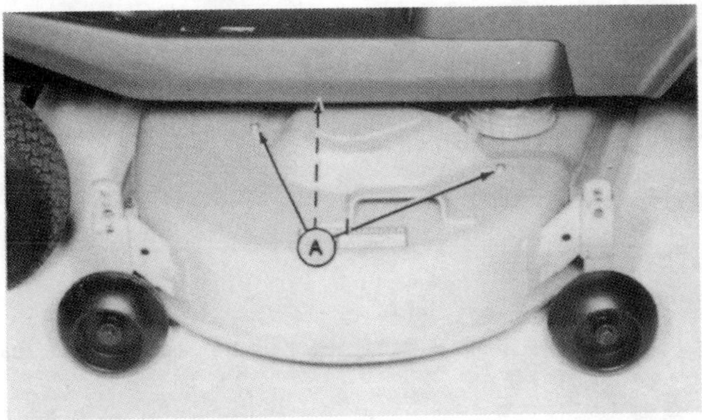

6-27 Check all belts after 25 hours of use. Reproduced by permission of Deere & Company. C19XX Deere & Co. All rights reserved.

Checking spark plugs

Check the spark plug annually. Make sure the engine is stopped and cool before checking the spark plug. Raise the engine shroud on SX75 and SX95 riding mowers. Remove the heat shield by removing the wing nuts on SX75 riding mowers. Disconnect the spark plug wire, then remove the spark plug. Clean the spark plug carefully with a wire brush. Inspect it for cracked porcelain, pitted or damaged electrodes, and other wear or damage (FIG. 6-28).

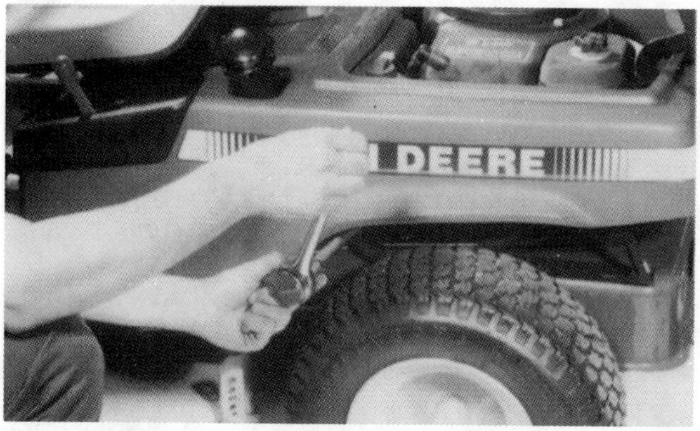

6-28 Inspect the spark plug for burned electrode. Reproduced by permission of Deere & Company. C19XX Deere & Co. All rights reserved.

Check the spark plug with a wire feeler gauge. Set the gap to 0.030 inches (A). To change the gap, move the outer electrode toward the center electrode (FIG. 6-29). Ground the spark plug electrode against the screw on the engine shroud. Turn the engine over and check for spark. Replace the spark plug if necessary. Install the new spark plug and tighten to 15 ft lb. Reconnect spark plug wire (FIG. 6-30).

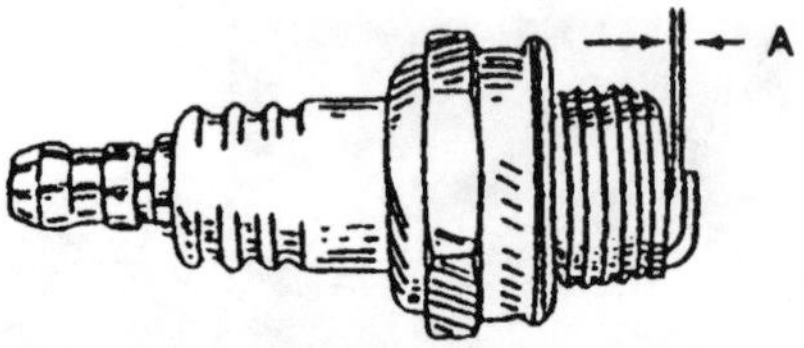

6-29 Adjust the spark plug gap to 0.030 inch and move the outer electrode towards the center. Reproduced by permission of Deere & Company. C19XX Deere & Co. All rights reserved.

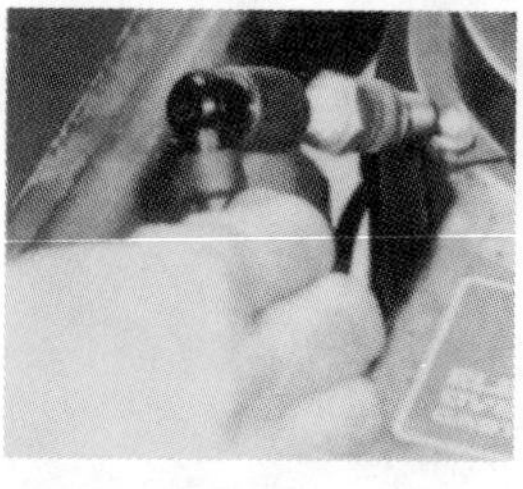

6-30 Install a new plug and reconnect the spark plug. Reproduced by permission of Deere & Company. C19XX Deere & Co. All rights reserved.

Sharpening blades

Raise mower to setting 4. Check the blade for sharpness and blade damage. Lower the blade to setting 1. Check for bent blade. Use a leveling gauge or short ruler and measure from the blade tip to the ground (A). Rotate the blade 180 degrees. Measure the opposite blade tip for dimension (A). The difference between the blades to ground should not be more than 1/4 inch. Install a new blade, if necessary. Always replace a damaged blade immediately.

To avoid being cut, wear gloves or wrap the blade with a rag when removing. Raise the mower with the lift lever as high as it will go. Put blocks under each side of the mower. Hold the blade with the rag and turn the cap screw counterclockwise (FIG. 6-31). Remove the cap screw, washer, and blade.

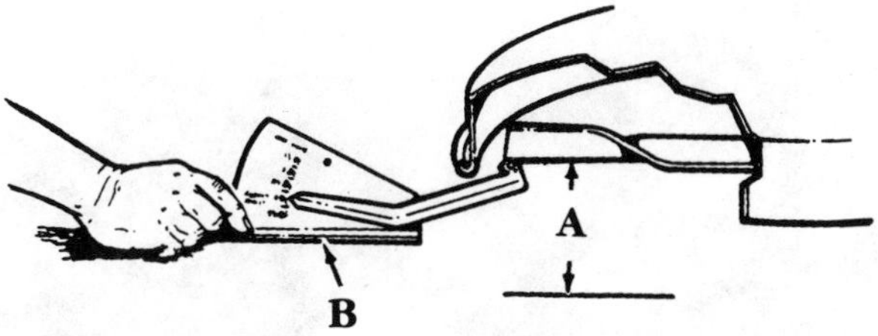

6-31 Raise the mower to the #4 setting and check the blade for sharpness.

Wear goggles and gloves when sharpening blades. Sharpen blades on a grinder, hand file, or electric blade sharpener. After blades are sharpened, they must be balanced. Keep the original blade level (A) when you grind or sharpen. Blades should have 1/64 inch cutting edge (FIG. 6-32).

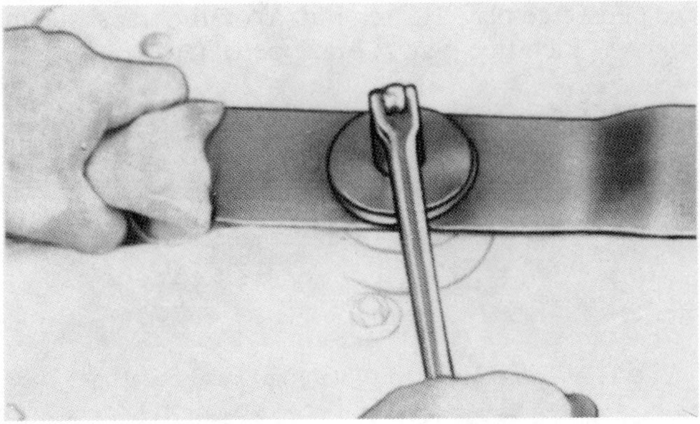

6-32 Remove the mower blade with a socket wrench.

Put the blade on a nail in a vise or on vertical wall stud and clean up. Turn the blade horizontally (FIG. 6-33). If the blade is not balanced, the heavy end of the blade will drop downward. Grind level the heavy end. Do not change blade level edge (FIG. 6-34).

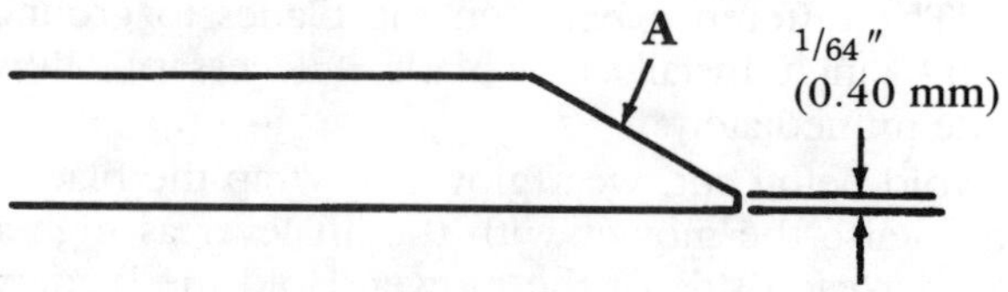

6-33 Keep the original blade level when sharpening. Reproduced by permission of Deere & Company. C19XX Deere & Co.

6-34 Balance the blade with a nail in a vise or vertically on a wall stud. Reproduced by permission of Deere & Company. C19XX Deere & Co.

Tightening brake pedal linkage

Check brake pedal free-play. Tighten nut (A) on the transaxle until there is approximately 3/4 inch free-play in brake pedal (FIG. 6-35).

6-35 Tighten nut A to tighten the brake pedal linkage. Reproduced by permission of Deere & Company. C19XX Deere & Co.

Adjusting speed control linkage

If your riding mower begins to lose speed, put the shift lever in the 7th speed position. Drive forward a short distance. Push in the clutch pedal fully and stop the engine. Release the clutch pedal. Lift up the seat and loosen nut (A). Move the shift lever to the number 1 speed and tighten the nut (FIG. 6-36).

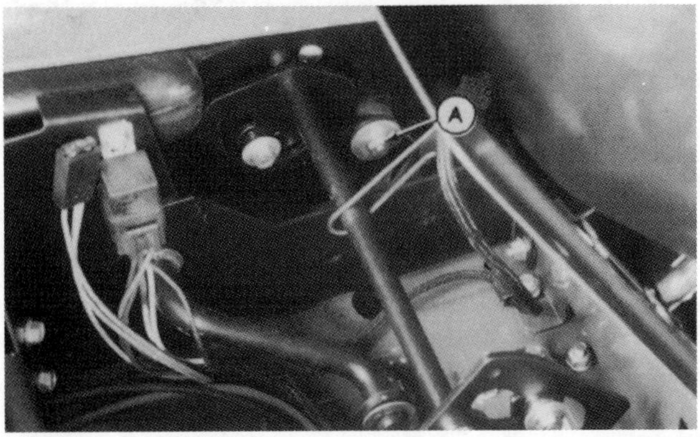

6-36 To adjust the speed control linkage, put the shift lever in #7 speed position, loosen nut (A), and then shift to #1 speed. Reproduced by permission of Deere & Company. C19XX Deere & Co. All rights reserved.

Replacing fuses

When engine will not crank, lift the seat and check the fuse. Replace the fuse. The overall troubleshooting chart for rear-engine riding mowers is found in TABLE 6-3.

Changing mower belts

To change mower belts, pull the PTO lever fully forward. Loosen nuts (A) and move the belt guides (B) away from the engine sleeve (FIG. 6-37).

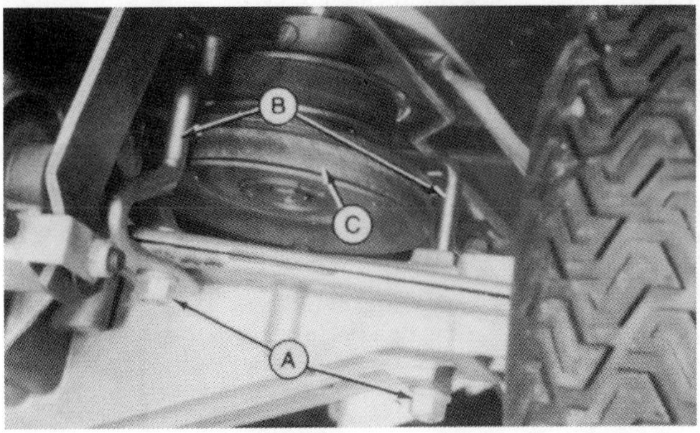

6-37 Pull the PTO lever fully forward before changing the mower belts. Reproduced by permission of Deere & Company. C19XX Deere & Co. All rights reserved.

Remove the mower belt (C) from the lower slot of the engine sleeve. Now, lower the mower deck to the number 1 setting with the lift lever. Remove the mower from the rear draft link by removing the cotter pin (or spring

Table 6-3 Troubleshooting RX75 and RX95 riding mowers.

Problem	*Solution*	**Section*
ELECTRIC START: Engine will not crank.	Pull PTO lever fully rearward.	–
	Put shift lever in N position.	–
	Clean battery cables.	Service
	Replace fuse.	
	Recharge or replace battery.	Service
Engine won't start	Check fuel.	–
	Turn fuel shutoff valve to ON position.	Operating engine
	Unplug tank vent cap.	–
	Replace spark plug.	Service
	Replace fuel filter.	Service
Engine runs rough.	Clean air intake screen.	Service
	Clean air cleaner.	Service
	Remove debris from mower spindles.	–
	Remove debris from under engine cowl.	–
	Adjust throttle cable.	Service
	Add oil to engine.	Service
	Replace spark plug.	–
Mower vibrates excessively.	Clean debris from mower deck.	–
	Remove debris from mower spindles.	–
	Adjust belt guides.	Service
	Sharpen and balance blades.	Service
	Replace damaged mower deck.	–
Clutch and/or shift levers vibrate	Replace drive belt.	Service
Riding mower makes clattering noise.	Adjust belt guides.	Service
Riding mower loses speed. Speeds 1-3 the same.	Adjust speed control linkage.	Service
Riding mower goes too slow in reverse	Adjust speed control linkage.	Service
Brake pedal has too much free-play.	Tighten brake linkage.	Service
Mowing unevenly.	Inflate tires.	Service
	Slow down. Mow in lower speed.	–
	Adjust mower wheels.	Operating mower
	Slow down when turning. Push in clutch pedal.	–
	Lever mower.	Operating mower
	Changing mowing pattern.	–
New riding mower or riding mower with new belts with not move—especially in cold weather.	Start engine. Move shift lever fully forward several times. Push clutch pedal in several times.	–

*Note: The Section column refers to the John Deere riding lawn mower owner's manual.

lock pin) (A). Put mower height adjustment lever at setting 4, then pull the mower belt away from the flat idler and V-idler. Loosen nut (B) and move the belt guide (C) away from belt (FIG. 6-38).

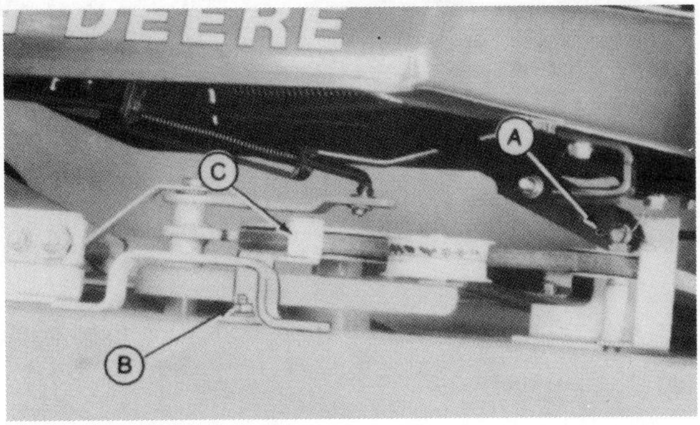

6-38 Loosen belt (B) and move the belt guide (C) away from the belt.

Put PTO lever fully forward. Put the belt between the sleeve and brake arm (A) (FIG. 6-39). Install the new belt in the engine sleeves. Move the shift lever fully forward. Put guides (A) and (B) next to the belt until there is approximately 1/16-inch clearance. The belt must go through loop (C) on the front belt guide (B) (FIG. 6-40). Tighten nuts (D).

Use FIG. 6-41 as a reference to installing new belts. Check the rear draft link that is connected to the mower with a cotter pin. Move the belt

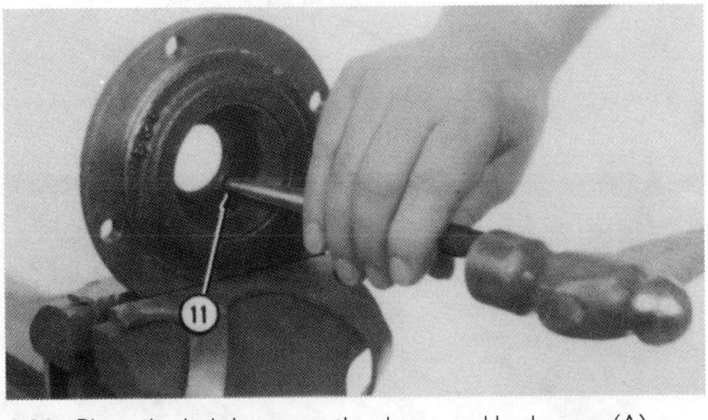

6-39 Place the belt between the sleeve and brake arm (A).

guide (A) as close to the belt as possible and tighten the nut. Recheck the PTO engagement rod adjustment after the new mower belt is installed.

Changing mower belt—SX95 Pull the PTO lever fully rearward. Loosen nuts (A) and move the belt guides (B) away from the engine sheave (FIG. 6-42). Remove the mower belt (C) from the lower slot sheave. Remove the

6-40 The belt must go through loop (C) in front of the belt guide (B). Reproduced by permission of Deere & Company. C19XX Deere & Co.

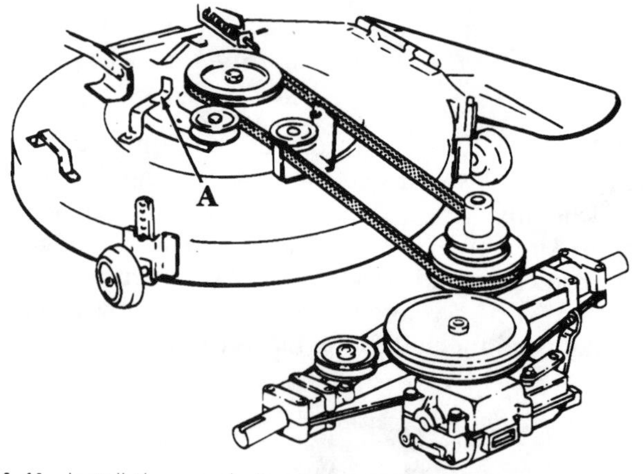

6-41 Install the new belt as shown. Reproduced by permission of Deere & Company. C19XX Deere & Co.

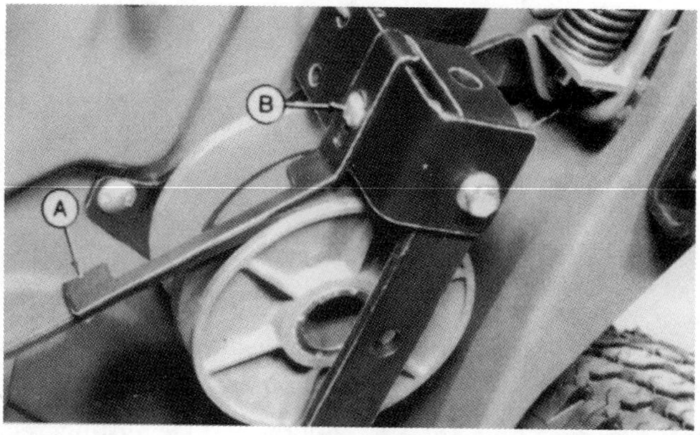

6-42 Remove the primary belt away from the lower sheave of the variator. Reproduced by permission of Deere & Company. C19XX Deere & Co.

mower belt from the lower slot of the engine sheave. Remove the mower from the riding mower. Remove the belt shield by removing the screws.

Loosen bolt and remove the belt from idler. Push the brake away from the sleeve and remove the belt. Loosen bolt. Pivot bracket to the right and remove belt. Pivot the strap to the left and remove the belt. Push the brake (D) away from the sheave and remove the belt (FIG. 6-43).

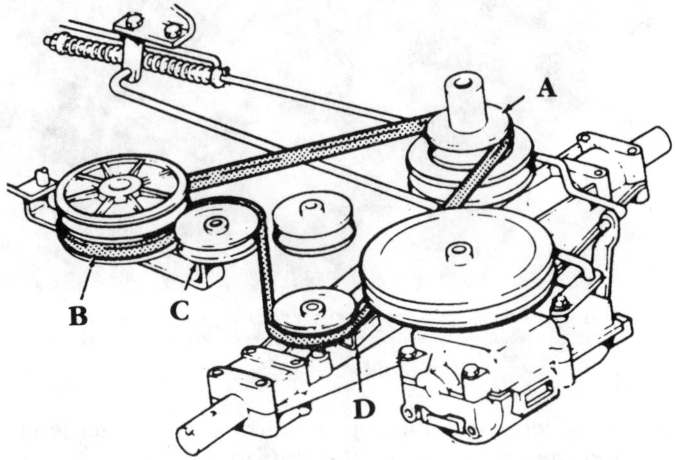

6-43 Install all belts as shown. Reproduced by permission of Deere & Company.

To install a new belt, put the belt between the guide bracket (A) and sleeve. Put the belt between the strap (B) and sheave. Pivot the strap to the right until it fits into the slot (FIG. 6-44). Tighten bolt (C) and place the belt inside the guide (D) and tighten the bolt (E). Install the shield (F) and fasten it with the bolt (G).

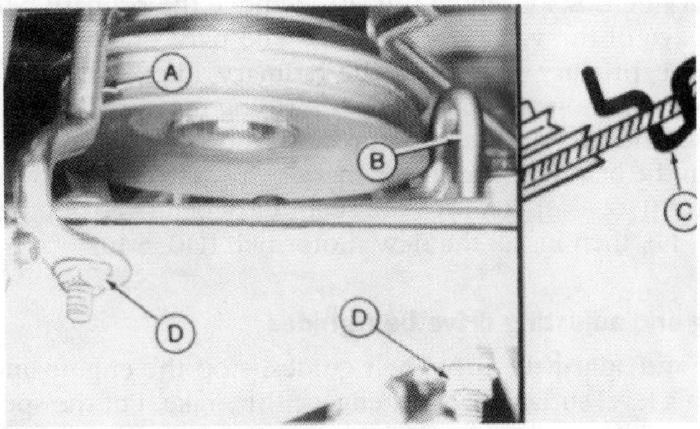

6-44 Remember that the belt guide must not rub on the engine sheave. Reproduced by permission of Deere & Company.

Install the belt on the engine sheave. Move the shift lever fully forward. Put the belt guides (A) and (B) next to the belt until there is approximately 1/16-inch clearance (FIG. 6-45). The belt must go through loop (C) in front of belt guide (B). Tighten nuts (D).

6-45 Adjust the speed control linkage for a shorter belt. Reproduced by permission of Deere & Company. C19XX Deere & Co. All rights reserved.

Adjust the speed control linkage to allow for a shorter length of new belt. First, start the engine. Move the shift to any forward speed setting. Drive forward several feet, and then push in the clutch. Stop the engine. Release the clutch pedal after the engine stops running. Lift the seat and loosen nut (A). Finally, move the shift lever to setting 1 and tighten the nut.

Changing primary and secondary belt Remove the secondary spring (A) from the frame with a screwdriver. Loosen the nuts and remove the belt guides away from the engine sleeve (FIG. 6-46). Remove the mower belt from the lower engine sheave. Move the variator belt guide (A) away from the primary belt by loosening nut (B). Remove the primary belt from the lower sheave of the variator (FIG. 6-47). The park brake must be locked. Remove the primary belt from the primary idler, V-idler, and engine sheave. Now, remove the belt from the riding mower.

Loosen nut (A) on the variator belt guide (B). Move the belt guide away from the belt. Remove the primary belt (C) from the lower sheave of the variator (FIG. 6-48). Remove the secondary belt (A) from the top variator (FIG. 6-49), then install the new motor belt (FIG. 6-50).

Checking and adjusting drive belt guides

To check and adjust the drive belt guides, stop the engine and park the mower on a level surface. Do not engage the brake. Put the speed control lever in the 7th speed notch. Using a hoist or safe lifting device, lift the rear wheels off the surface. Loosen nut (A) under the axle to adjust the front guide (B) (FIG. 6-51).

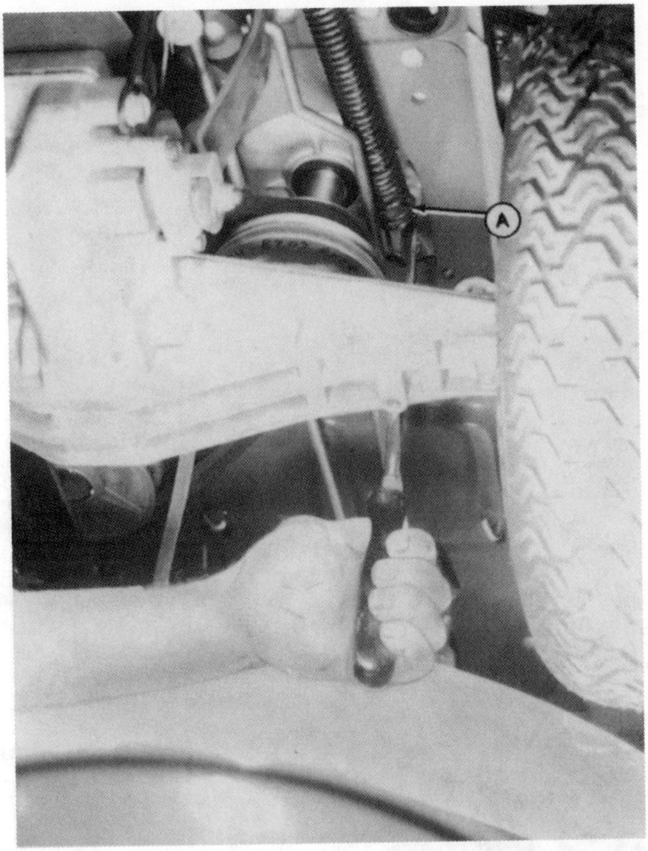

6-46 Remove the secondary spring (A) with a large screwdriver.

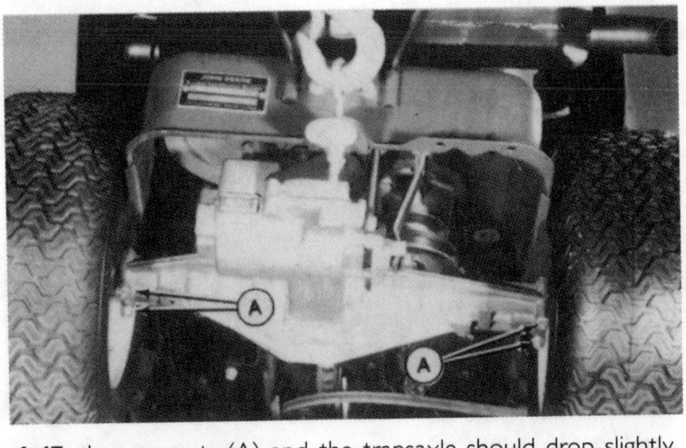

6-47 Loosen nuts (A) and the transaxle should drop slightly.

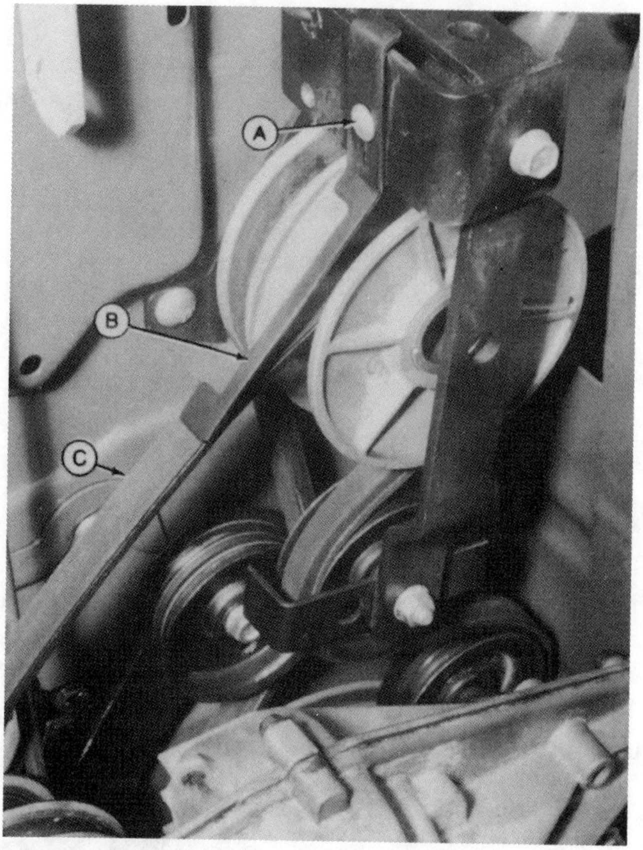

6-48 Remove the primary belt (C) from the lower sleeve of the variator. Reproduced by permission of Deere & Company.

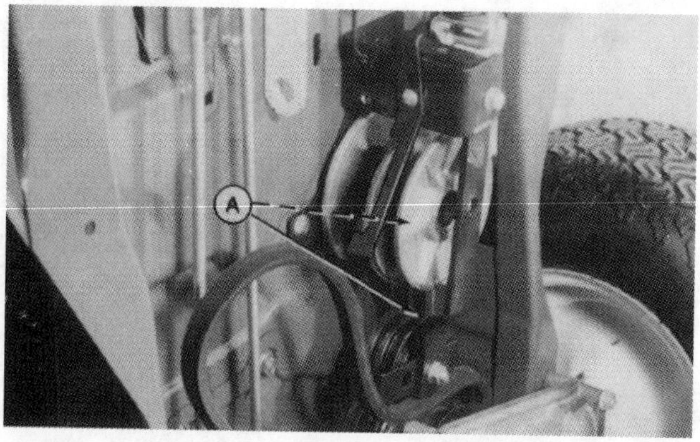

6-49 Pull the belt off of the rear transaxle and off of the left rear-corner of the mower. Reproduced by permission of Deere & Company.

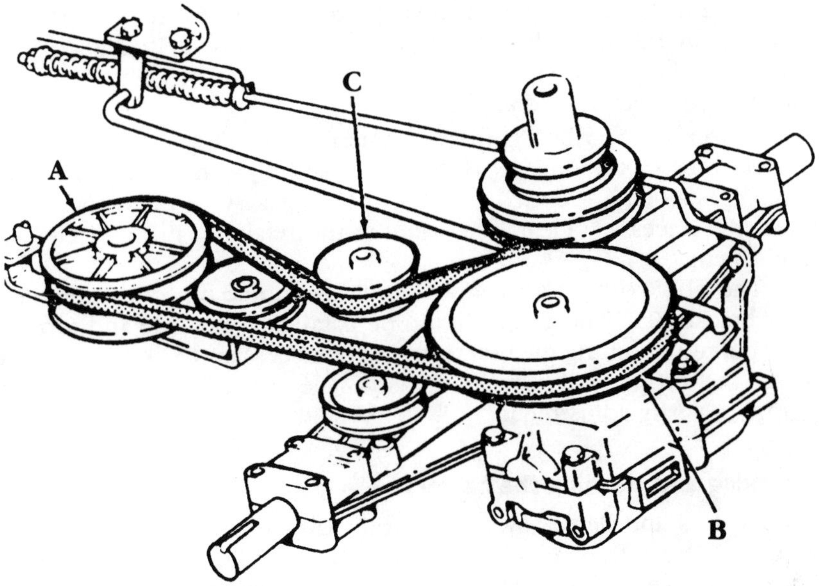

6-50 Install a new mower belt as shown. Reproduced by permission of Deere & Company. C19XX Deere & Co. All rights reserved.

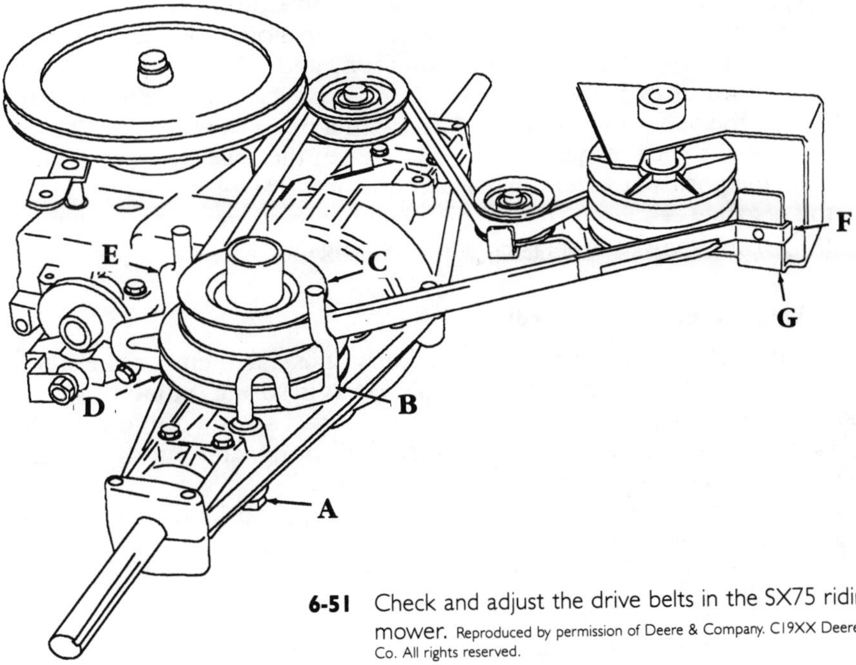

6-51 Check and adjust the drive belts in the SX75 riding mower. Reproduced by permission of Deere & Company. C19XX Deere & Co. All rights reserved.

Move the guide as close as possible to the primary drive belt but not pushing on the jack sheave (C). Less than 3/16-inch clearance is best between the top of the front guide and the jack sleeve. Tighten the retaining nut and check the adjustment.

Loosen the rear belt guide retaining nut (D). Slide the rear belt guide (E) rearward to the end of its slot. Check the clearance to the traction drive upper belt—3/16 inch. It might be necessary to bend the guide to attain the necessary clearance. Tighten the retaining nut and check the adjustment.

The tab (F) of the variator belt guide (G) should be contacting the variator bracket (H). The guide should be parallel to the side and top of the belt, but not touching the belt. It might be necessary to bend the guide to attain the proper adjustment. Operate the mower after adjusting the guides to verify adjustments.

Checking and cleaning the battery

Keep sparks and flames away from the battery because battery gas can explode. Check the electrolyte level with a flashlight. Do not check the battery for spark by placing a screwdriver blade across the posts. Instead, check with a voltmeter, DMM, or hydrometer. Always remove the ground (−) battery clamp first and replace it last.

To check or remove the battery, tip the seat forward, and remove the springs and battery cover. Remove the cell cap. Check the electrolyte level, then reinstall the cell cap.

To clean the battery, disconnect the negative (−) cable and positive (+) cable. Remove the battery. Remove any corrosion from the terminals with a wire brush. Clean the battery with a damp cloth. For excessive corrosion, use a solution of one part baking soda and four parts water. Keep the solution out of cells, however. Rinse with clean water and let dry. Clean out the vent holes in the cell cap with a piece of wire.

Reinstall the battery under the seat. Fasten the positive (red) battery cable to the positive (+) terminal. Fasten the negative (black) battery cable to the negative (−) terminal. Put petroleum jelly or grease on terminals, install a battery cover, and fasten it with springs.

Checking the battery electrolyte

Check the battery level after every 25 hours of use. Remember, the sulfuric acid in battery electrolyte is poisonous. It is strong enough to burn skin, eat holes in clothing, and cause blindness if splashed into eyes. To get at the battery, lift up the seat, remove the spring, and put the battery cover to one side. Remove the cell cap.

Check all the cells. The electrolyte must be 1/4 to 1/2 inch above the plates. Do not fill cells to the bottom of the filler neck. If necessary, add distilled water to the cells. Reinstall the cell cap and lower the seat.

Part 2

Servicing Engines

Chapter 7

Briggs & Stratton Engines

This chapter covers how to maintain, repair, service, and lubricate Briggs & Stratton engines. Remember to remove the spark plug wire before doing any service work on the engine. If you have not read chapter 1 on safety, do so now before beginning any service or engine work.

Maintenance involves keeping the air cleaner free of dirt and dust, cleaning up the cooling system, and replacing or cleaning up the spark plug to keep the engine operating smoothly. Each process usually only takes a few minutes.

FUEL AND LUBRICATION REQUIREMENTS

A high-quality detergent oil classified as SC, SD, SE, SF, and SG is recommended for Briggs & Stratton engines. Detergent oils keep the engine cleaner and retard gum and varnish deposits. For temperatures of 0 to 100 degrees, use 10W 30 or 10W 40 motor oil when 10W 30 is not available. Use 5W 20 or SW 30 oil in colder temperatures of 20 to -20 degrees.

To check the oil, make sure the engine is level and locate the fill plug or oil level. If the engine has an oil-minder and extended oil fill, remove and wipe oil from the dipstick with a clean cloth. Screw dipstick firmly into place. Remove to check oil level.

CONTROL ADJUSTMENTS

Manual controls require no adjustment. To increase or decrease engine speed, move the speed adjusting rod (FIG. 7-1). To check equipment controls, move the governor control lever in a direction that will elongate the governor spring to obtain maximum recommended speed.

7-1 To compensate for fuel, temperature, altitude, and load, you might need to make minor carburetor adjustments.

To adjust equipment control, loosen casing clamp screw on carburetor and move casing in or out to obtain proper speed. Do not exceed maximum speed recommended by the manufacturer of equipment. Retighten screw.

Connect control adjustment is necessary for good engine performance. To check the operation of CHOKE-A-MATIC control remove air cleaner cover and element. With equipment control lever in the CHOKE position, choke valve should be fully closed.

With equipment control lever in FAST position, loosen casing clamp screw on carburetor or control plate. Move casing and wire until washer just touches bell crank. Tighten casing clamp screw. Bell crank on carburetor or governor control lever on control plate must make good contact with stop switch, if so equipped. Reassemble air cleaner.

Remote choke control

Move remote choke control lever to the CHOKE position. The carburetor choke should be closed. To adjust the remote choke control, place the remote control lever to FAST (high-speed position). Loosen the casing clamp screw on the carburetor. Move the casing and wire forward or backward until the lever just touches the choke operating link. Tighten the casing clamp screw on the carburetor.

Recheck controls after adjustment. Move control lever to STOP position. Lever must make good contact with the stop switch, if so equipped. Replace air cleaner.

Throttle control

The acceptable operating range for the throttle is 1,800 to 3,600 RPM, and the idle speed is 1,750 RPM. Do not exceed the manufacturer specified TOP NO-LOAD RPM.

Governor control

The governor control lever has been adjusted to permit the top no-load speed specified by the equipment manufacturer. Do not bend the governor control lever.

Carburetor

More carburetors are rendered useless by neglect and abuse than all operational ills combined. A carburetor has but one task to perform, to mix fuel with air and feed it into the combustion chamber—at all speeds. The operational efficiency of a carburetor can be compromised by any foreign material (solid or liquid) that retards this flow of air or fuel. There are only three areas of carburetor malfunction: it is too lean; it is too rich; or it leaks.

Minor carburetor adjustments might be required to compensate for differences in fuel, temperature, attitude, or load. The air cleaner and air cleaner cover must be assembled on the carburetor when running the engine. The best carburetor adjustment is obtained when the fuel tank is approximately half full.

Gently turn the needle valve clockwise until it just closes. You could inadvertently damage the valve turning it in too far. Next, open the needle valve 1½ turns counterclockwise (FIG. 7-2). This initial adjustment will permit the engine to be started and warmed up (approximately 5 minutes) prior to final adjustment.

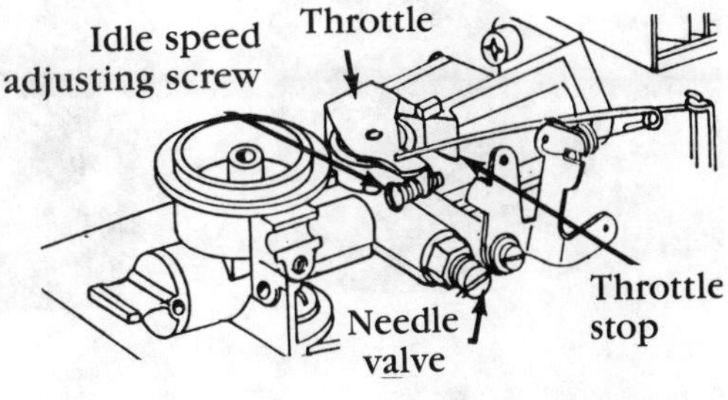

7-2 Before making the final adjustment, open the needle valve 1½ turns counterclockwise and run the engine for 5 to 10 minutes.
Briggs & Stratton Corp.

For the final adjustment, place the equipment control lever in the FAST position. Turn the needle valve in until the engine slows (clockwise-lean mixture). Then, turn it out past the smooth operating point until the engine runs unevenly (rich mixture). Now, turn the needle valve mid-point between rich and lean until the engine runs smoothly. Next, adjust idle RPM. Rotate the throttle counterclockwise and hold it against stop while adjusting the idle speed adjusting screw until you obtain 1,750

RPM. Release the throttle. The engine should accelerate without hesitation or sputtering. If the engine still does not accelerate smoothly, the carburetor should be adjusted to a slightly richer mixture.

MAINTENANCE

Maintenance involves keeping the air cleaner free of dirt and dust, cleaning up the cooling system, and replacing or cleaning up the spark plug to keep the engine operating smoothly. Usually, each process takes only a few minutes.

Air cleaners

There are several different air cleaners found on Briggs & Stratton engines. These air cleaners should be inspected and cleaned every 25 hours, usually before the season starts. Service cartridge cleaners every 100 hours or every season if it is equipped with a pre-cleaner. If the cartridge cleaner is not equipped with a pre-cleaner, service it every 25 hours. Clean up more often under dusty conditions (FIG. 7-3). When servicing the air cleaner, check the mounting and gaskets for worn or damaged mating surfaces. Replace any worn or damaged air cleaners.

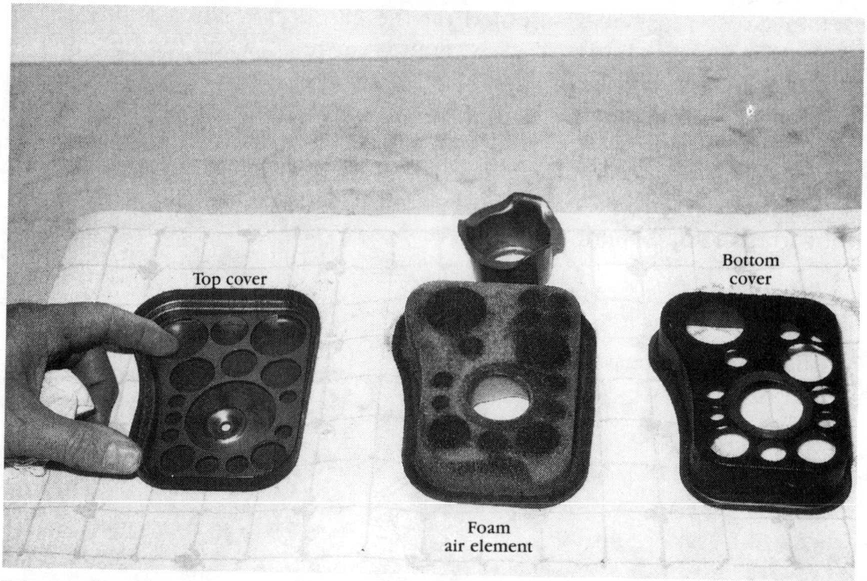

7-3 Notice the dirty foam cleaner on this Briggs & Stratton garden tiller engine.

Dual-cartridge air cleaners Dual-cartridge air cleaners are found on older 3 to 5 HP engines. To service, loosen screws and remove the cover (FIG. 7-4). Carefully remove the pre-cleaner and wash it in liquid detergent and water. Squeeze dry in a clean cloth. Saturate it in engine oil, then squeeze in clean, absorbent cloth to remove all excess oil.

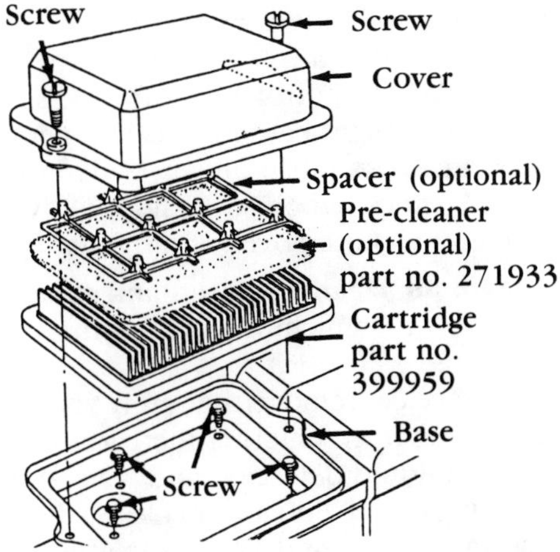

7-4 Remove the metal cover to get at the pre-cleaner and cleaning cartridge on dual air cleaners. Briggs & Stratton Corp.

To service the cartridge, carefully remove it and clean it by tapping lightly on a flat surface. If it is very dirty, replace it or wash it in a nonsudsing detergent and warm water solution. Rinse thoroughly with water flowing from the mesh side until the water is clear. Allow the cartridge to stand and air dry thoroughly before reinstalling.

Dual element/cartridge air cleaner Remove and service the pre-cleaner, if so equipped, every 25 hours or every season, whichever occurs first. Service cartridge every 100 hours, if not equipped with pre-cleaner.

To service, remove the knob and cover (FIG. 7-5). Carefully remove pre-cleaner and wash in liquid detergent and water. Squeeze dry in a clean cloth. Saturate in engine oil. Squeeze in clean absorbent cloth to remove all excess oil.

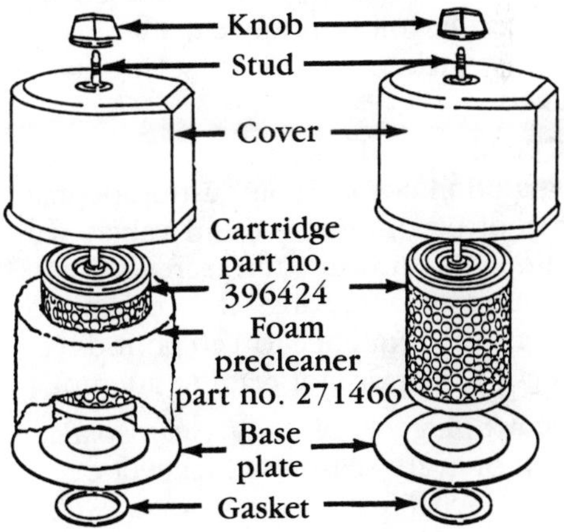

7-5 The dual element/cartridge of a Briggs & Stratton engine. Briggs & Stratton Corp.

To service cartridge, carefully remove cartridge by pulling it off the stud. Clean by tapping gently on a flat surface. If very dirty, replace or wash in a nonsudsing detergent and warm water solution. Rinse thoroughly with flowing water from inside out until water is clear. Allow cartridge to stand and air dry thoroughly before using.

Do not use petroleum solvents, such as kerosene, to clean the cartridge. This might cause the cartridge to deteriorate. Do not oil the cartridge, and do not use pressurized air to clean or dry cartridge. Reinstall the pre-cleaner (when so equipped) over the cartridge. Reinstall the cartridge on the stud, cover, and tighten knob securely.

Oil-foam air cleaner Clean and reoil foam element every 25 hours or every season, whichever occurs first. Service more often under dusty conditions.

To service, remove the screw and carefully remove the air cleaner to prevent dirt from entering the carburetor. Take the air cleaner apart and wash it in liquid detergent and water. Squeeze dry in a clean cloth. Saturate in engine oil. Squeeze in clean, absorbent cloth to remove excess oil. Reassemble parts and fasten securely to the carburetor with the screw. The screw hole is sometimes hard to locate and it might take you several attempts.

Engine

Preventive maintenance can keep your engine in tip-top shape, and perhaps keeping an engine clean might just be the most important part of its maintenance. Start by removing any dust and debris from around the engine's cooling system with a cloth or brush. Cleaning with a forceful spray of water is not recommended around the fuel system. Brush off debris from rack and pinion controls, governor linkage, and springs. Periodically clean the muffler area to remove all grass, dirt, and combustible debris.

Spark arrestor screen If the engine is equipped with a spark arrestor screen assembly, remove it after every 50 hours of operation or every season, whichever occurs first, for cleaning and inspection. Replace if damaged.

Cylinder head Remove the cylinder head after every 100–300 hours of operation. Scrape combustion deposits from the cylinder, cylinder head, top of piston, and around valves with a wire brush. Reassemble gasket and cylinder head. Turn screws down finger-tight with three long screws around exhaust valve, if so equipped. Torque cylinder head screws in a staggered sequence to 140 pounds (15.82 Nm). If you don't have the correct tools or do not want to attempt a repair, leave it to the professionals.

Spark plug Replace or clean spark plug after every 100 hours of operation or every season, whichever occurs first. Remove the spark plug with a $^3/_4$-inch plug ($1^1/_2$ cm) or a $^{12}/_{16}$-inch plug (2 cm) deep-well socket wrench. Do not try to remove spark plug with a pair of pliers.

Clean off deposits with a pocketknife or sharp instrument. Be careful not to break electrodes or proclaim insulator. If the electrodes are burned or deeply pitted, replace the spark plug. Scrape off with a wire brush and wash out with a commercial cleaning solvent.

After cleanup, check the spark plug gap. Using a wire feeler gauge, adjust the gap by bending or opening the side electrodes to .030 inch. Double check the gap adjustment (FIG. 7-6).

7-6 After cleaning up the spark plug, adjust the plug gap with a feeler gauge.

Inspect the plug threads and clean off with cleaning fluid. Sometimes oiling the plug thread lightly helps. Tighten the plug up firmly. Do not over-torque the plug. Most spark plugs are torqued to about 15 pounds.

Chapter 8

Clinton engines

Clinton engines are found in lawn mowers, chain saws, garden tillers, paint sprayers, posthole augurs, tractors, sprayers, compressors, weed cutters, and drilling equipment. This chapter covers how to maintain, repair, service, and lubricate Clinton engines. Remember to remove the spark plug wire before doing any service work on the engine. If you have not read chapter 1 on safety, do so now before beginning any service or engine work.

If you are unsure of the engine type, check the nameplate. In older models, the mylar nameplate with the engine model and serial number are stamped on the cylinder air deflector. These numbers are next to the mylar nameplate. The first digit is used to identify the engine, 4-4 cycle and 5-2 cycle engines. The second and third digits identify the basic series. The odd numbers are used for vertical shaft engines and even numbers for horizontal engines. The 405 indicates a 4-cycle vertical shaft series and the 406 horizontal shaft. The fourth digit identifies the starter:

0 Recoil starter.
1 Rope starter.
2 Impulse starter.
3 Crank starter.
4 12-volt electric starter.
5 12-volt starter generator.
6 110-volt electric starter.
7 12-volt generator.
8 Not assigned to-date.
9 Short block.

The fifth digit identifies bearing usage; the sixth digit identifies auxiliary power takeoff and speed reducers; the seventh digit indicates a major design change; and the eighth, ninth, and tenth digits identifies model variations.

Maintenance involves keeping the air cleaner free of dirt and dust, cleaning up the cooling system, and replacing or cleaning up the spark plug to keep the engine operating smoothly. Each process usually only takes a few minutes. Check the troubleshooting chart in TABLE 8-1 to help pinpoint the specific cause when a problem arises.

Table 8-1 Troubleshooting Clinton engines.

ENGINE FAILS TO START OR STARTS HARD	
Cause	*Correction*
1. No fuel in tank.	Fill tank with clean, fresh fuel.
2. Fuel shutoff valve not open.	Open fuel shutoff valve.
3. Fuel line to carburetor blocked.	Clean fuel line or remove and replace with new.
4. Water or foreign liquid in tank.	Drain tank, clean carburetor, and fuel lines, and dry spark plug points. Fill tank with clean, fresh fuel.
5. Stale fuel in tank.	Drain tank. Clean carburetor and fuel lines. Dry spark plug points. Fill tank with clean, fresh fuel.
6. No fire or insufficient fire to spark plug.	Check points, condenser, coil, high-tension lead, and flywheel keyway and magneto charge. Rework or replace as necessary.
7. Spark plug fouled or defective.	Replace spark plug with new.
8. Stop device in the OFF position.	Move stop device to on position.
9. Engine flooded.	Open choke. Remove air cleaner, clean and service.
10. Choke valve not completely closing in carburetor.	Adjust control cable travel and/or speed control lever.
11. Carburetor idle needle or power needle not properly adjusted.	Reset idle and power needles to the recommended preliminary settings.
12. Carburetor throttle lever not open far enough.	Move speed control lever to fast or run position; check for binding linkage or unhooked governor spring.
13. Low or no compression.	Check the following: Blown head gasket; damaged or worn cylinder; and valves stuck open, burned, not properly adjusted, or bad seats. Rework or replace as necessary.
14. Not cranking engine over fast enough.	Impulse starter spring broken or weak. Too much drag on driven equipment.

Table 8-1 Continued.

	Replace broken or weak spring, and remove belts, chains, and/or release clutch.
15. Carbon blocking exhaust ports (two-cycle engine).	Remove muffler and clean carbon from ports.
16. Reed broken off (two-cycle engine).	Replace reed or reed assembly.
17. Oil seals leaking (two-cycle engine).	Replace oil seals with new.
18. Carburetor dirty.	Remove and clean carburetor in a recommended cleaning solvent.
19. Loose blade (vertical shaft engines).	Tighten blade.
ENGINE MISSING UNDER LOAD OR LACK OF POWER	
1. Weak or irregular fire to spark plug.	Check points, condenser, coil, high-tension lead wire, flywheel, keyways, and flywheel charge.
2. Defective spark plug.	Remove and replace with new.
3. Choke not completely open.	Open lever to full choke position.
4. Carburetor idle or power needle not properly adjusted.	Reset idle and power needle to the recommended preliminary settings.
5. Restricted fuel supply to carburetor.	Clean tank, open gas tank cap vent, or clean and/or replace fuel lines.
6. Valves not functioning properly.	Reseat or reface valves, clean guides and stems of valves, and reset valves to tappet clearance.
7. Stop device not in the positive on position.	Move stop device to the ON position and/or adjust.
8. High-tension lead wire loose or not connected to spark plug.	Adjust high-tension lead wire terminal and/or connection to spark plug.
9. Air cleaner dirty or plugged.	Clean and/or replace air cleaner element.
10. Not enough oil in crankcase (four-cycle engine).	Drain and refill with the proper type and quantity.
11. Improper fuel oil mix (two-cycle engine).	Drain tank and carburetor, and refill with clean, fresh correct fuel mix.
12. Engine needs major overhaul.	Overhaul engine.
13. Too much drag on driven equipment.	Adjust clutches, pulleys, and/or sprockets on driven equipment.
14. Obstructed exhaust system or muffler not the type designed for engine.	Remove obstruction and/or replace muffler with correct one.
15. Weak valve springs (four-cycle (engine).	Replace weak valve springs with new.
16. Reed valve assembly not functioning properly (two-cycle engine).	Replace and/or adjust reed assembly.
17. Crankcase gaskets or seals leaking (two-cycle engine).	Replace gaskets and/or seals in question.

Table 8-1 Continued.

ENGINE NOISY OR KNOCKS	
1. Piston hitting carbon in combustion chamber.	Remove head and clean carbon from head and top of cylinder.
2. Loose flywheel.	Torque flywheel nut to recommended torque.
3. Loose or worn connecting rod.	Replace rod and/or crankshaft if tightening rod bolt won't correct.
4. Loose drive pulley blade or clutch on power take-off end of crankshaft.	Replace, tighten, or rework as necessary.
5. Rod lock or rod bolt hitting cam gear or block.	Crimp rod lock and/or tighten rod bolt.
6. Main bearings worn.	Replace worn bearings and/or crankshaft if necessary.
7. Rivet holding oil distributor to cam gear hitting counterweight of crankshaft.	Replace cam gear and/or grind head of rivet off.
8. Rotating screen hitting flywheel housing.	Center screen on flywheel.
ENGINE SURGES OR RUNS UNEVENLY	
1. Fuel tank cap vent hole obstructed.	Remove obstruction and/or replace with new cap.
2. Carburetor float level set too low.	Reset float level.
3. Restricted fuel supply to carburetor.	Clean tank, fuel lines, and/or inlet needle and seat of carburetor.
4. Carburetor power and idle needles not properly adjusted.	Readjust carburetor power and idle needles.
5. Governor parts sticking or binding.	Clean, and if necessary, repair or replace governor parts.
6. Engine vibrates excessively.	Check for bent crankshaft and/or out of balance condition on blades, adaptors, pulleys, sprockets, and clutches. Replace or rework as necessary.
7. Carburetor throttle linkage or throttle shaft and/or butterfly binding or sticking.	Clean, lubricate, or adjust linkage and deburr throttle shaft or butterfly.
OVERHEATING	
1. Carburetor settings too lean.	Reset carburetor to proper setting.
2. Improper fuel.	Drain tank and refill with clean, fresh correct fuel mix.
3. Overspeeding and/or running engine too slow.	Reset speed control and/or adjust governor to correct speed.
4. Overloading engine.	Review the possibility of using larger horsepower engine.

Table 8-1 Continued.

5. Not enough oil in crankcase (four-cycle).	Drain tank and refill with the proper type and quantity.
6. Improper fuel mix (two-cycle).	Drain tank and refill with correct clean, fresh mix.
7. Air flow to cooling fins and head and block obstructed.	Clean debris from rotating screen and/or head cylinder cooling fins.
8. Engine dirty.	Clean grease and/or dirt from cylinder block and head exterior.
9. Too much carbon in combustion chamber.	Remove head and clean carbon deposits from combustion chamber.
10. Obstructed exhaust system or muffler not the correct type designed for engine.	Remove obstruction and/or replace muffler with correct type.
11. Engine out of time (four-cycle engine).	Time the engine.
ENGINE VIBRATES EXCESSIVELY	
1. Engine not mounted securely.	Tighten mounting bolts.
2. Bent crankshaft.	Replace crankshaft with new.
3. Blades, adaptors, pulleys, and sprockets out of balance.	Rework or replace parts involved.
CAUSES OF ENGINE FAILURE	
1. Broken or damaged connecting rods and scored pistons.	Engine run low on oil (four-cycle engine).
	Rod bolt locks not crimped securely.
	Engine operated at speeds above the recommended RPM.
	Oil pump, line, and passage obstructed, with debris (four-cycle vertical shaft engines).
	Oil distributor broken off (four-cycle horizontal engine).
	Not enough oil in fuel mix (two-cycle engine).
	Oil in crankcase not changed often enough (four-cycle engine).
2. Excessive wear on parts. This covers valves, valve guides, cylinders, pistons, rings, rods, crankshafts, and main bearings.	Air cleaner not serviced often enough.
	Oil not changed often enough in crankcase.
	Air cleaner element improperly installed in air cleaner body or element needs replacing.

Table 8-1 Continued.

	Air cleaner body not making good seal to carburetor. Engine run low on oil.
3. Main bearing failure.	Excessive side loading of crankshaft. Oil in crankcase not changed often enough (four-cycle engine). Blades, adaptors, pulleys, and sprockets out of balance.

Clinton Engines

FUEL AND LUBRICATION REQUIREMENTS

Some Clinton engines have a float carburetor with a fuel filter in the tank to the fuel line adaptor. This adaptor might have a shutoff valve. Filtration is handled by a 120-mesh, bronze wire screen. To clean up, remove the adaptor from the tank, soak in cleaning solvent, and blow dry.

On larger horizontal shaft engines, the standard fuel filter is mounted below the tank with the filter screen, a sediment bowl, and a shutoff valve (FIG. 8-1). To service, close the valve and then disassemble the filter for inspection and cleaning. Check for chipped edges on the glass bowl and warped sealing edges on the body of the sealing gasket. Replace if damaged.

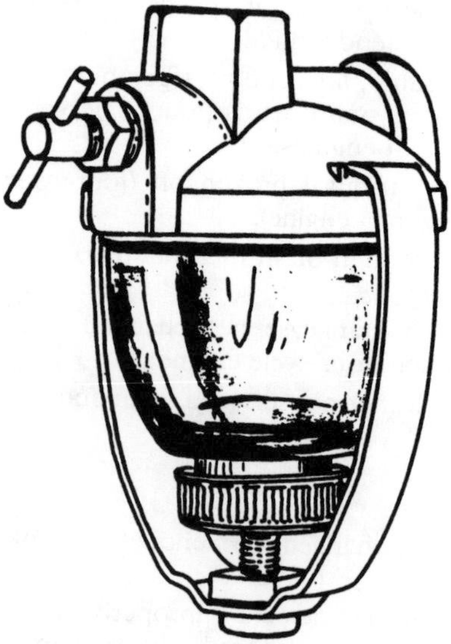

8-1 Large, horizontal shaft engines are equipped with a sediment bowl, filter screen, and shutoff valve. Clinton Engine Corp.

Engines with left-type carburetors have a ''built-in'' fuel filter on the bottom of the pickup pipe or standpipe assembly. This bronze screen is 100 or 200-mesh, or a combination of both. Clean the filter after removing the standpipe of the carburetor. Soak it in cleaning solvent and blow dry with compressed air. Remove any foreign material from the entire pipe (FIG. 8-2).

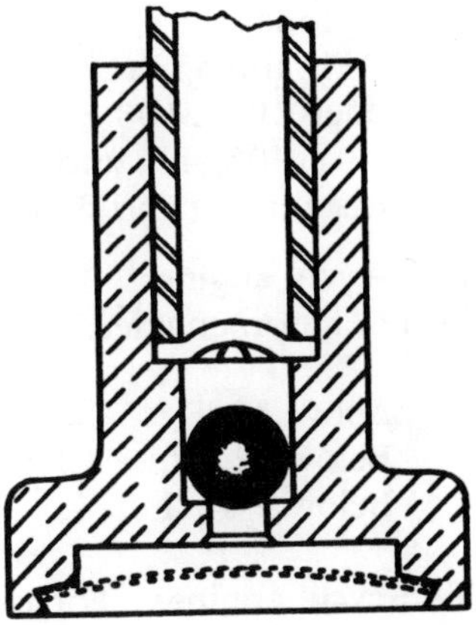

8-2 Blow out all rust and foreign material from the entire pipeline. Clinton Engine Corp.

Fuel lines and tanks

To service the fuel lines and tanks, first inspect for any hardness of the neoprene line in the area of the engine muffler. Flexible line hardness is usually followed by a fracture, so if there are signs of hardness, the line must be replaced. Cut replacement neoprene line to length, and allow adequate clearance around muffler and exhaust pipes, avoiding any sharp bends.

Suspect excessive rust particles if the carburetor keeps flooding. If water enters the tank for any length of time, it can cause internal rusting, and the sediment becomes trapped in the tank's filter. A fine, powderlike dust might pass through the filter. All steel tanks can be soldered. If the fuel tank is plastic, rust will, obviously, not form, but should repair be necessary, apply standard epoxy cement. Plastic tanks employ a nonremovable 120-mesh filter that requires no service.

Lubrication

All oil containers have a rating of ML, MM, MS, DC, and DM on the container. ML-marked oil is not to be used. An MM oil rating is acceptable but is the minimum rating to use. The MS rating is adequate under most operations. It is a high-additive oil that might have some detergent additive.

DG and DM ratings are high-detergent oils. DG oil is used in automobiles and can be used in Clinton engines but it is not recommended. An MS oil is preferable. DM oil should not be used and the warranty is voided if this grade of oil is used.

Always check the oil level in the crankcase with the engine on level ground. On some tillers with vertical shaft engines, you might have to block up the rear wheels to level the engine. Fill the crankcase with 1 pint of oil for models V-100, VS-100, A-300, 650, VS-2100, VS-3100, and VS-4100. Models 401, 403, 4059, 4079, 408, 4119, 415, and 417. Models 429, 431, and 435 require 1 3/4 pints of oil. To properly fill the crankcase of models 100, 2100, 3100, H-3100, and 4100, use 1 1/4 pints. Models 400, 402, 404, 406, 424 and 426. Different motors might have different ways of measurement and filling, so check the owner's manual.

Four-cycle engines The following grades of oil should be used in four-cycle Clinton engines:

Above 32 °F	Use SAE 30 of MM or MS rating.
Below 32 °F to −10 °F	Use SAE 10W of MM or MS rating.
Below −10 °F	Use SAE 5W of MM or MS rating.

Two-cycle engines For two-cycle engines, use an SAE 30, high-quality outboard motor oil or its equivalent in an SAE 30 or 40 viscosity with a minimum MM rating. Do use DM or DS-rated oils. For a sleeve-bearing engine, the correct two-cycle fuel mixture consists of 3/4 pint of oil to each gallon of gasoline. For needle-bearing engines, 1/2 pint of oil to each gallon of gasoline.

MAINTENANCE

Maintenance involves keeping the air cleaner free of dirt and dust, cleaning up the cooling system, and replacing or cleaning up the spark plug to keep the engine operating smoothly. Each process usually only takes a few minutes.

Air cleaners

Air cleaner systems on air-cooled engines must completely filter dust and dirt to protect the engine. It must also deliver a full volume of clean air to ensure correct carburetion. The frequency with which a cleaner must be serviced depends on the operating conditions. Extreme dusty conditions, such as garden tilling, might require daily service. The cleaner on a reel-type mower normally requires service after several weeks.

Check the dust inside the carburetor or cleaner body after removing the air cleaner. If dust is present, it had to come through the element or it was leaked by a sealing gasket in the system. Use factory-specified part numbers to replace air cleaners.

Metallic-mesh air filter A metallic-mesh air filter should be regularly cleaned. All of the air for the carburetor must pass through this filter to remove dust and moisture. Loosen the air cleaner screw and remove the cleaner element. Wash the air cleaner in solvent (do not use gasoline) and agitate vigorously to remove all dirt and dust (FIG. 8-3). Dip the air cleaner in oil, then replace and tighten. If the air filter becomes damaged or is lost, replace.

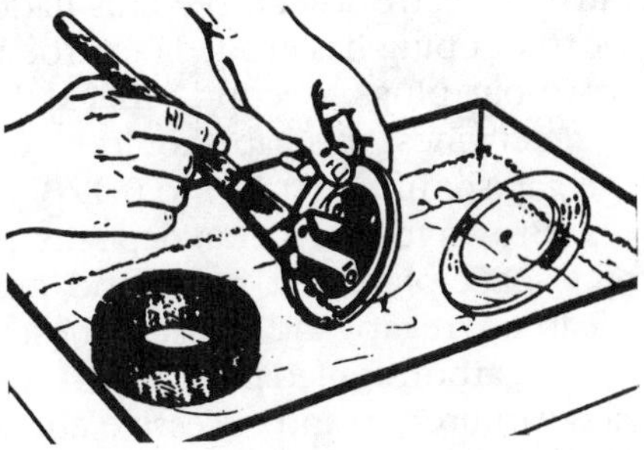

8-3 Clean the metallic mesh cleaner in solvent. Clinton Engine Corp.

Dry-type paper air filter A dry-type paper air filter can be cleaned with a bristle brush (not wire). After brushing off, blow dirt from the inside to the outside of the cleaner with an air hose. Do not wet or soak this type of cleaner in solvent or gasoline. Make sure the gasket is in place when reinstalling.

Oil-bath air filters Disassemble and thoroughly wash out oil-bath air filters in solvent (FIG. 8-4). If the bowl is plastic, make certain that there are no cracks, especially around the sealing areas. Repair cracks with epoxy, if possible. Blow out any remaining solvent from the mesh filter in the cover with compressed air. Fill to the correct level with SAE 30 engine oil.

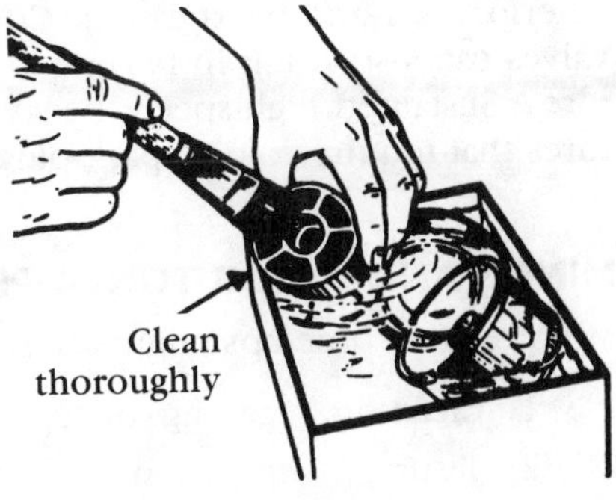

8-4 Wash out the oil bath cleaner in solvent and inspect the plastic body for cracks. Clinton Engine Corp.

Polyurethane air filters Polyurethane air filters require regular cleaning and reoiling. Wash the filter out in hot soapy water to remove dust, dirt, and original oil. Make sure the element is dry. Use SAE 30 engine oil to cover the face of the filter, about one tablespoon depending on the size of the filter. In addition to doing an excellent cleaning job, warm water will expand the element, providing a better seal around the edges when it is reinstalled in the container.

Spark plugs

Defective spark plugs can cause an engine not to start or to misfire when the engine is running. Make a visual check first. Look for carbon buildup, burned electrodes, cracked insulation, and carbon between electrodes. A worn-out plug has eroded electrodes and a pitted insulator. Replace these worn-out plugs. Second, check the gap between electrodes. For two-cycle engines, this gap should be 0.028 to 1.033. For four-cycle engines, the gap should be 0.025 to 0.128.

Brown to grayish tan deposits and slight electrode wear indicates correct spark plug heat range and mixed periods of high and low speed. Clean up, regap, and reinstall these types of spark plugs.

A carbon-fouled plug has dry, black deposits that can result from over rich carburetion and excessive choking. In this case, suspect a clogged air filter. A clogged air filter restricts the air flow, causing a rich carburetor mixture.

Poor ignition output with faulty breaker points, a weak coil or condenser, and worn ignition cables can reduce voltage and cause misfiring. Excessive idling at slow speeds and no-load can keep plug temperature so low that normal combustion deposits are not burned off.

An oil-fouled plug has wet oily deposits. Some electrode erosion can be caused by oil pumping past worn rings. Usually, these plugs can be cleaned up and reinstalled. Excessive valve stem guide clearances can also cause oil fouling.

Excessive burned electrodes on the spark plug with a burned or blistered insulator nose and badly eroded electrodes are indications of spark plugs overheating. Improper spark timing or low octane fuel can cause deterioration and overheating. Cooling system obstructions or sticking valves can also result in burned electrodes. Check for lean air fuel mixtures. Sustained high-speed, heavy-load service produces high temperatures that require colder spark plugs.

MINOR AND MAJOR TUNE-UPS

Minor engine tune-ups might consist of:

1. Cleaning, regaping, or replacing the spark plug.
2. Testing compression.
3. Cleaning the air filter.
4. Adjusting the carburetor.
5. Cleaning the fuel tank, line, and filter.
6. Adjusting governor speed.

Major engine tune-ups might consist of:

1. Cleaning, regaping, or replacing the spark plug.
2. Testing compression.
3. Removing the carburetor and overhauling.
4. Cleaning the oil filter.
5. Cleaning the fuel tank, line, and filter.
6. Adjusting governor speed.
7. Inspecting the reed valve on two-cycle engines.
8. Testing the capacitor.
9. Testing the coil.
10. Installing new breaker points.
11. Cleaning carbon from the muffler and exhaust parts on two-cycle engines.

If an engine is using oil and the compression is low, consider overhauling the engine. Leave the overhaul jobs to the professional mechanic. The remainder of the chapter focuses on servicing carburetors and starters.

Carburetors

More carburetors are rendered useless by neglect and abuse than all operational ills combined. A carburetor has but one task to perform, to mix fuel with air and feed it into the combustion chamber—at all speeds. The operational efficiency of a carburetor can be compromised by any foreign material (solid or liquid) that retards this flow of air or fuel. There are only three areas of carburetor malfunction: it is too lean; it is too rich; or it leaks.

There are many different carburetors on Clinton engines—501 left carburetors, LMG, LMB, and LMV types, H.E.W., U.T., and Carter carburetors. First, try to determine if the carburetor requires minor readjustment or major service as a detached unit. For older carburetors that might require considerable service, check the throttle shaft to maintain casting tolerance. An oversized or worn hole is not repairable and must be replaced.

If the carburetor is equipped with a bowl drain, start by looking for puddles of water. Press the valve and let a small amount of fuel leak into a container. If water is in the fuel, suspect a defective fuel tank, fuel line, or main casting of the carburetor. If the engine reacts poorly when the speed is changed, it might indicate a poor setting. Otherwise, the orifice in the carburetor is restricted by dirt or corrosion.

If the carburetor must be overhauled, it is advised that the engine be thoroughly tuned to handle the revised fuel distribution from correct metering.

501 engine carburetors To overhaul a 501 engine carburetor, first remove the carburetor from the engine (FIG. 8-5). Remove the choke assembly and the air filter. Remove the adjusting screw and spring and the bolt, lock nut, washer, and upper-body gasket. Remove the body assembly and lower the cover gasket. Remove the bolt and jet assembly and bolt gasket. Remove the bowl (bowl drain) assembly and float pin, float assembly, and bowl ring gasket. Remove pin, spring, and gasoline intake needle.

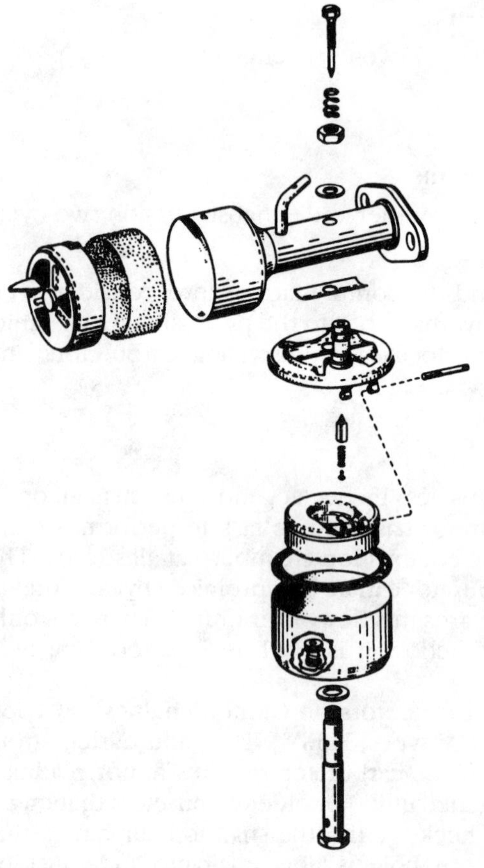

8-5 A 501 engine carburetor.
Clinton Engine Corp.

Install the new bowl cover, needle pin, spring, and seat assembly.

Clean all parts in solvent, and blow dry. Replace worn or damaged parts. Use new gaskets. Check to make sure the atmospheric vent is open. To reassemble, reverse the procedure. Once the carburetor is reassembled, adjust the needle one turn from the seat start engine. Check engine performance after a few minutes of operation. If mixture is too rich, turn 1/16 turn at a time to correct. Remember that this engine will not operate at speeds below 300 RPM with no load.

Lift carburetors To overhaul a lift carburetor, remove the throttle shaft by drilling through the expansion plug at the rear of the carburetor body.

Insert drift punch into the drilled hole, force out the expansion plug. Remove plastic plug and throttle valve, lift out the throttle shaft assembly.

To reassemble the shaft assembly, insert the throttle shaft into the carburetor body. Fasten the throttle valve to the shaft and torque the screw from 5- to 6 1/2-inch points. Make sure the throttle valve does not bind. Insert the plastic plug from the rear. Insert a new metal expansion plug into its seat, and strike the plug in the center until it expands and does not drop out. Seal the contact area between the plug and carburetor body with Gasolia sealer or equivalent.

Choke shaft assembly. The throttle shaft assembly might be assembled and disassembled at the front of the carburetor by removing the air filter cover and filter element.

Standpipe assembly. The standpipe is press-fitted into the carburetor body. To remove, clamp the standpipe into a vise and pull on the carburetor body. Reassemble the standpipe to the carburetor body by using a plastic hammer, tapping lightly on the bottom of the pipe. Slowly tap the standpipe into the carburetor body until the end of the pipe is 1.94 (plus or minus .045) inches from the bottom of the carburetor body. Seal the contact area between the standpipe and the carburetor body with the recommended sealer.

Idle needle bushing, idle screw, and idle setting. Remove the idle needle from bushing in a counterclockwise direction. Remove the bushing with a large screwdriver. Apply a light coat of recommended sealer to external bushing threads before installing the idle needle bushing. Install the idle bushing from 40- to 50-inch pound torque. Insert the idle screw into the metal bushing or carburetor casting until the screw seats, then open the screw from 4 to 4 1/4 turns (fine-thread screw). *Note:* when metal idle bushing is not used in the carburetor, turn open the idle screw 1 1/2 turns (course-thread screw).

Idle jet. Remove the expansion plug from the bottom of the carburetor. Remove the idle needle bushing. The idle jet is located in the passage connecting the fuel well. Remove the idle jet by pushing a piece of 1/16-inch diameter drill rod through fuel well and up the idle passage until the jet is pushed out of the passage and into the idle fuel reservoir.

To install the jet, scribe a mark on the 1/16-inch diameter drill rod exactly 1 1/4 inches from the end. Place the new jet on the end of the drill rod. Insert the rod through the main well and up into the passage until the mark on the rod is exactly in the center of the main fuel wall (FIG. 8-6). Remove the rod and install the idle needle bushing, if applicable. Insert the new expansion plug and seal it with Gasolia sealer or equivalent.

High-speed screw and main nozzle. Remove the screw and inspect for damage of taper. Replace if damaged. The power needle in some models might be changed. Check to see if the main nozzle has been tapered or split. This main nozzle cannot be removed. If it is split, a complete carburetor must be replaced. Turn the high-speed screw clockwise until it seats, but do not force. Open 3/4 to 1 turn. On carburetors having screws with straight taper and no shoulder, turn 1 1/4 to 1 1/2 turns.

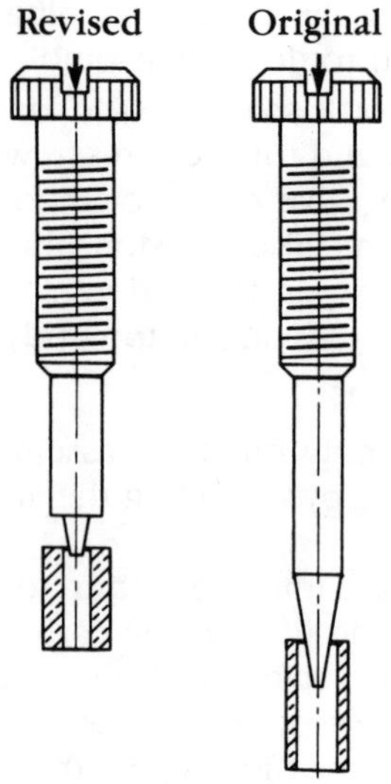

8-6 The revised and original power needle and nozzle found in lift-type carburetors.

Air leading into the fuel system might cause the carburetor to malfunction, which can sometimes be corrected by applying recommended sealer to the standpipe to carburetor body, the external threads of the idle needle bushing to the carburetor body, and the expansion plug to the carburetor body.

LMG, LMB, and LMV-type carburetors (FIG. 8-7) To overhaul an LMG, LMB, or LMV-type carburetor, remove the governor link from the throttle lever, and tie a short wire in the hole to ensure that you reinstall the link correctly. Soak the unit in a cleaning solution.

Remove the air cleaner, power adjustment needle assembly, gasket and bowl, float shaft, float assembly float valve, float valve seat, and gasket. Check the float for pinholes on the float bracket.

Remove the bowl ring gasket, idle adjusting needle, and spring assembly. Remove the throttle valve screws, valve, throttle shaft, and lever assembly, if necessary. Remove choke valve screws, valve, choke shaft, and lever assembly.

Do not adjust or remove the main nozzle for cleaning. Discard the nozzle if it is removed. Wash out the carburetor body with cleaning solvent. Blow out all passages. Check for worn parts. Install new gasket. Use a "repair kit" overhaul assortment, a new valve seat, and needle assembly. Always use a new gasket kit when reassembling. Make sure the atmospheric vent is open. Do not install old nozzle, replace with new one. To reinstall:

1. Install choke shaft and valve. Install with the part number towards the outside and the valve in the closed position.
2. Install the throttle shaft and valve and idle adjusting needle. Seat firmly and back off (CCW) 1¼ turns. Install a new needle if it is worn.

3. Install float valve seat, gasket, float valve, float, and float shaft.
4. Set float setting with a clearance of $^5/_{32}$ inch between outer rim of casting and nearest part of float at opposite side from the hinge.
5. Install the bowl ring gasket so that it nestles in the groove. Install the bowl with fiber gaskets on the inside and outside of bowl.
6. Install the power adjusting needle assembly with the gasket in place. Back out needle before tightening.
7. Seal power adjusting needle very lightly by turning clockwise and back off (CCW) $1^1/_4$ turns as a preliminary setting.
8. Install a new flange gasket to install the carburetor on the engine.
9. Assemble the throttle control and governor linkage at original location.

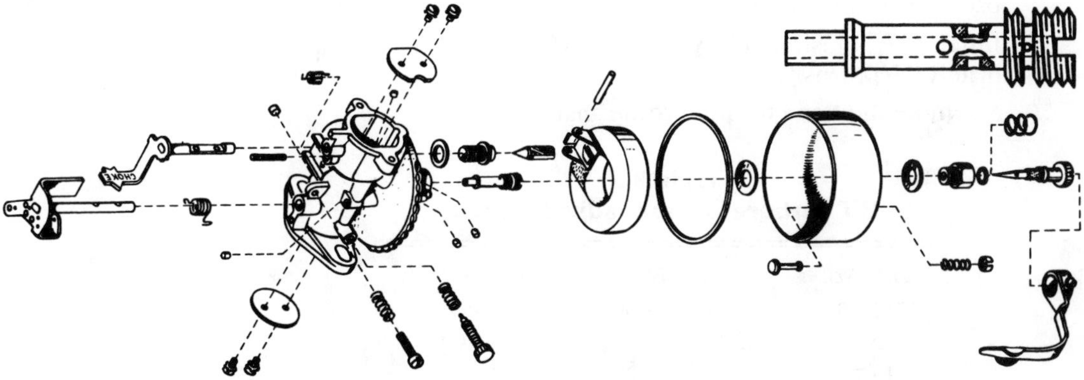

8-7 LMG, LMB, and LMV-type carburetors. Clinton Engine Corp.

UT carburetors To overhaul a UT carburetor, remove the carburetor from the engine. Remove the bowl screws, float pin, float needle, and needle seat. Check the float for dents, leaks, and wear on the float tip pinholes. Remove the bowl gasket and idle and high-speed adjustment screw assembly and springs. Remove the nozzle and idle jet tube, throttle valve screws, valve, and shaft assembly.

Do not remove the choke valve and shaft unless parts must be replaced. A spring-loaded pin keeps the choke in the open position. Take care not to lose the pin and spring.

Clean all parts in a cleaning solvent, and blow out all passages in the carburetor. Examine parts for wear and damage. Always use new gaskets when reassembling. To reassembly:

1. Install the throttle shaft and valve assembly. Install with the trademark on the side toward the idle part when viewing from the mounting flange side.

2. Install new screws. With the valve screws loose and the throttle lever stop screw backed out, seat the valve by tapping lightly with a small screwdriver. Hold in place while tightening screws.
3. Install the main nozzle, make sure it seats correctly in the casting.
4. Install the needle seat, needle, float and float pin.
5. Set the float level. With carburetor casting inserted, the float should be resting lightly against the needle in its seat and the bowl gasket removed. There should be clearance between the float seam and throttle body. See TABLE 8-2. Adjust by bending the lip of the float with a small screwdriver.
6. Install the bowl gasket, making sure the atmospheric vent and the idle jet passages are not blocked by the gasket.
7. Install the idle jet tube.
8. Install the high-speed screw assembly. Turn it until it seats, then back out 1¼ turns.
9. Install idle adjustment screw finger-tight, then back out approximately 1½ turns.
10. Assemble the bowl to the throttle shaft assembly.

Table 8-2
UT carburetor float adjustments.

Ident. No.	*Part No.*	*Float Setting*
2712–S	39–143–500	19/64
2713–S	39–144–500	19/64
2714–S	39–140–500	1/4
*2908–S	39–147–500	1/4
2336–S	39–146–500	1/4
2336–SA	39–146–500	1/4
2377–S	39–145–500	1/4
2337–SA	39–145–500	1/4
2230–S	39–343–500	17/64
2217–S	39–344–500	11/64

*When resilient seat is used, set float level at .9/32+or−1/64.

Clinton Engine Corp.

Carter carburetors To overhaul a Carter carburetor, remove the carburetor from the engine and remove the bowl nut, gasket, and bowl. Remove the float pin, float, needle, and needle seat. Check the float for dents, leaks, and wear on the float lip or in float pinholes. Remove bowl ring gasket, low-speed jet, and high-speed adjusting needle assembly and spring. Remove the idle adjustment screw and spring.

Remove the nozzle, throttle valve screws, valve and shaft, and lever assembly. Do not remove the choke valve and shaft unless these parts must be replaced. A spring-loaded ball retains the choke in a wide-open position. Be sure to use a new bolt and spring when replacing the choke shaft and lever assembly. Hold a screwdriver handle or a small piece of wood over the threaded hole in the air horn (side opposite choke lever) to prevent the ball from flying out when the shaft is removed.

Clean all parts in solvent, making sure all carbon accumulation is removed from the bore, especially where the throttle seats in the casting. Blow out all passages. Replace worn or damaged parts. Replace with new gaskets. To reassemble:

1. Install the throttle shaft and valve. Install the valve with the trademark on the side towards the idle port when viewing from the flange side.
2. Install new screws. With valve screws loose and throttle lever set screw backed out, seat valve by tapping lightly with a small screwdriver.
3. Install the nozzle, making sure it seats in the casting.
4. Install the needle seat, needle, float, and float pin. Set the float level. With carburetor casting inverted, the float should rest lightly against the needle in its seat. Leave $^{3}/_{16}$-inch clearance between machine surface of casting and free end of float. Adjust by bending the lip of the float with a small screwdriver.
5. Install the bowl ring gasket, bowl, bowl nut gasket, and bowl nut. Tighten securely after making sure the bowl is centered in the gasket.
6. Install the low-speed jet and high-speed needle assembly. Turn in until it seats in the nozzle, then back out 2 turns.
7. Install the idle adjusting screw tight. Back out approximately $1^{1}/_{2}$ turns.

Starters

This section provides information on servicing three types of starters—recoil starters, heavy-duty die cast impulse starters, and stamped-metal impulse starters.

Recoil starters A recoil troubleshooting chart is shown in TABLE 8-3. To repair a recoil starter, first disassemble by removing the recoil assembly from the engine. Slowly release the spring tension. Remove the rope pulley assembly— rope from pulley and recoil spring.

Clean parts in a cleaning solvent. Inspect all recoil parts for worn or damaged parts. Check for a bent, damaged, or broken recoil spring; a worn rope pulley bearing; a bent, cracked, or damaged housing; a bent, worn, or broken panel; and a broken, worn, or frayed rope or cable. Replace all damaged or worn parts.

Coat the recoil spring, the inside dome of the housing and the rope pulley shaft with grease. Install the recoil spring, making sure that it is

Table 8-3 Troubleshooting recoil starters.

Problem	*Possible cause*	*Correction*
Rope does not recoil	1. Spring bent.	1. Replace with new spring.
	2. Broken spring.	2. Replace with new spring.
	3. Spring disengaged.	3. Replace with new spring.
	4. Not enough end play.	4. Remove shims.
	5. Starter housing damaged.	5. Replace with new housing.
	6. Binding starter pulley.	6. Replace with new housing.
	7. Broken rope.	7. Replace with bulk rope.
	8. Insufficient tension on spring.	8. Rewind spring.
Noisy when running.	1. Hub rubbing on cap.	1. Use additional washers.
	2. Too much end play.	2. Use shim stock to get clearance.
		3. Replace pulley assembly.
Starter frozen up; will not pull.	1. Starter spring broken and jammed hub.	1. Replace spring with new. Check hub for damage and replace.
	2. Improper lubrication or dirty.	2. Disassemble and clean and lubricate.

wound in the right direction. Install the rope pulley, making sure the spring hooks into the pulley. Check to see if the rope must be installed before the pulley is in place (FIG. 8-8).

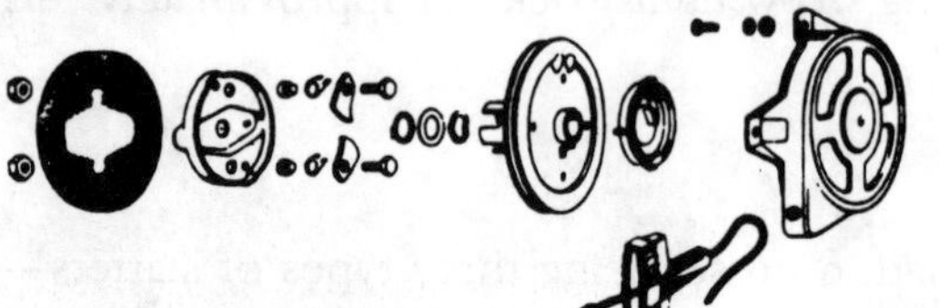

8-8 Top view of parts layout in recoil starter assembly.
Clinton Engine Corp.

Assemble the panels or washer to the recoil housing shaft or rope pulley. Wind the recoil spring by turning the rope pulley. The spring can be wound completely tight and then backed off 1 turn. Install the starter rope and handle while holding the pulley to keep it from unwinding. If the recoil spring is wound in the wrong direction, the spring will fall on the first pull of the rope.

Heavy-duty die cast impulse starters Heavy-duty die cast impulse starters (265-135-500) have waffled tops that are $2^3/_4$ inches from the bottom of the legs to the top of the housing (FIG. 8-9). Heavy-duty starters are used in engines up to, and including, $4^1/_2$ BHP. Standard starters are used on vertical shaft engines under $3^1/_2$ BHP and should not be used on installations that impose a heavy starting load on the engine.

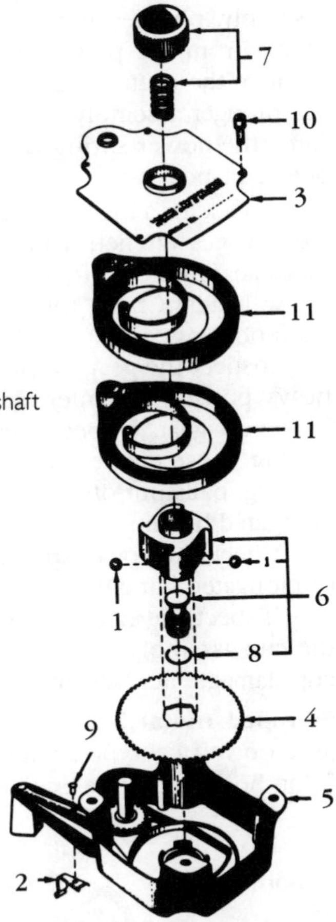

8-9 The standard impulse starter found in vertical-shaft Clinton engines. Clinton Engine Corp.

The compact, or low file, 265-206-500 starter is 2 1/4 inches from the bottom of legs to the top of the starter housing and has a waffled top. The only way to tell the difference is the overall height of the standard starter because it is taller. The low-profile starter is used on horizontal and vertical engines under 3 1/2 BHP and should not be used on installations that impose a heavy starting load on the engine.

The main housing assembly is serviced as a complete assembly and includes the handle, shaft, small gear, panel, and spring assembly.

To service a defective starter, first disassemble the starter spring. Remove the ratchet with a 3/8-inch Allen wrench. Turn in a counterclockwise direction. If ratchet is broken or will not unscrew, skip this operation.

Remove the screws holding down the cover assembly to the starter housing. Grasp starter housing top and lightly tap starter assembly (legs down) on a clean workbench, holding the starter at arm's length with fingers on the main housing assembly only.

Tap lightly to remove the bottom cover assembly spring and cup assembly, plunger assembly, and large gear. Do not remove the power spring from the power spring cap. These must be serviced separately. Remove the bottom cover assembly from the internal assembly. Remove the plunger assembly from the power spring and cup assembly. Do not force the power spring upward. Wash out all parts in a cleaning solvent before inspecting.

Check for a broken or cracked housing; a rounded corner where handle engages ratchet; a broken pawl spring; small gear-tooth damage; a loose gear in the shaft; a shaft grooved by the bottom cover; and stripped screw heads. Check for large gear teeth that might be cutting into the main housing.

Inspect the gear for broken or damaged teeth, peening, grooving, or heavy burring of center plunger hole of gear. Check closely where balls lock into gear. Inspect the plunger assembly for damaged or broken ratchet, loose ratchet or bushing, damaged plunger, frozen plunger, balls missing, balls out of round or peened, missing retainer, or damaged and elongated bushing.

Check the power spring assembly for lack of tension, a broken spring or elongated handle shaft hole of the power spring cup.

Inspect the ratchet spring kit for damaged teeth on ratchet. Check the cup assembly for lazy pawls, a broken pawl spring, bent pawls, and cup damage. Replace all broken, bent, or damaged parts.

Stamped metal impulse starter Stamped metal impulse starters are used on vertical-type engines up to, and including, $4^1/_2$ HP. They will not fit on horizontal type engines (FIG. 8-10).

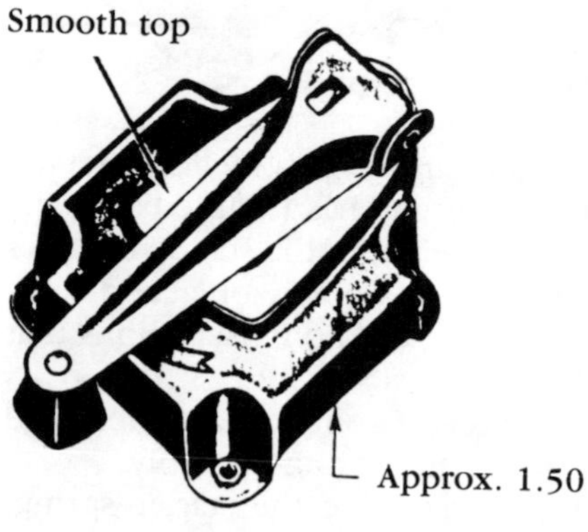

8-10 Layout assembly of die cast impulse starter assembly. Clinton Engine Corp.

Disassembly of stamped metal impulse starters is limited only to the handle. The main power spring and drive gear are not serviceable. Replace complete starter. To disassemble the handle, remove the center screw holding the handle to the starter body. When the screw is removed, the handle can be lifted from the starter body. This will expose the starter locking pawls and springs. The starter handle, pawls, or pawl springs can be serviced.

To reassemble, coat pawls and handle gear with grease. To assemble handle to starter, starter pawls have to be held out away from the center so the handle gear will fit into place. After handle is in place, install the center screw.

Chapter 9

Jacobsen engines

This chapter covers how to maintain, repair, service, and lubricate Jacobsen engines. Remember to remove the spark plug wire before doing any service work on the engine. If you have not read chapter 1 on safety, do so now before beginning any service or engine work. Jacobsen 123V and A984H engines are used in commercial lawn equipment. The two-cycle 123V has a vertical crankshaft while the A984H engine has a horizontal shaft. The vertical shaft engine has the recoil starter on top and the horizontal engine with starter along the side.

Maintenance involves keeping the air cleaner free of dirt and dust, cleaning up the cooling system, and replacing or cleaning up the spark plug to keep the engine operating smoothly. Each process usually only takes a few minutes.

123V TWO-CYCLE ENGINES

The vertical shaft engine (123V) is usually found on lawn mowers with a revolving mower blade at the bottom of the mower (FIG. 9-1). If the engine power decreases, suspect a defective carburetor or air intake system. The air cleaner consists of an outer and inner element.

Air cleaners

To remove the cleaning element, open the spring clip and remove the air filter cover and then the element and back plate (FIG. 9-2). Wash the inner and outer element in detergent and warm water. Rinse and dry thoroughly. Do not use compressed air, a dryer, or light bulb to dry elements.

Replace the cement if damaged. Soak the foam element in light engine oil. Squeeze the element to remove excess oil. Do not oil the inner fiber element.

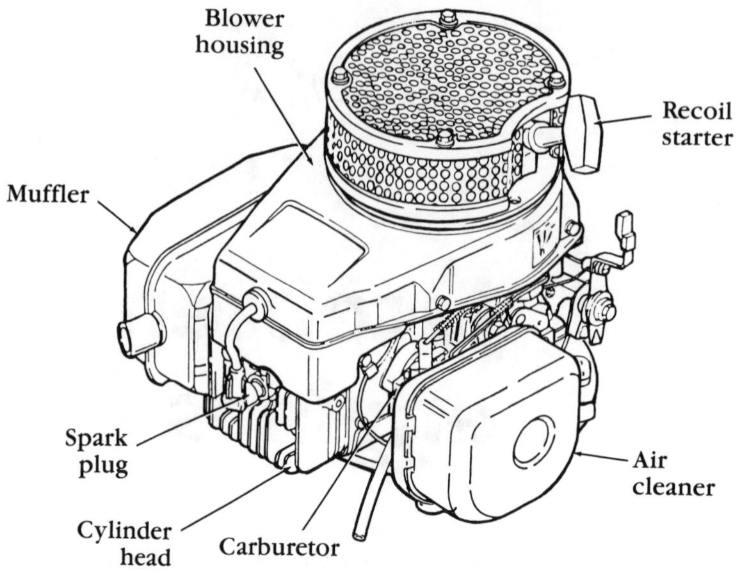

9-1 Jacobsen Model 123V vertical crankshaft engine. Jacobsen Division of Textron Inc.

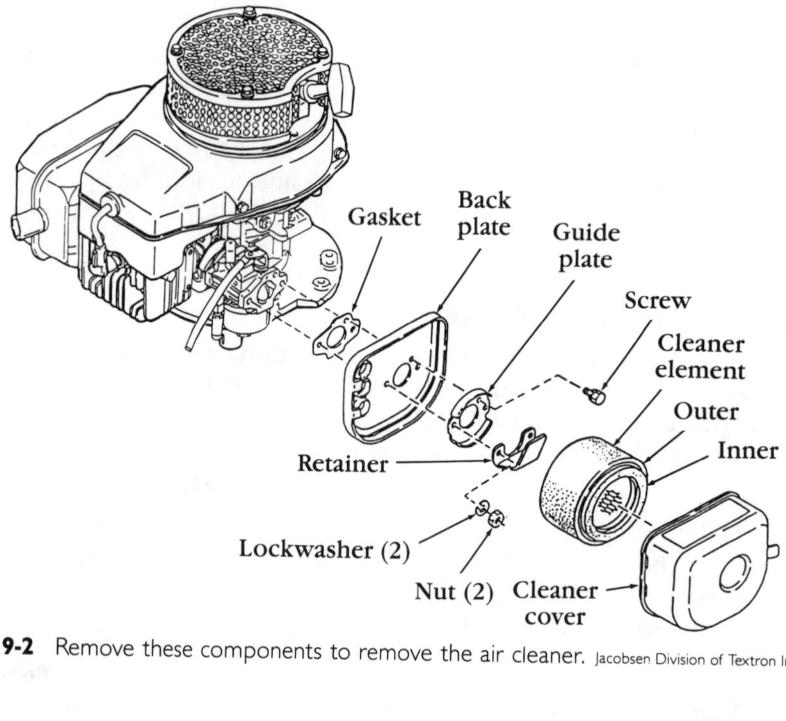

9-2 Remove these components to remove the air cleaner. Jacobsen Division of Textron Inc.

Install a new gasket and back plate to the carburetor. Install the outer element around the inner element. Place the element on the back plate. Position the cover and close the spring clip.

Recoil starters

To service a recoil starter, remove the recoil starter components. If the rope, springs, and/or ratchet require replacement, remove the entire starter unit. While maintaining pressure on the friction plate, remove the nut and friction plate. Remember, there is considerable amount of tension on the spiral spring. Insert the rope in the slot on the reel and rotate four to five turns to release tension prior to disassembly of recoil starter.

Note the position of the ratchet and return spring. Remove the ratchet, return spring, friction spring, and washer. Remove the rope reel and rope. Do not remove the spiral spring if it is not broken or defective. If the spiral spring is broken, remove it. Be careful; the spiral spring could be under tension.

Install a new spiral spring and a new rope by threading the rope through the reel, knotting the end, and pulling tight. Install the handle and knot the other end of rope. Wind the rope on the reel, leaving about 14 inches of rope loose. Install the reel, washer, friction spring, and ratchet. Install the friction plate and nut. Place the rope in the rope groove of the reel. Wind the reel 5 turns clockwise to tighten the spiral spring. Pull on the rope to ensure that it is properly installed. Install the recoil starter on the engine assembly.

Exhaust systems

Inspect the muffler for cracks or damage. Clean off the muffler with a metal brush. Small muffler cracks can be repaired with auto muffler mend repair kits. If the muffler is dented and damaged, replace. Remove the nuts, lockwashers, and screw washer to remove the muffler.

Carburetors

The 123V carburetor has a fixed, gravity-fed main type jet carburetor that does not require replacement. To service, remove the air cleaner and back plate, governor, throttle linkage, carburetor outer gasket, spacer, and inner gasket (FIG. 9-3). Inspect all parts for wear, and damaged or broken parts. Replace all defective parts. Clean all parts in a carburetor cleaning solvent such as Stoddard or equivalent. To reinstall, install the:

1. Main jet to the carburetor body.
2. Needle valve, spring, and float. Fasten with the float pin. Install the round end of the float pin into the body holes, but do not force the end with the flat through the holes.
3. Flat chamber gasket, chamber gasket, and bolt.
4. Seal, seal retainers, spring, and choke shaft.
5. Spring by hooking and turning the shaft 1/2 turn.
6. Choke plate.
7. Throttle shaft seal, throttle shaft, and throat-leakage.

8. Pilot jet. Tighten firmly to prevent fuel leakage.
9. Throttle stop screw and spring.
10. Carburetor with new gasket, governor, and throttle linkage, and air cleaner. Fasten carburetor in place. Governor linkage might be necessary after carburetor replacement.

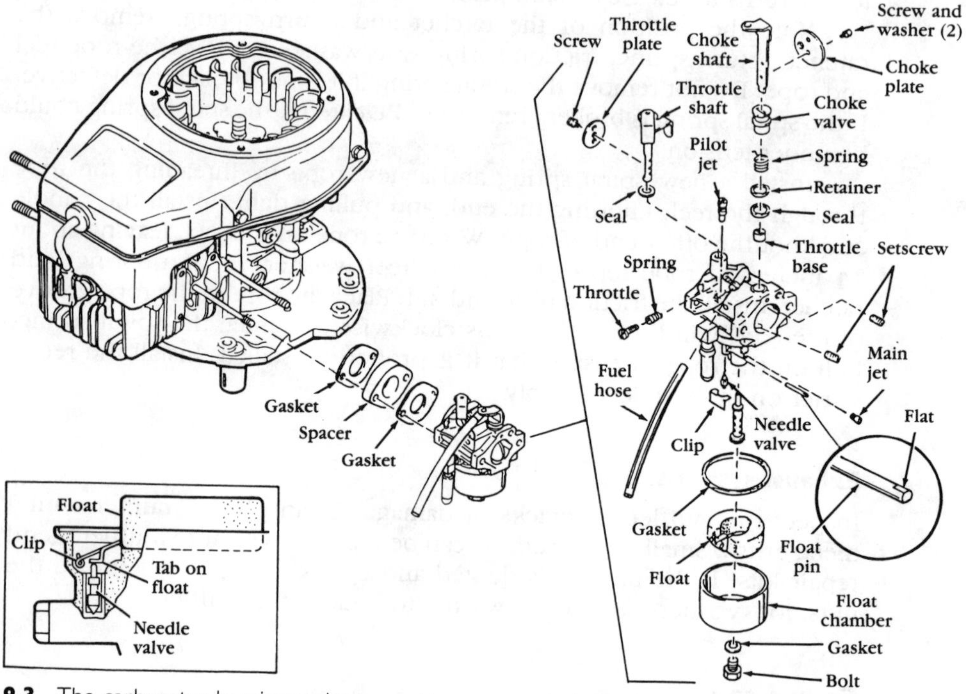

9-3 The carburetor housing and reassembly on a vertical engine. Jacobsen Division of Textron Inc.

Governors

Governor flyweight mechanisms are located in the bottom of the crankcase and are lubricated by the fuel/oil mixture. Governor adjustments can be made without removing the engine and separate block (FIG. 9-4).

To make standard governor adjustments, slightly loosen both the governor control shaft nut and the adjustable Phillips screws (FIG. 9-5). Push the adjusting plate down as far as it will go and tighten the Phillips screw. Set the speed control lever in the high-speed position and tighten the governor control shaft nut.

If the speed control lever and speed control handle were not removed for high-speed governors, no adjustment is necessary. If the speed control linkage was removed, adjust as follows:

1. Start the engine, and loosen the speed control lever linkage screw.
2. Position a tachometer on the engine.

3. Manually move the speed control lever down until the recommended full throttle of RPM is obtained (.3600 RPM).
4. When the proper RPM is obtained, tighten the speed control linkage screw.

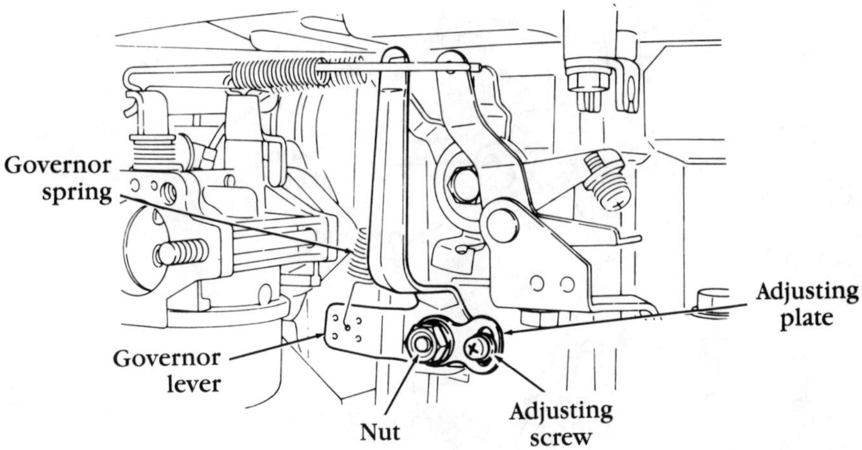

9-4 The location of the governor linkage adjustment on 123V engines. Jacobsen Division of Textron Inc.

Ignition systems

The ignition system of two-cycle engines is composed of a flywheel, coil with built-in TCI (Transistor Control Ignition), module, spark plug, primary load, and a high-tension, secondary spark plug lead (FIG. 9-6). The flywheel must be removed to install a new ignition coil with a built-in TCI.

Checking the coil The coil does not have to be removed to be tested. If the coil is defective, it can be removed without removing the flywheel. Disconnect the primary leads from the stop switch and the secondary lead from the spark plug (FIG. 9-7). Connect the spark plug lead to a suitable spark plug tester.

Pull the recoil starter several times. If a good strong spark occurs, the ignition coil might not be at fault. If the spark is weak or there is no spark, check it using a multimeter. Set the multimeter (DMM) to the 20K ohm range. Connect the meter leads between the secondary lead connector (spark plug lead) to ground (FIG. 9-8). The reading should be around 9K ohms. If the coil is open with no measurement, the spark plug connector is faulty or the high-tension lead is bad. A very low measurement indicates a shorted coil.

Setting the coil gap To set the coil gap, place a thickness gauge between the ignition coil and the flywheel assembly. Set the coil at a thickness of 0.016–0.020 inches (0.4–0.5 mm). See FIG. 9-9.

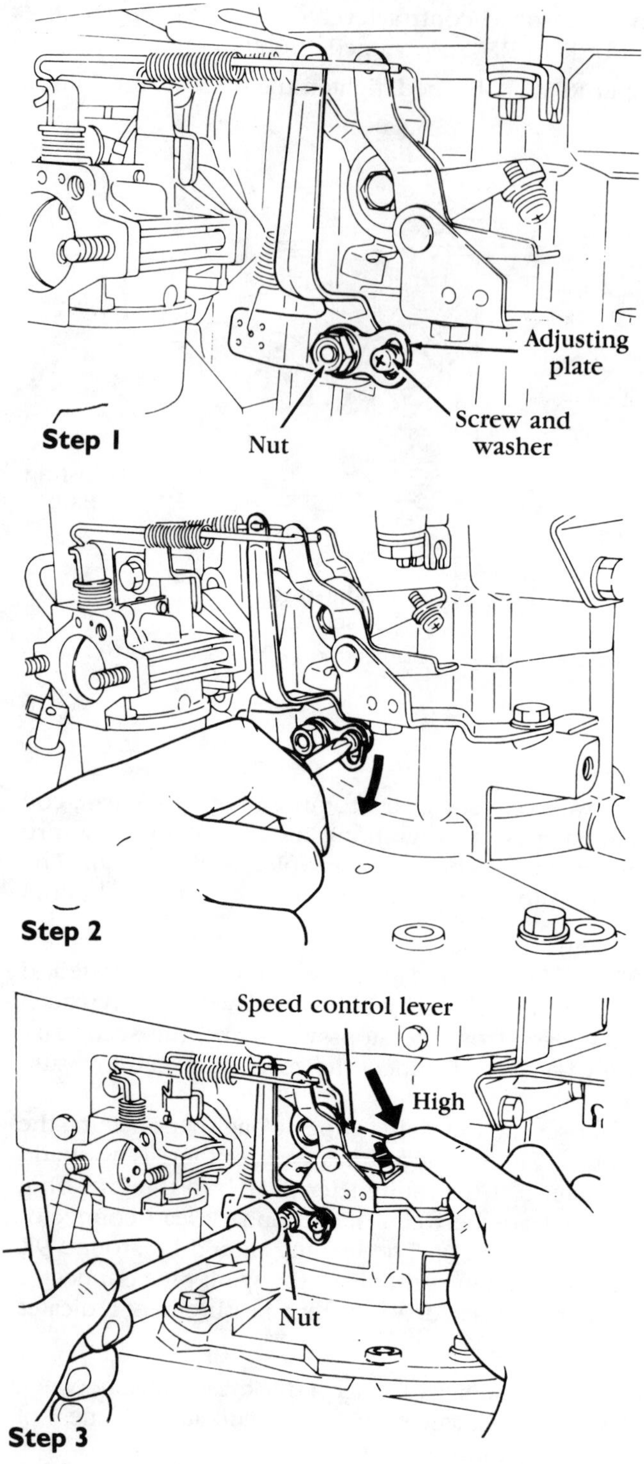

9-5 The standard governor linkage adjustment on 123V engines. Jacobsen Division of Textron Inc.

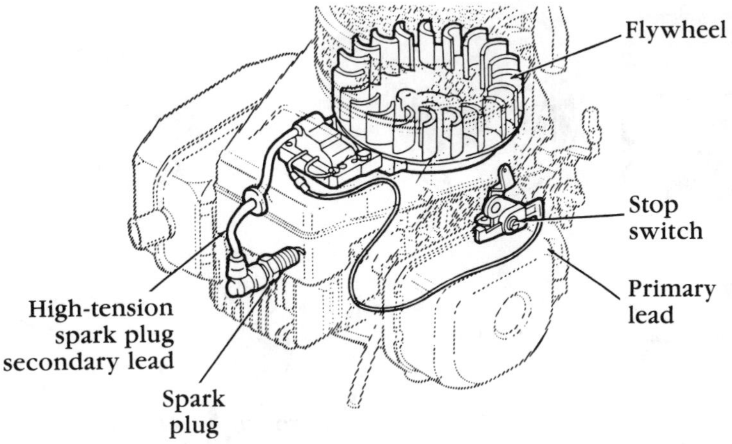

9-6 Ignition system components of 123V vertical engines. Jacobsen Division of Textron Inc.

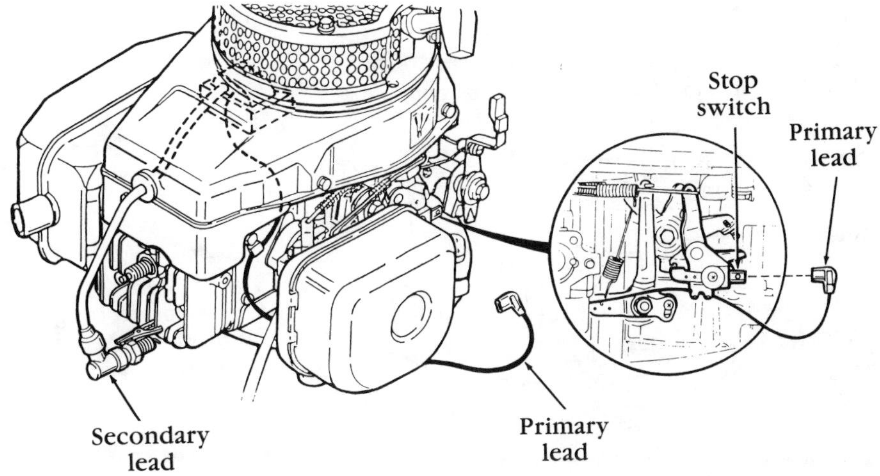

9-7 The coil wiring of the 123V vertical Jacobsen engine. Jacobsen Division of Textron Inc.

Replacing block assembly, pistons and crankcase assembly should be done by the professional repair shop or factory repair depot.

Adjusting the spark plug To adjust the spark plug, remove the spark plug and check the points for damage or wear. Replace the defective plug. Set the spark plug gap at 0.019 to 0.023 inch. (0.5–0.6 mm) (FIG. 9-10). Install the spark plug torque to 18–22 ft lbs (24–30 Nm).

A984H TWO-CYCLE ENGINES

The A984H is a two-cycle horizontal shaft engine. The recoil starter and rope are located on one side of the engine (FIG. 9-11). The engine layout is shown in FIG. 9-12.

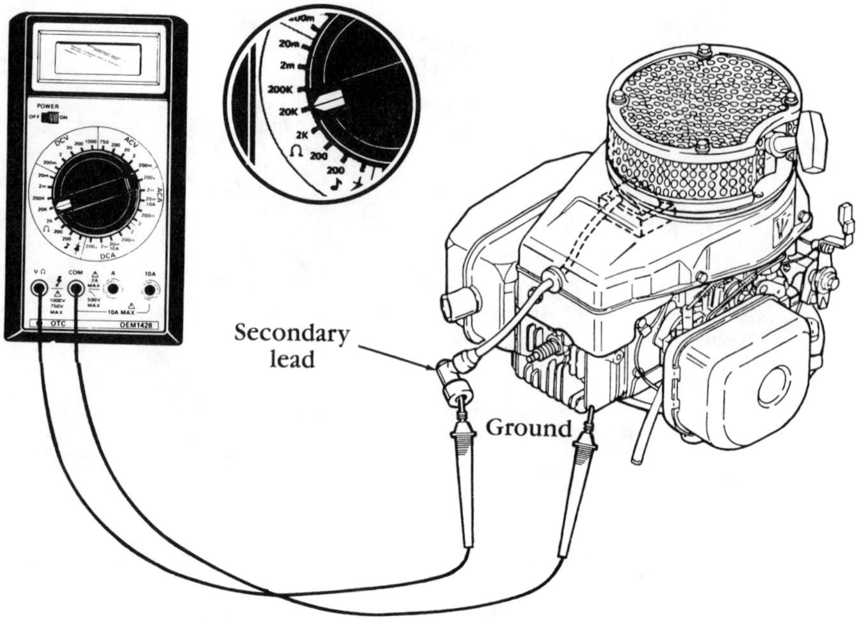

9-8 A coil test with a DMM set at the 20k ohms range.

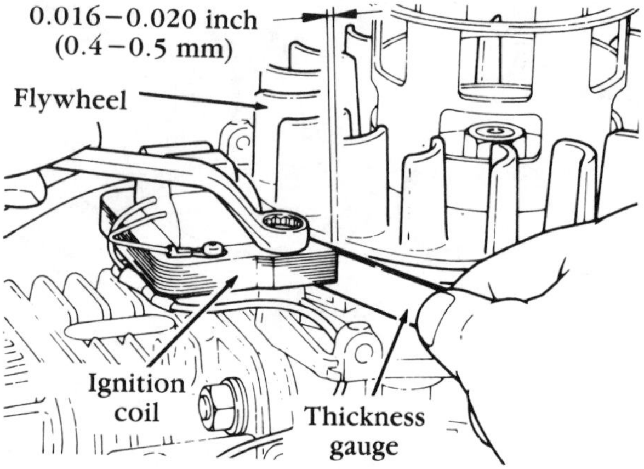

9-9 The correct coil gap adjustment between the ignition coil and flywheel. Jacobsen Division of Textron Inc.

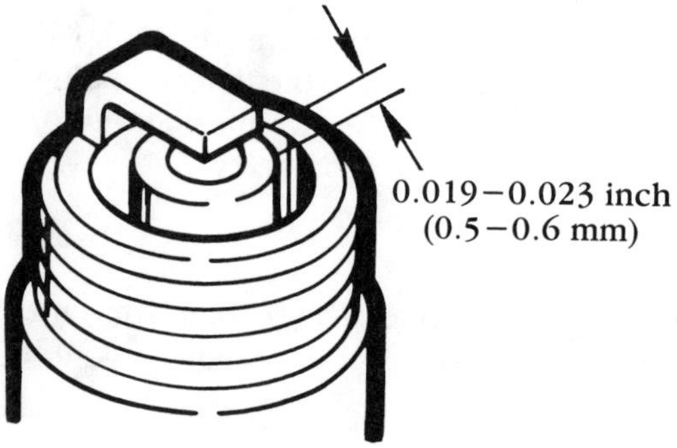

9-10 The correct spark gap adjustment on 123V engines. Jacobsen Division of Textron Inc.

9-11 Jacobsen A984H, two-cycle horizontal engine on a commercial greens lawn mower. Jacobsen Division of Textron Inc.

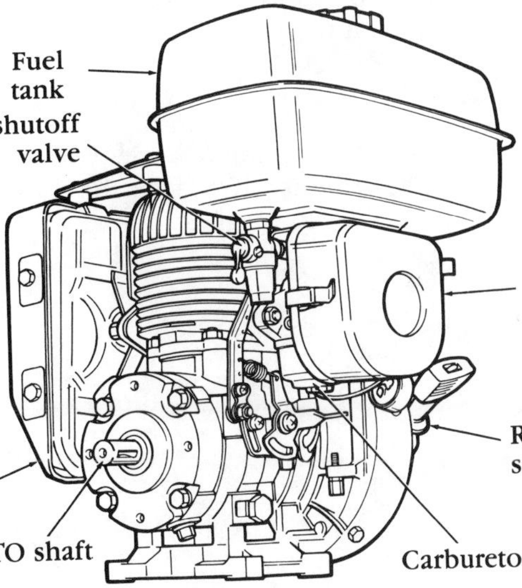

9-12 Components in the Jacobsen A984H engine. Jacobsen Division of Textron Inc.

Air cleaners

The air cleaner is a two-stage, high-efficiency system consisting of an outer and inner element. To service, remove the air cleaner by opening the spring clip and removing the air cleaner (FIG. 9-13). Remove the back cover.

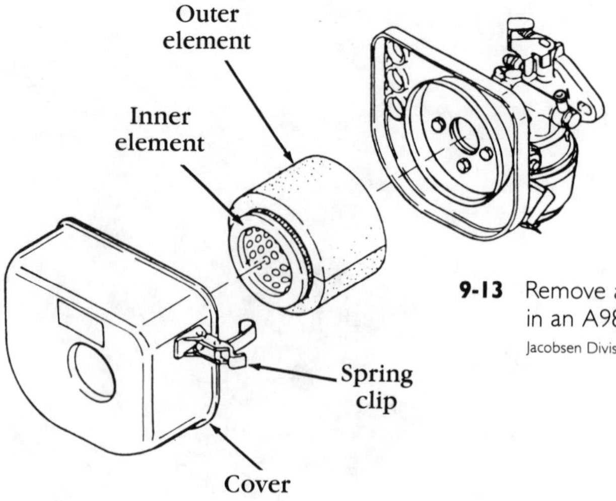

9-13 Remove and install the air cleaner in an A984H Jacobsen engine. Jacobsen Division of Textron Inc.

Wash elements in detergent and warm water. Rinse and air dry thoroughly. If the element is damaged or coming apart, replace. Soak the foam element in light engine oil, and then squeeze to remove excess oil. Replace the back plate with the element and cement in reverse order.

Recoil starters

Recoil rope-type starters are mounted horizontally on one end of the engine (FIG. 9-14). If the rope is broken or the parts inside the starter, remove the screws from the blower housing.

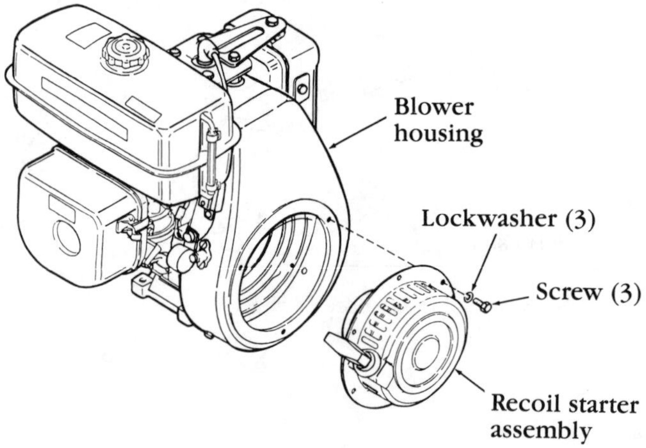

9-14 Remove the recoil starter on a Jacobsen A984H two-cycle engine. Jacobsen Division of Textron Inc.

Remove the recoil starter to replace the rope, springs, and ratchet. Release the reel pressure by inserting the rope in the slot on the wheel and rotating the reel 4 to 5 turns. While maintaining pressure on the friction plate, remove the clip and thrust washer. Remove the friction plate. Remove the ratchets, return spring, and friction spring. Remove the rope reel.

Do not remove the spiral spring if it is not broken or defective. If it is defective, remove the coil spring. The spring could be under tension, so use caution when removing. Install the spiral spring as shown in FIG. 9-15. The spiral spring might also be under tension, so use caution.

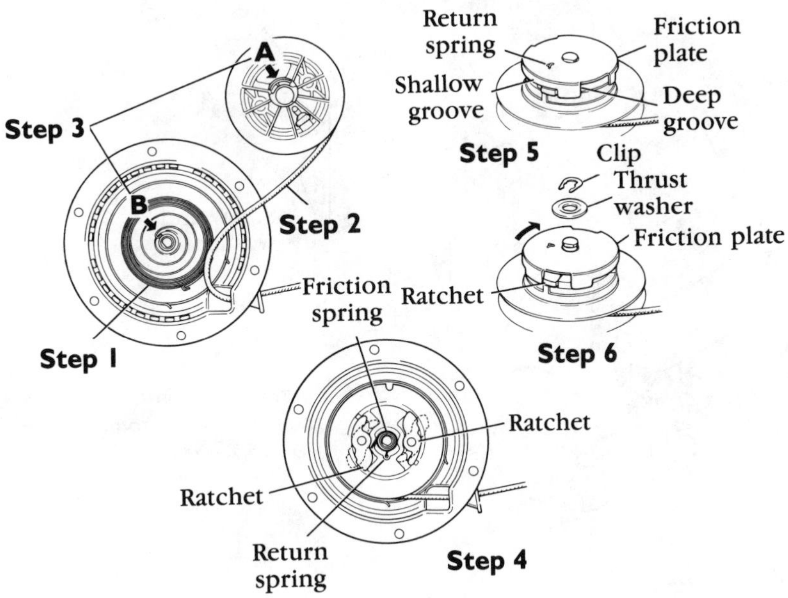

9-15 Install the recoil starter. Jacobsen Division of Textron Inc.

Thread a new rope through the reel, knot the end, and pull tight. Install the handle and knot the other end of the rope. Wind the rope on the reel, leaving approximately 14 inches of rope loose. Install reel, friction spring, return spring, and ratchets.

Install the friction plate with the end of the return spring through the notch in the friction plate. Turn the friction plate clockwise until the deep grooves of the friction plate are over the ratchets. Apply pressure to the friction plate to expose the groove in the mounting stud. Install the thrust washer and snap the clip in place using pliers.

Place the rope in the rope groove of the reel. Wind the reel 5 times clockwise to tighten the spiral spring. Pull on the rope to ensure proper installation, and reinstall the recoil starter engine assembly.

Exhaust systems

To service the exhaust system, remove the muffler by removing the top and side screws (FIG. 9-16). Inspect the muffler for cracks or damage. Repair small cracks with an auto muffler mend kit. If the muffler is faulty, replace. Clean off with a metal brush and wash out with Stoddard or equivalent solvent.

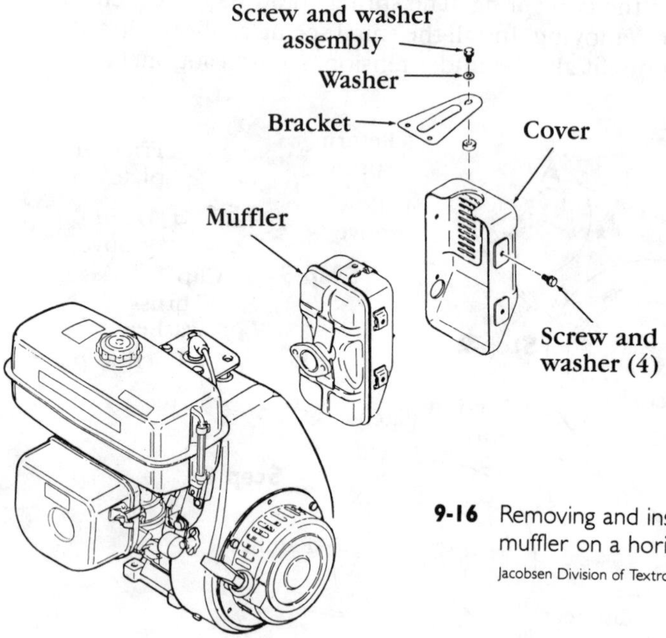

9-16 Removing and installing a repaired muffler on a horizontal engine.
Jacobsen Division of Textron Inc.

Fuel systems

The fuel tank is a metal tank with a sight tube that indicates fuel level. The tank has a strainer located under the tank cap that filters fuel as it goes into the tank (FIG. 9-17). Another finer strainer is located at the bottom post of the tank.

To remove the tank, shut off the fuel supply. Remove the banjo fitting and fuel line from carburetor (FIG. 9-18). Remove the lower tank support cap screw and the two top bracket cap screws from the engine head. Remove the tank and two spacers. Repair and clean up the tank. If it is too damaged, replace. To reinstall, reverse the procedures. Connect the fuel line and the banjo fitting on the carburetor. Tighten all three screws of tank to 18 ft lbs (24.4 Nm).

The fuel outlet strainer consists of a strainer screen sediment bowl and shutoff valve. Clean the strainer screen and bowl and replace all damaged parts. The shutoff valve cannot be serviced and if damaged, it must be replaced.

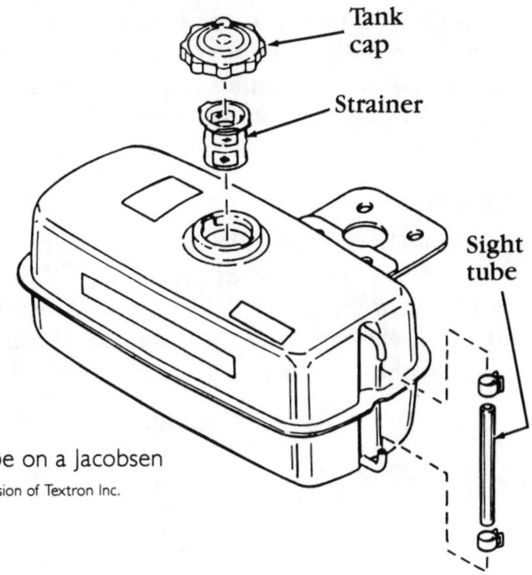

9-17 The fuel tank and sight tube on a Jacobsen two-cycle engine. Jacobsen Division of Textron Inc.

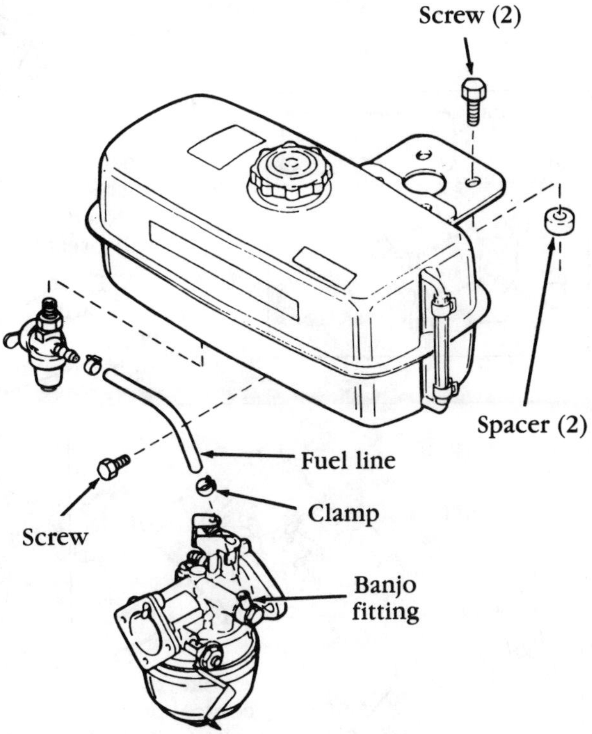

9-18 Fuel tank removal and installation on a horizontal drive engine. Jacobsen Division of Textron Inc.

If the carburetor keeps flooding, suspect excessive rust particles. If water entered the tank for any length of time, it can cause internal rusting, and the sediment becomes trapped in the tank's filter. A fine, powderlike dust might pass through the filter. All steel tanks can be soldered. Plastic tank's can be repaired with standard epoxy cement.

Carburetors

The A984H carburetor has a fixed, main jet, gravity-fed type carburetor. To service, remove the air cleaner, back plate, and fuel tank. Disconnect the governor and throttle linkage. Remove the two carburetor mounting nuts, lock washers, other washers, and carburetor assembly, outer gasket, spacer, and inner gasket (FIG. 9-19).

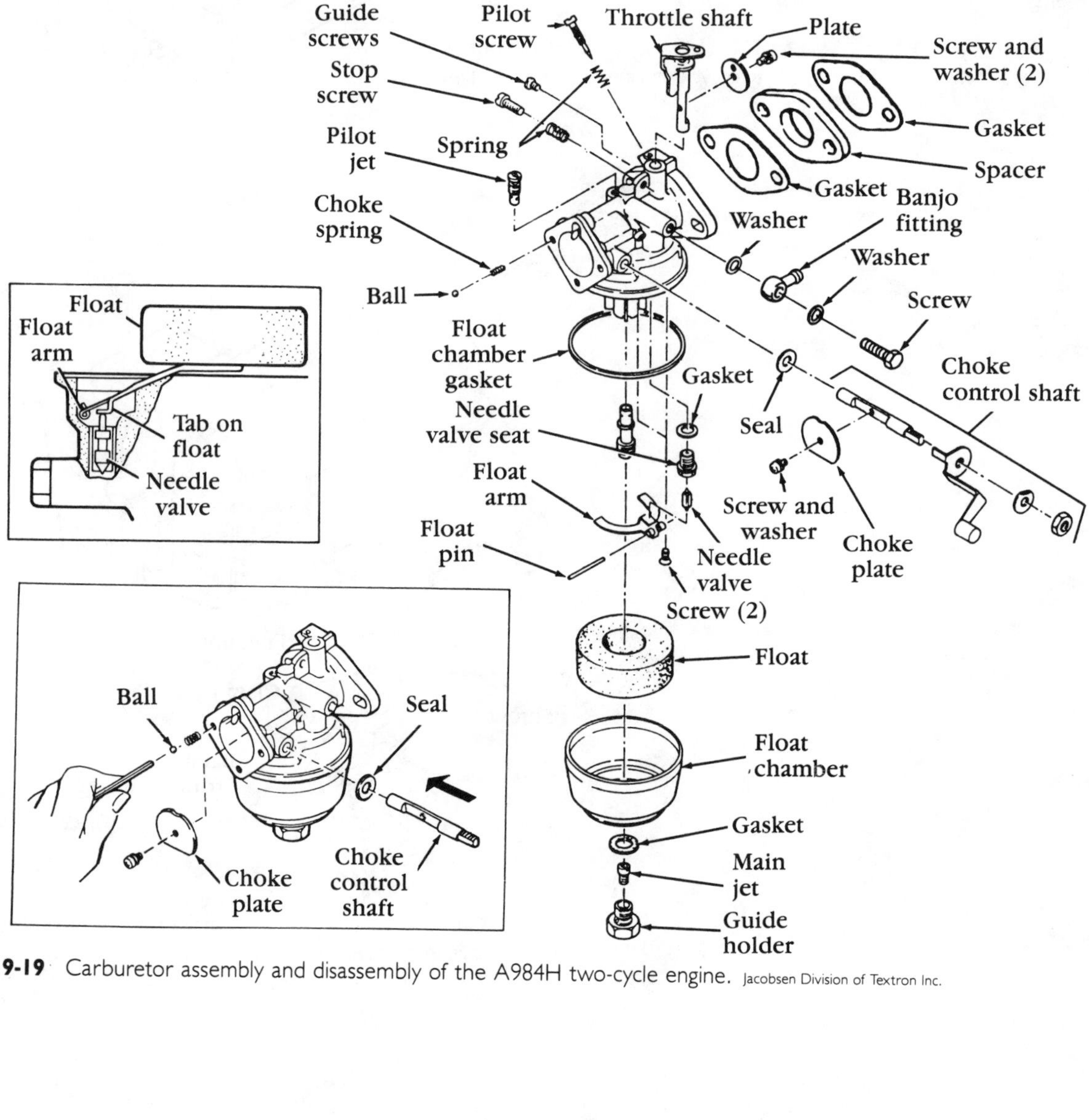

9-19 Carburetor assembly and disassembly of the A984H two-cycle engine. Jacobsen Division of Textron Inc.

Inspect all parts for wear and damaged or broken parts. Replace any defective parts. Clean all parts in a solvent and dry.

Adjusting the carburetor To adjust the carburetor, turn the pilot screw clockwise until it gently bottoms on its seat. Do not overtighten the pilot screw when closing it fully. The needle point might become damaged. Turn the pilot screw counterclockwise 1 turn. You might have to adjust the screw after the engine is started and warmed up.

Replacing the carburetor To replace the carburetor, install the main jet to the guide roller and the needle seat valve seat and gasket. Install the float pin. Notice if the center is spring-loaded and free to move. Install the float arm pin, float chamber gasket, chamber, guide holder, and gasket.

Install the pilot screw and spring. Do not jam taper of screw against seat. Install choke spring and ball. Depress ball with a small wrench. At the same time, push on the choke control shaft. Maintain pressure on the ball to keep it from flying out of housing because of spring tension.

Install the choke plate and pilot jet and tighten firmly to prevent fuel leakage. Install throttle stop screw and spring, throttle shaft, throttle screw, and throttle plate with screws and washers.

Install a new inside gasket, spacer, and new outside gasket over the carburetor studs on the engine. Position the carburetor on the engine and fasten with flat washers, lock washers, and nuts, Connect the governor rod and spring.

Governors

The governor flyweight mechanism is located in its own housing and has its own oil sump. The oil level can be checked by using the governor oil-level gauge. When removing the governor lever, do not loosen the Phillips screws on the adjusting plate. Mark the hole where spring connects to the governor lever. Remove the governor spring, rod, and rod spring from the governor control. Mark how the governor spring and rod, are positioned for correct assembly.

To install the linkage, connect the governor rod and spring on the governor arm. Connect the other end of governor rod and spring to the throttle control on the carburetor. Position the governor arm over the governor shaft, and fasten the lock washer and nut. Never apply torque against the governor stop. Place a block of wood between governor arm and the carburetor.

Install the stop plate and governor control lever to the engine using a large flat washer, lock-washer, and Phillips screw. Do not tighten. Loosely install the screw and washer through the stop plate into the engine block.

To make standard governor adjustments, push the governor control lever down to the high speed position. Loosen the governor control arm lock nut and the Phillips screw on the adjusting plate. Push the adjusting plate to the right as far as it will go. Tighten the set screw and governor control shaft nut.

If the speed control lever and stop plate were not removed for high-speed governors, no adjustment is necessary. If it was removed, loosen the stop plate screw slightly and rotate the stop plate completely counter-clockwise. *Note*: the engine must be installed on the equipment before adjustment.

Start the engine, and using a tachometer, slowly advance the throttle control until the recommended high-speed RPM is obtained. As the throttle is advanced and the governor control is moved clockwise, so will the stop plate turn clockwise. Tighten the stop plate screw.

Ignition systems

The ignition system consists of a flywheel, spark plug, transistor control (TCI), interlock module, coil, and primary and secondary leads (FIG. 9-20).

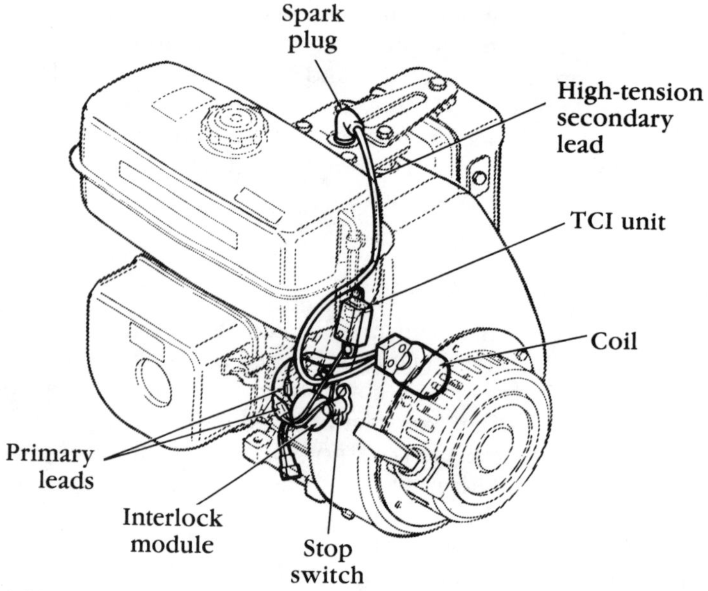

9-20 The ignition system components found in the horizontal engine.
Jacobsen Division of Textron Inc.

Checking the coil The coil does not have to be removed to test it. If the coil is defective, however, the flywheel must be removed first. Disconnect the primary leads from the stop switch, interlock module, and TCI module. Disconnect the secondary lead from the spark plug. Set the multimeter to 200 ohms. Measure the resistance between primary leads and ground (1.1 to 1.5 ohms) (FIG. 9-21). Set the multimeter to the 20K ohm range and measure the resistance between the secondary lead and the ground, 10 to 14K ohms.

When replacing defective coils, be sure dowel pins are properly located on both sides of the coil before tightening the screws.

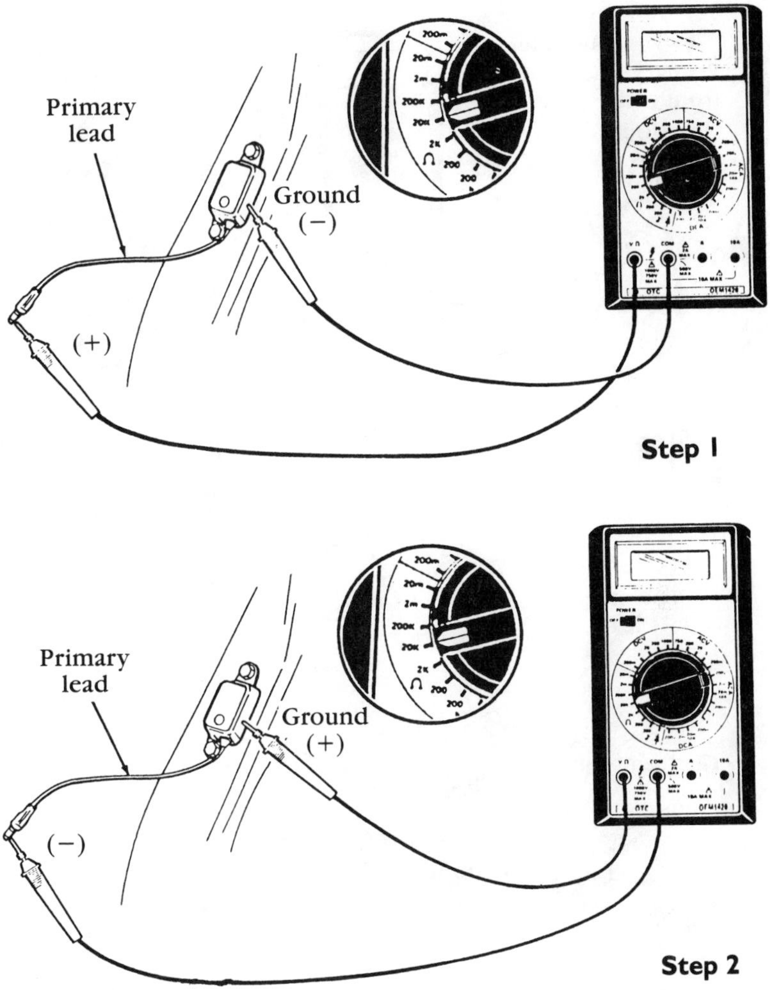

9-21 Checking the transistor module with a multimeter. Jacobsen Division of Textron Inc.

Checking the TCI module The TCI module can be checked without removing it from the engine. Set a multimeter to the 20K ohm range and connect the positive terminal of the tester to the primary lead (FIG. 9-22, Step 1). Connect the negative terminal of the tester to the TCI unit casing (8 to 9K ohms).

Connect the negative terminal of the tester to the primary lead (Rep 2) and the positive terminal of the tester to the unit seating (8 to 9K ohms). If the module is open with no measurement or is less than 8K ohms, suspect a shorted TCL module. In this case, replace the entire module.

Checking the interlock module If the engine cannot be started or shut down, suspect a defective interlock module. The interlock module is a

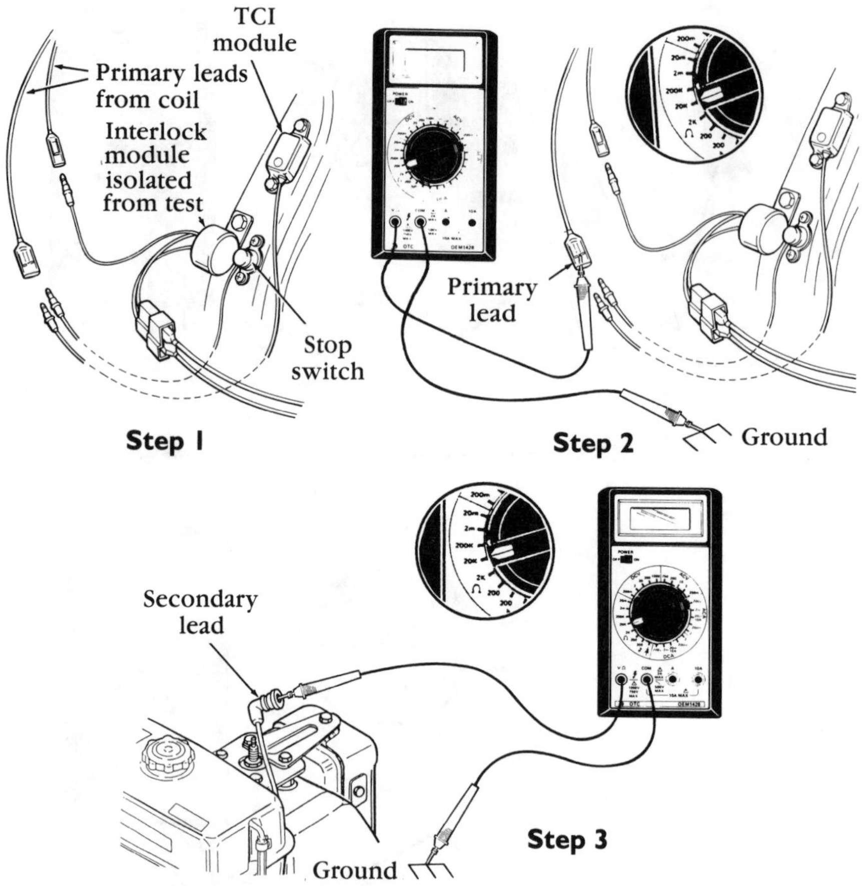

9-22 Checking the primary and secondary tests of the coil with a DMM. Jacobsen Division of Textron Inc.

solid-state component and must be replaced as a unit. Never allow the engine to operate with the interlock module disconnected.

To service, disconnect the module plug from the tractor interlock switch, and install a jump wire (FIG. 9-23). If the engine does not start, disconnect the positive (+) lead from the primary coil lead. Try starting the engine. If the engine starts and does not shut down, replace the defective interlock module.

Checking the push button If the push (stop) button is erratic or does not stop the engine, check for continuity with a 200 ohm range of DMM. Replace if it is open or erratic.

Adjusting the spark plug To adjust the spark plug, first remove it and check for signs of damage or wear. If it is excessively pitted, replace the plug. Set the spark plug gap setting at 0.019–0.023 inches (0.5–0.6 mm).

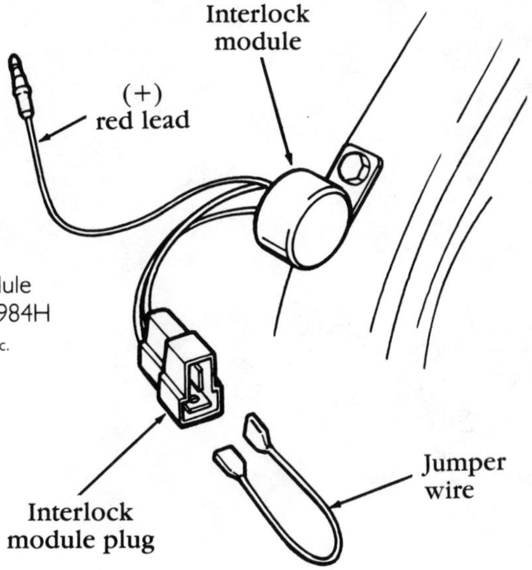

9-23 Checking the interlock module with a jumper wire in an A984H engine. Jacobsen Division of Textron Inc.

Install a new spark plug with the correct spark plug wrench.

Repairs of the block assembly, pistons, flywheel, and crankcase should be left to the professional small engine technician.

Chapter 10

Tecumseh engines

This chapter contains information on how to maintain, repair, service, and lubricate Tecumseh TVS/TVXL840 two-cycle engines and four-cycle engines. Remember to remove the spark plug wire before doing any service work on the engine. If you have not read chapter 1 on safety, do so now before beginning any service or engine work.

Maintenance involves keeping the air cleaner free of dirt and dust, cleaning up the cooling system, and replacing or cleaning up the spark plug to keep the engine operating smoothly. Each process usually only takes a few minutes.

TVS/TVXL840 TWO-CYCLE ENGINES

If you are unsure of the engine type, check the blower housing. Tecumseh numbers are stamped on the TVS and TVXL840 blower housing.

Fuel and lubrication requirements

Fresh, clean, unleaded regular gasoline is recommended for all engines. Unleaded gasoline burns cleaner, extends engine life, and promotes good starting by reducing the buildup of carbon deposits. Leaded gasoline or gasohol containing no more than 10 percent ethanol can be used if unleaded fuel is not available. Never use gasoline containing methanol, gasohol containing more than 10 percent ethanol, gasoline additives, premium gasoline, or white gas because engine/fuel system damage could result.

Make sure that gasoline and oil are stored in a clean, covered rust-free container. Dirty fuel can clog small pacts and passages in the carburetor. Gasoline stored for long periods of time develops a gum that fouls up spark plugs, fuel lines, carburetors, and fuel screens. Using fuel that is not fresh will also make it difficult to start engines, especially in cold temperatures. Clean the gas cap, tank, and fuel container spout when filling the fuel tank to ensure that dirt does not get into the system.

Use a two-cycle, air-cooled oil rated SAE 30 or SAE 40. Do not use multiscasity oil. Use the correct fuel/oil mix listed in the owners manual, and disregard conflicting instructions found on oil containers. The correct fuel/oil mix for the TVS 840 engine is 32:1. Engines equipped with a Kleen-Aire, dual-stage canister air cleaner can use the fuel/oil mixture in TABLE 10-1.

Table 10-1 Tecumseh fuel and oil mixtures.

	U.S. Gallons		*Imperial Gallons*		*Metric*	
	Fuel (Gallons)	*Oil (Ounces)*	*Fuel (Gallons)*	*Oil (Ounces)*	*Petrol (Liters)*	*Oil (Liters)*
32:1	1	4	1	5	4	.125
	3	12	3	15	12	.375
	5	20	5	25	20	.625
	6	24	6	30	24	.750

Tecumseh Products

To ensure that oil and gasoline are thoroughly mixed, fill the gasoline container 1/4 full, add the recommended oil, shake the container vigorously, and then add the remainder of gasoline. Do not mix directly in the engine or equipment tank. Some models have a cup attached to the underside of the air cleaner cover to ensure proper fuel/oil mixture (FIG. 10-1).

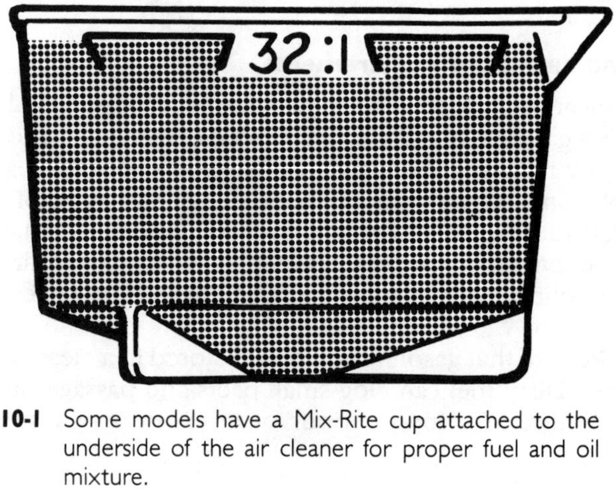

10-1 Some models have a Mix-Rite cup attached to the underside of the air cleaner for proper fuel and oil mixture.

Air cleaner

Service the air cleaner frequently to prevent the element from clogging and the screen to prevent dust and dirt from entering the engine. Dust entering through a damaged air filter can quickly damage the engine. Keep covers and air cleaner connections tight to prevent dirt from entering. Suspect a clogged air filter when excessive carburetor adjustments must be made or there is loss of power (FIG. 10-2).

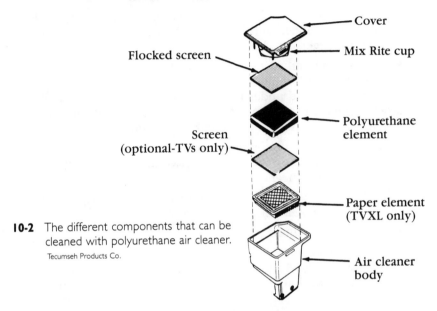

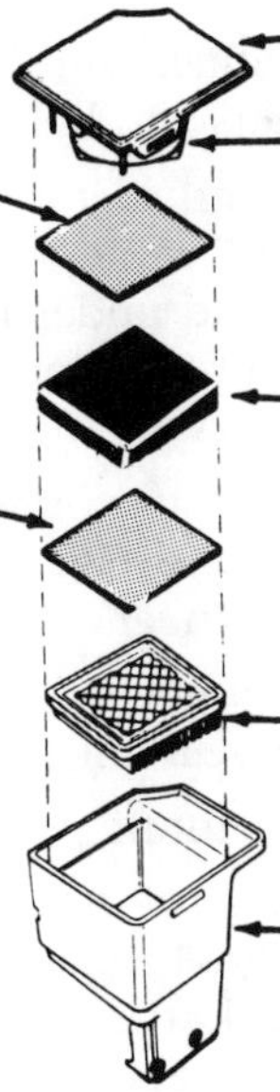

10-2 The different components that can be cleaned with polyurethane air cleaner.
Tecumseh Products Co.

Polyurethane air cleaners Wash out polyurethane air cleaners in detergent and water. Squeeze (don't twist) until all dirt is removed. Rinse thoroughly. Wrap in a clean cloth and squeeze until completely dry. Clean up the air cleaner body and cover.

Reoil the filter with a generous quantity of engine oil to all sides. Squeeze and work oil in and then remove excess oil. Replace in the reverse order.

Flacked screen elements can be cleaned by blowing compressed air through the screen from the back side. Replace if it will not clean up. *Note*: Polyurethane filters lose effectiveness if they are stored for extended periods of time because oil migrates out of the filter.

Paper air cleaners Paper air cleaners are found on TVS and TVXL840 engines. Never clean or oil this type of filter. Instead, replace once a year. Never run the engine without the complete air cleaner installed.

Kleen-Aire Canister dual-stage air cleaners Kleen-Aire air cleaners consist of a paper-type element with a polyurethane pre-cleaner around it. Clean up and oil like the polyurethane air cleaner. Clean off base arcs and cover before installing filter.

Note: When installing a new foam pre-cleaner, always turn it inside out before installing it around the paper element to prevent gaps between the paper element and the pre-cleaner.

Tune-ups

A tune-up might consist of the following.

1. Service or replace the air cleaner, if necessary.
2. Remove the blower housing, and clean all dirt, grass, or debris from the air intake screen, cylinder cooling fins, and carburetor governor levers and linkage.
3. Remove the carburetor and clean. Install a carburetor kit, and make preset adjustments where needed. Carburetor preset adjustments are found under the carburetor. Make sure the fuel tank, fuel filters, and fuel lines are clean. If the fuel line and filter are removed, use a new fuel line during reassembly.
4. Reinstall the carburetor, replacing any worn or damaged governor springs or linkage. Make proper governor adjustments. Consult the owner's manual.
5. Remove the flywheel with an approved flywheel puller (670306). Check the oil seal linkage. Do not use a knock-off tool.
6. Replace the spark plug.
7. Make sure all ignition wires are properly routed, so they will not rub on the flywheel. Inspect all ignition wires for abrasion or damage. Check the flywheel key, reinstall the flywheel, and torque the flywheel nut to specifications. Set the air gap between the solid-state module and flywheel at .0125 with air gap gauge 670297.
8. Mount the engine firmly to the equipment. On rotary lawn mowers, make sure the blade is properly balanced and correctly torqued.
9. Make sure all remove linkage is properly adjusted for proper operation.
10. Fill tank with proper fuel-oil mix.
11. Rim the engine, adjust the carburetor, and set the RPM according to recommendations.

Carburetors

More carburetors are rendered useless by neglect and abuse than all operational ills combined. A carburetor has but one task to perform, to mix fuel with air and feed it into the combustion chamber—at all speeds. The operational efficiency of a carburetor can be compromised by any foreign material (solid or liquid) that retards this flow of air or fuel. There are only three areas of carburetor malfunction: it is too lean; it is too rich; or it leaks.

Both the TVS and TVXL840 engine has a series V1 carburetor. The series V1 has a high-speed, fixed-idle system. The model and code date number of the carburetor are on the carburetor body. Use the engine model number and type number for ordering repair parts (FIG. 10-3). If the engine model number is not available, use the carburetor model number. Cross-reference the carburetor model number with a service part number using the Master Parts manual.

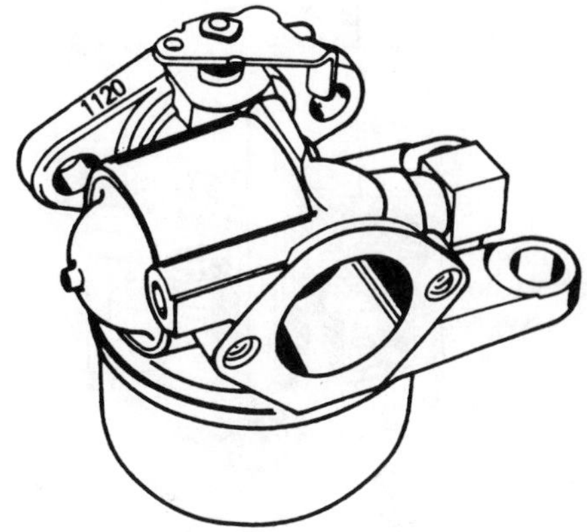

10-3 Use the engine model and type numbers to locate the correct part. Tecumseh Products Co.

In the start position, fuel fills the prime well in the bowl nut to the level maintained by the float. This provides the rich mixture required to start a cold engine. It takes about 5 seconds for the prime well to refill each crank or when the engine is stopped (FIG. 10-4). The primer bulb can be used to provide a richer mixture under cold weather conditions.

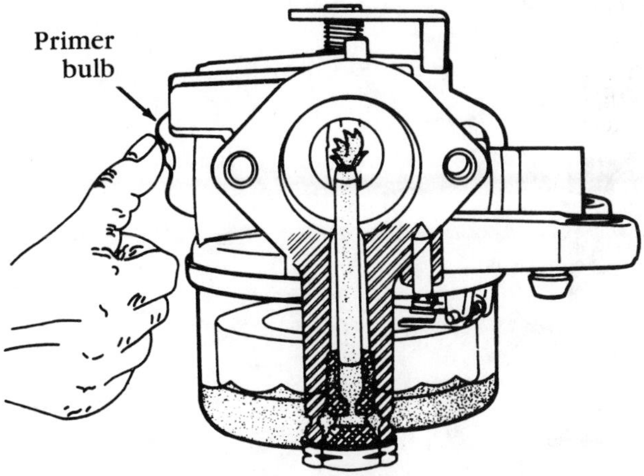

10-4 Push the power bulb to fill the carburetor, especially in cold weather. Tecumseh Products Co.

When the engine starts and runs, the fuel level in the bowl and prime well stabilizes, and air from the air bleed and fuel from the main jet are pulled up the main nozzle for engine operation.

Do not exceed the manufacturers recommended RPM. Excessive RPM or speed will cause the carburetor fuel mixture to lean out and the engine might overheat and eventually fail. At idle or low-load running, the fuel is drawn up the fixed idle passage (FIG. 10-5).

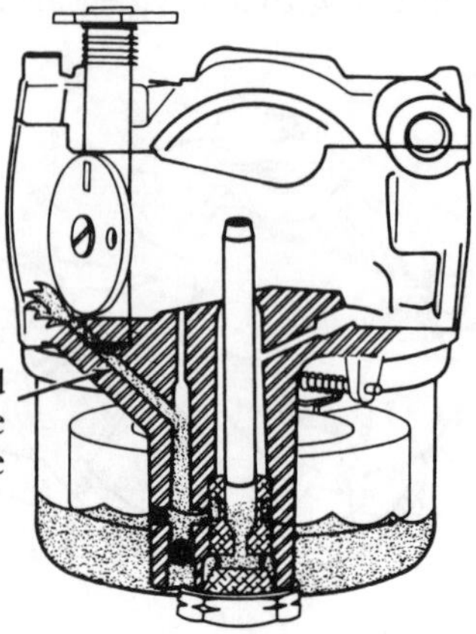

10-5 During idle running, the fuel is drawn up the fixed idle passage of the carburetor. Tecumseh Products Co.

To service the carburetor, first remove it and the primer bulb from the engine. Grasp the primer bulb and roll the primer bulb out with a pair of needlenose pliers. Wear safety glasses or goggles when removing the retaining ring that holds the primer bulb in place (FIG. 10-6).

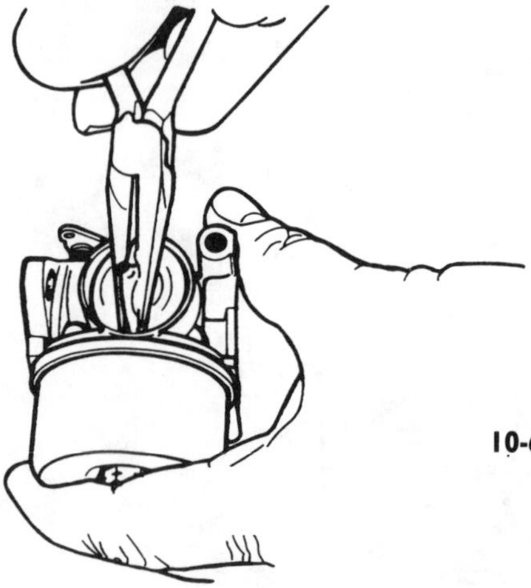

10-6 Removing the retaining ring in the carburetor. Tecumseh Products Co.

Remove the bowl nut. This bowl nut has a left-handed thread on the carburetor. The letter L identifies it as the left-handed thread. Also, the head of the bowl nut is notched. This is the same identification used in many industries for left-handed nuts.

If the bowl nut is turned the wrong way, it will break off in the center leg where the fuel pick-up passages are drilled. If this happens, fit a screw-driver into the bowl nut and turn out in the correct direction. Remove the throttle plate and shaft with the dust seal and spring. Remove the inlet seat (FIG. 10-7).

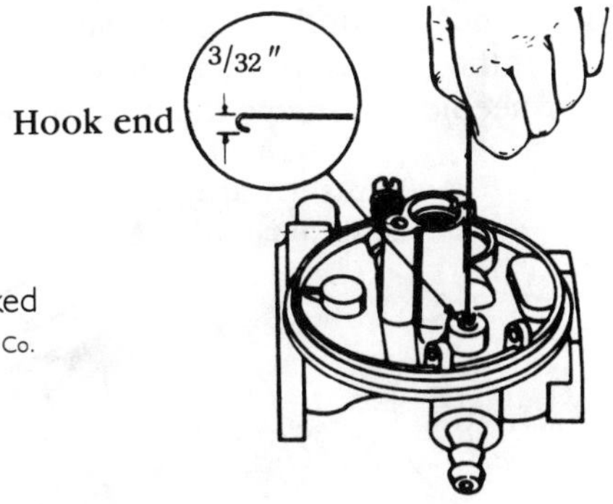

10-7 Remove the inset slot with the hooked wire of the carburetor. Tecumseh Products Co.

Soak the carburetor body and bowl nut in a commercial cleaner no longer than 30 minutes, even less if the cleaner is extremely toxic. Notice the strength of the cleaner used. The fuel fitting can stay when soaking the carburetor. All passages can be probed with soft tag wire and blown out with compressed air, if handy.

Rebuilding the carburetor To rebuild a carburetor, replace the viton seat into the carburetor body. The side of the viton seat with the groove in it goes into the carburetor body so that the smooth side can be seen. Place a drop of oil onto the seat and press it in with a flat punch or a point plunger until it seats. Be careful not to scratch the polished inlet bore (FIG. 10-8).

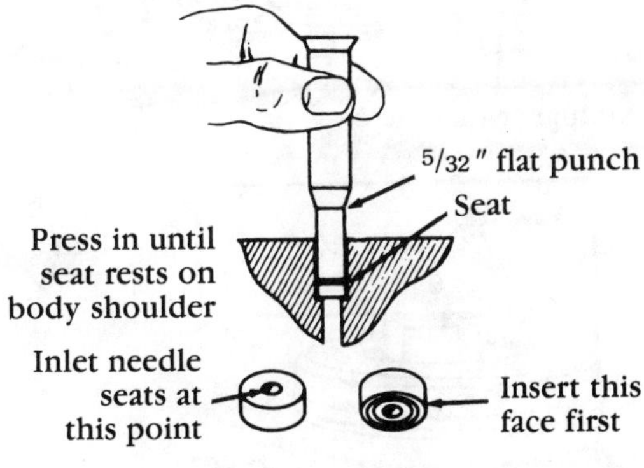

10-8 When rebuilding the carburetor, install a new inlet needle seat and press into place. Tecumseh Products Co.

Place the inlet needle and spring clip into the float and set in place. The long end of the spring clip must point towards the choke end of the carburetor. This ensures that the inlet needle drops and raises in a straight line.

The carburetor uses a damping spring on the float, and the short leg hooks onto the carburetor body. The longer end points towards the choke end (FIG. 10-9). To set the correct float height, use a Tecumseh float starting tool (670283A). The gauge is a go-no-go type. Pull the tool in at 90 degrees to the hinge pin (FIG. 10-10). The toe of the float, end opposite the hinge, must be under the first step and can touch the second step without gap. If the float is too high or too low, carefully bend the tab holding the inlet needle to achieve the proper height. Recheck with the gauge.

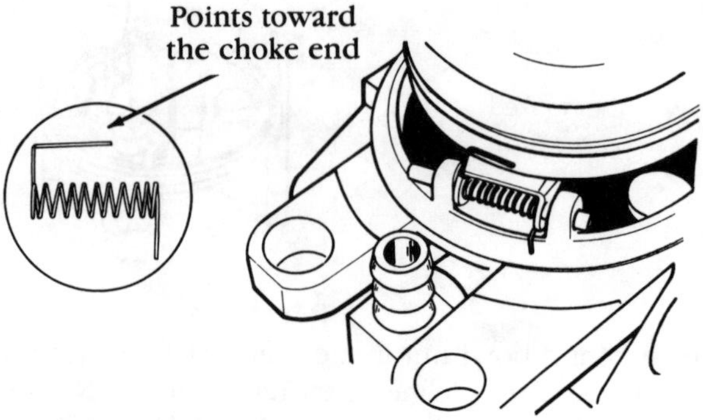

10-9 Hook the damping spring on to the float. The longer end points toward the choke end. Tecumseh Products Co.

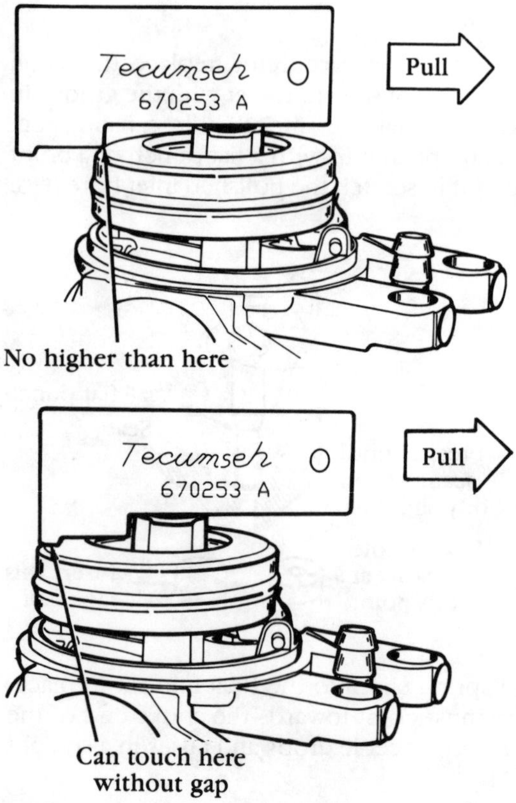

10-10 Use the Tecumseh 670253H float setting tool for float adjustment. Tecumseh Products Co.

Install a new O bowl ring. Place the bowl into the carburetor with the flat area of the bowl over the hinge pin and parallel to the hinge pin. Insert the bowl nut with the fiber washer between the bowl and the nut. Remember, this is a left-handed bowl nut.

Install the throttle shaft and shutter. The scribe mark on the shutter is in the twelve o'clock position. Any other position might cause the throttle to stick. Use a new throttle shutter screw to ensure that the screw does not come loose during operation. A new dust seal should also be used (FIG. 10-11).

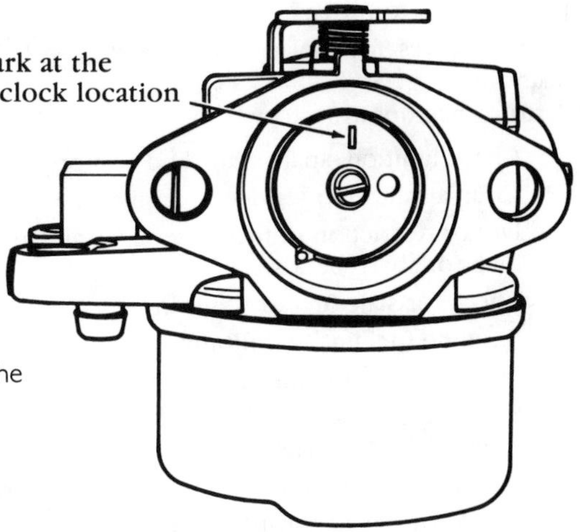

10-11 Place the scribe mark at the twelve o'clock position. Tecumseh Products Co.

Place the primer bulb with the retainer ring into a $^3/_4$-inch-deep reach socket. Check FIG. 10-12 for the various carburetor parts, then check the parts, troubles, and corrections in the troubleshooting chart shown in TABLE 10-2.

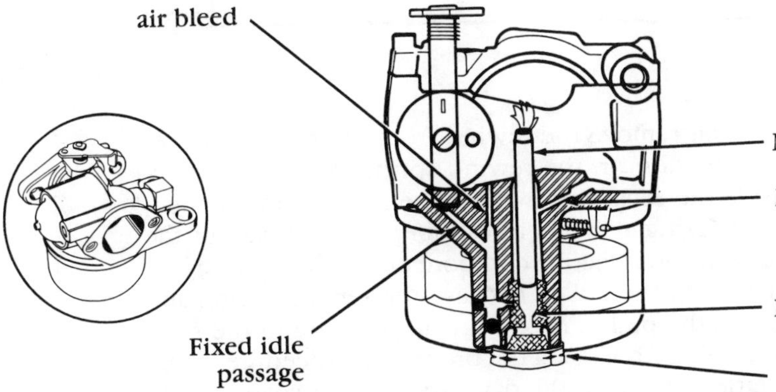

10-12 The various parts found inside the TVS/TVXL840 two-cycle engine. Tecumseh Products Co.

Table 10-2 Troubleshooting carburetors.

Trouble	*Corrections*
Engine will not start.	1, 2, 3, 4, 7, 9
Engine will not accelerate.	1, 2
Engine hunts (at idle or high-speed).	2, 3, 7, 8, 9, 14, 15
Engine will not idle.	3, 7, 8, 9, 13, 14, 15
Engine lacks power at high speed.	1, 2, 5, 7, 13, 14
Carburetor floods.	3, 6, 11, 14, 15
Carburetor leaks.	5, 6, 12
Engine overspeeds.	7, 8, 9, 12, 13
Idle speed is excessive.	7, 8, 9, 12, 13
Engine starves for fuel at high speed (leans out).	2, 3, 5, 11, 14
Performance unsatisfactory.	1, 2, 3, 4, 5, 6, 7, 8, 10, 11, 12, 13, 14

1. Check ignition, spark plug, and compression.
2. Clean air cleaner; service as required.
3. Dirt or restriction in fuel system. Clean tank and fuel strainers, check for kinks or sharp bends.
4. Check for stale fuel or water in fuel. Fill with fresh fuel.
5. Examine fuel line and fittings.
6. Check and clean atmospheric vent holes.
7. Examine throttle shaft for binding or excessive play. Remove all dirt or paint and replace shaft.
8. Examine throttle return spring for operation.
9. Check for a bent throttle plate.
10. Clean carburetor after removing all non-metallic parts that are serviceable (Exception: plastic fuel fitting). Probe all passages.
11. Check inlet needle and seat for condition and proper installation.
12. Check sealing of welch plug, primer bulb, fuel fitting and gaskets.
13. Adjust governor linkage.
14. Adjust float setting.
15. Check float shaft for wear and float for leaks or dents.

Tecumseh Co.

Recoil starters

To service the recoil starter, remove the rewind from the engine blower housing and release the tension on the rewind spring. Place a 3/4-inch-deep reach socket inside the retainer pawl. Set the rewind on a bench, supported on the socket. Using a 5/16-inch roll pin punch, drive out the center pin. Replace all worn or defective components.

Take care when handling the pulley because the rewind spring and cover is held by bosses in the pulley. Make sure all parts are in the right order to replace. Reassemble by reversing the preceding procedure, keeping in mind that the starter days with the day springs must snap back to the center of the pulley. Always replace the center pin with a new pin on reassembly. Also, add an additional plastic washer (total of two). This washer is provided with the new center pin.

Check retainer pawl for wear or damage, and replace if necessary. Tap the new center pin in until it is within 1/8 of an inch of the top of the starter. Do not drive the pin in too far or the retainer pawl will bind and the starter dogs will not engage the starter cup. TABLE 10-3 lists Tecumseh RVS/TVXL840 engine motor specifications.

Table 10-3 TVS/TVXL840 engine specifications.

		TVS840 Inches	*TVXL840 Inches*
Bore		2.437 / 2.438	2.437 / 2.438
Stroke		1.812	1.812
Cubic inch displacement		8.46	8.46
Spark plug gap		.030	.030
Piston ring end gap		.007 / .017	.007 / .017
Piston diameter		2.4320 / 2.4326	2.4320 / 2.4326
Piston ring groove width	Top	.0645 / .0655	Half keystone ring
	Bottom	.0645 / .0655	.0645 / .0655
Piston ring width	Top	.0615 / .0625	Half keystone ring
	Bottom	.0615 / .0625	.0615 / .0625
Crank pin journal diameter		.9710 / .9715	.9710 / .9715
Crankshaft P.T.O. side main bearing diameter		.9833 / .9838	.9833 / .9838
Crankshaft magneto side main bearing diameter		.7864 / .7869	.7864 / .7869
Crankshaft end play		.0004 / .0244	.0004 / .0244

Tecumseh Co.

FOUR-CYCLE ENGINES

The model numbers of the Tecumseh overhead-valve rotary mower and medium-frame, four-cycle engine are stamped into the blower housing or are located on a nameplate or tag on the engine (FIG. 10-13). The OVM (overhead valve vertical medium) frame engine has the model number at the end, while the overhead valve rotary mower has the number stamped into the blower housing. The first letter designation in a model number indicates basic type of engine:

V	Vertical Shaft
LAV	Lightweight Aluminum Vertical
VM	Vertical Medium Frame
TVM	Tecumseh Vertical (Medium Frame)
VH	Vertical Heavy Duty (Cast Iron)
TVS	Tecumseh Vertical Styled
TNT	Toro N'Tecumseh
ECV	Exclusive Craftman Vertical
OVM	Overhead Valve Vertical Medium Frame
H	Horizontal Shaft
HS	Horizontal Small Frame
HM	Horizontal Medium Frame
HHM	Horizontal Heavy Duty (Cast Iron) Medium Frame
HB	Horizontal Heavy Duty (Cast Iron)
ECH	Exclusive Craftman Horizontal

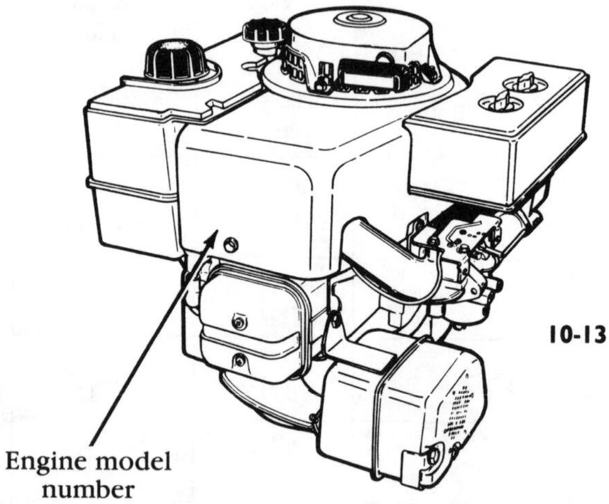

10-13 A Tecumseh overhead valve medium engine.
Tecumseh Products Co.

For instance, Tecumseh engines found in Craftsman (Sears, Roebuck & Co.) begin with ECV, ECH, OVM, and OVRM. The Tecumseh engines found in Toro machines might start with TVT letters. Tecumseh engines can be found in Toro, Jacobsen, Montgomery Ward, and Sears power equipment.

The number following the letter indicates the horsepower or cubic inch displacement. The specification number follows the model number. The last three numbers of the specification number indicate a variation to the basic engine specification. The serial number indicates the production date.

Using model number QVM120 - 202008, serial number 7310D, as an example, it would interpreted as follows:

OVM120 202008	The model and specification number.
OVM	Overhead valve medium frame.
120	A 12-cubic-inch displacement.
202008	The specification number used to identify engine parts.
7310D	The serial number.
7	First digit is the year of manufacture (1987).
310	The calendar day of that year, (310th day, November 1987).
D	The line and shift on which the engine was built at the factory.

Fuel and lubrication requirements

Always use fresh, clean unleaded regular gasoline in all Tecumseh engines. Unleaded gasoline burns cleaner, extends engine life, and reduces the buildup of combustion chamber deposits. Leaded gasoline or gasohol containing no more than 10 percent ethanol can be used if unleaded is not available. Never use gasoline containing methanol, gasohol containing more than 10 percent ethanol, gasoline additives, premium gasoline, or white gas because engine/fuel system damage might result.

Use a clean, high-quality detergent oil. Be sure the original container is marked A.P.1. service SE or SF. Do not use SAE 10W 40 oil. For temperatures above 32 degrees, use SAE 30 oil. SAE 10W 30 is an acceptable substitute. Use SAE 10W 30 oil in high temperatures and for high loads. Using multigrade oil might increase oil consumption. For temperatures below 32 degrees, use SAE 5W 30 oil. SAE 10W is an acceptable substitute. Only use SAE OW 30W or an acceptable substitute in temperatures below zero degrees.

Change the oil after every 25 hours or more often under dusty or dirty conditions. Check the oil every five hours or each time the equipment is used. Always position the machine level when checking the oil.

Air cleaners

Tecumseh engines have foam, polyurethane, and paper air cleaners. Before removing the air cleaner, make sure all excess dirt is removed around it. Air cleaners should be serviced frequently to prevent dust and dirt from entering the engine. Dust mixed with oil form an extremely abrasive compound that quickly wears out an engine.

Suspect a clogged air filter when carburetor adjustment is excessive or there is a loss of power. Replacing a clogged air filter should improve engine performance immediately. Always use factory recommended air filters. Make certain the covers and air cleaner connections are tightly sealed to prevent entry of dirt after replacement.

Polyurethane air cleaners Polyurethane air cleaners use an element that can clog up with use. Wash the element in detergent and water, and squeeze (do not twist) until all dirt is removed. Rinse thoroughly, and wrap in a clean cloth until dry.

Clean the air cleaner housing and cover and dry thoroughly. Reoil the element on both sides of the unit. Squeeze vigorously to distribute oil and to remove excess oil. Some polyurethane elements have a flocked screen attached to them.

Paper air cleaners Dry-type paper air cleaners are found on many Tecumseh engines. These air cleaners have treated paper elements with rubberlike scaling edges. The edges must seal properly to prevent dirt leakage.

Replace these air filters once a year or more often in extremely dusty or dirty conditions. Do not attempt to clean or oil paper filters. Clean up the base and cover before installing the new paper cleaner.

Serious damage to the engine can result if the correct filter is not used. Never run the engine without the air cleaner installed.

Dual-stage air cleaners Dual-stage air cleaners consists of a paper-type element with a foam pre-cleaner around it. Try knocking and brushing out all dirt and dust from the air cleaner before replacing it. If the air cleaner cannot be cleaned up properly, install a new foam pre-cleaner. Always turn it inside out before installing a new filter around the paper element to prevent gas from entering between the paper element and pre-cleaner.

Tune-ups

To tune-up the engine, first remove the spark plug wire before doing any work on the engine. Service or replace the air cleaner, if necessary. Inspect the level and condition of oil, and change or add oil as required. Remove the blower housing, clean all dirt, grass, or debris from the intake screen, head and cylinder cooling fins, and carburetor governor levers and linkage. Make sure fuel tank, fuel filters, and fuel line are clean. Replace any worn or damaged governor springs or linkage. Make proper governor adjustments and carburetor presets where required.

Replace the spark plug with the proper plug. Notice the reach on the overhead valve spark plug is longer than the standard L-head spark plug because of the style of head and the spark plug location. The wrong plug will cause performance problems. Set the proper spark plug gap.

Install the spare plug in the engine and tighten to 15-foot-pounds torque. If a torque wrench is not available, screw the spark plug in by hand as far as possible and use a regular spark plug wrench to turn the plug 1/8 to 1/4 turns farther, reusing the spark plug or 1/2 turns farther with a new spark plug.

Make sure all ignition wires are free of abrasions and breaks and are properly routed so as not to rub on the flywheel. Properly reinstall the blower housing, gas tank, and fuel lines, and then check for spark as stated in the ignition section later in this chapter.

Finally, make sure all remote cables are properly adjusted for proper operation. Run the engine and adjust the carburetor. Set engine RPM as specified in the owner's manual.

OVM carburetion The series 6 carburetor is totally nonadjustable. It is designed for use on the overhead valve rotary mower engine (OVRM). The carburetor contains the fuel inlet, main nozzle, main nozzle air bleed, dual fuel orifices (bowl nut and center leg of carburetor), main jet, idle transfer passage (bowl nut and center leg of carburetor), fixed idle drilling, idle air bleed, atmospheric vent, and primer passage (FIG. 10-14).

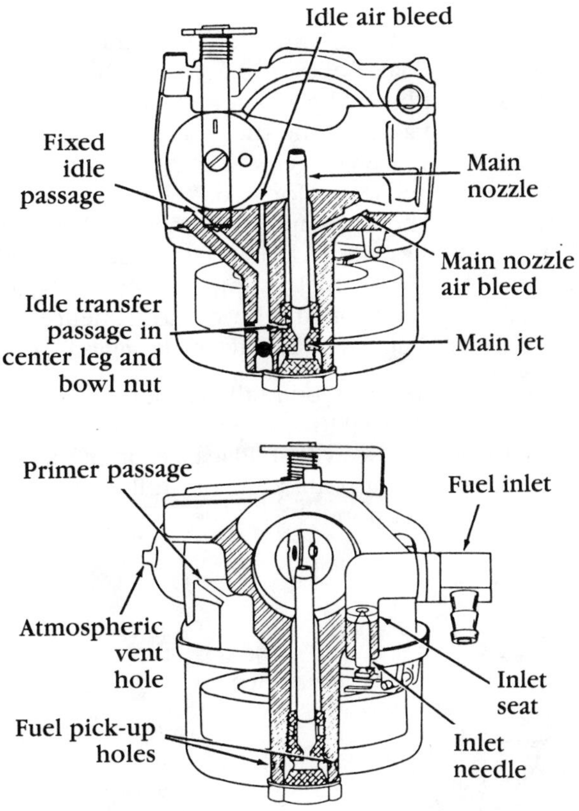

10-14 The different parts found in an OVRM Tecumseh carburetor.. Tecumseh Products Co.

After the carburetor has been removed from the engine, remove the primer bulb. Grasp the primer bulb with needlenose pliers and roll the primer bulb out. After the primer bulb is removed, remove the retaining ring. Use a screwdriver to carefully pry the retainer out of the carburetor body.

Remove the retaining ring that holds the primer bulb in place. Be sure to wear safety glasses or goggles. Remove the bowl nut (FIG. 10-15). The main jet and idle transfer passages are in the bowl nut. Be sure to soak the bowl nut with the carburetor body.

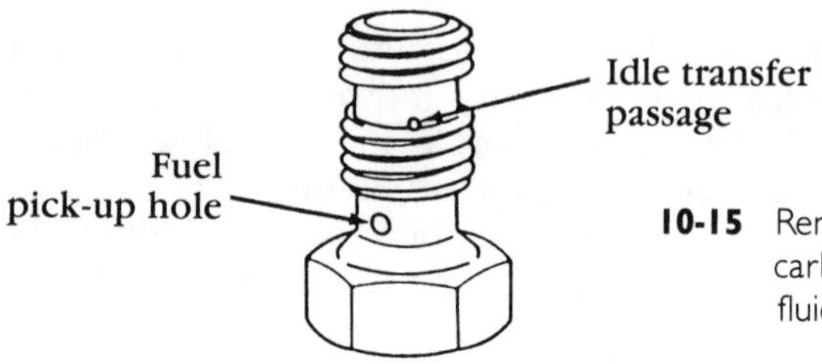

10-15 Remove the bowl nut and soak the carburetor in a commercial cleaning fluid. Tecumseh Products Co.

Remove the throttle plate, throttle shaft, dust seal, and spring. Remove the hinge pin, float, needle, and spring clip. Remove the inlet seat. This can be accomplished by a variety of methods. One method is by blowing compressed air into the fuel fitting. Another method is to use a piece of hooked wire. Be extremely careful not to scratch the polished bore where the inlet seat is located.

Soak the carburetor and bowl nut in a commercial carburetor cleaner no longer than 30 minutes. Be sure to follow the instructions on the cleaner container. The plastic fuel fitting will not be harmed by the cleaner. All passages can be probed with monofilament fishing line and compressed air to open plugged or restricted passages.

Rebuilding the carburetor To rebuild the carburetor, install a new inlet seat into the carburetor body (FIG. 10-16). The grooved side of the inlet seat goes into the carburetor body first. Place a drop of oil on the seat and press it in with a flat punch or point plunger until it seats. Be careful not to scratch the polished inlet bore.

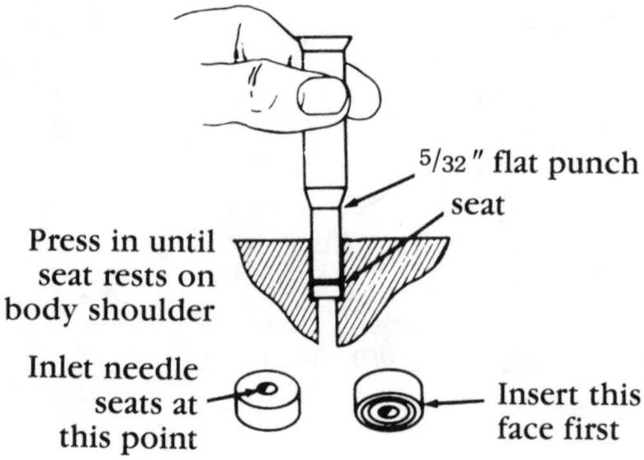

10-16 Rebuild the carburetor by installing a new inlet seat. Tecumseh Products Co.

Place the inlet needle and spring clips onto the float as shown in FIG. 10-17. The long end of the spring clip must point towards the choke end of the carburetor to ensure that the inlet needle moves up and down in a straight line.

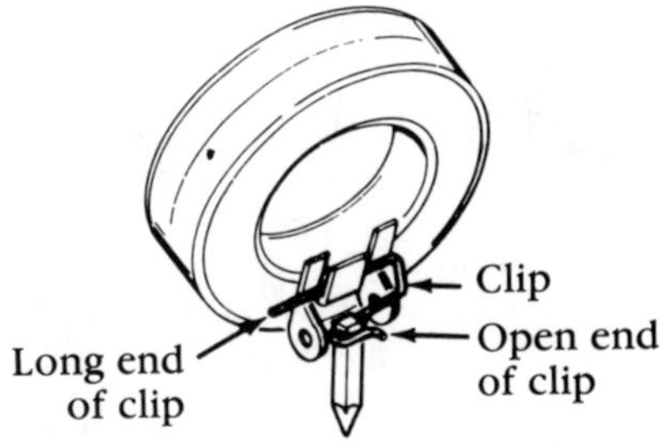

10-17 Place the inlet needle and spring clip into the float. Tecumseh Products Co.

Use the Tecumseh float setting tool (part No. 670253A) to set the correct float height. The gauge is a go-no-go type (FIG. 10-18). Pull the tool in at 90 degrees to the hinge pin. The toe of the float, end opposite the binge, must be under the first step and touch the second step without gap. If the float is too high or low, carefully bend the tab holding the inlet needle to achieve the proper height. Recheck with the gauge.

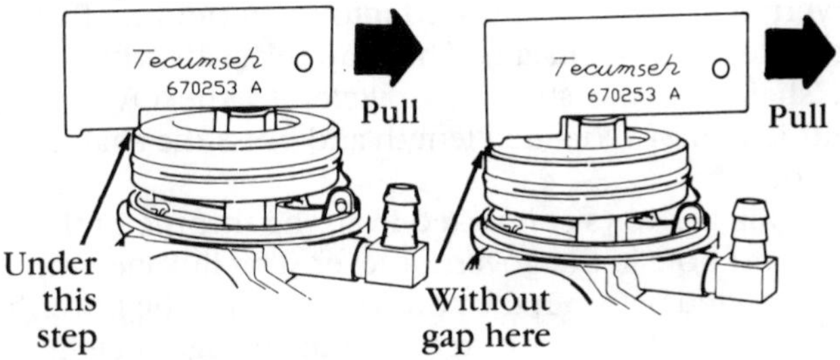

10-18 For correct float height, use the Tecumseh float setting tool #670253A. Tecumseh Products Co.

Install a new O bowl ring. Place the bowl onto the carburetor with the flat area of the bowl over the hinge pin and parallel to the binge pin. Insert the bowl nut with the fiber washer between the bowl and nut.

Install the throttle shaft and shutter. A new dust seal should also be used. The scribe mark on the shutter is in the twelve o'clock position. When the shutter is in place, no light should be seen around the edges of the shutter. If there is, position the shutter so that it closes without binding and without light showing. Any other position might cause the throttle to stick. Use a new throttle shutter screw to ensure that the screw does not come loose during running.

Place the primer bulb with the retainer ring into a 3/4-inch-deep reach socket. Press into the carburetor body until the primer bulb and retainer are seated (FIG. 10-19).

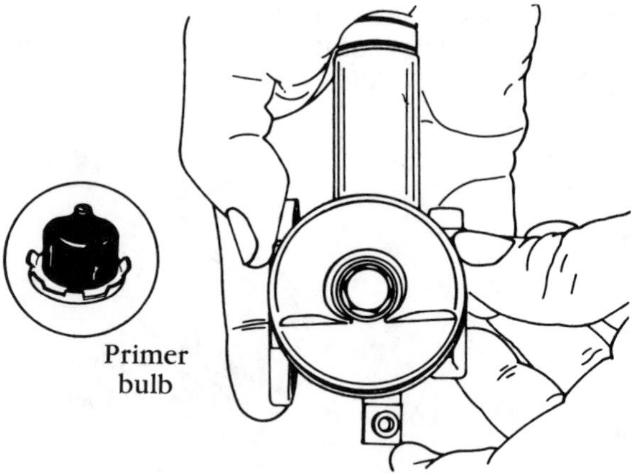

10-19 Replace the primer bulb with retainer ring in four-cycle carburetors.
Tecumseh Products Co.

OVRM governors and linkage

All Tecumseh four-cycle engines are equipped with mechanical-type governors. There are several types of speed controls. Vertical shaft engines most commonly have a control mounted above the carburetor similar to the one above. The standard governor assembly is characterized by a plastic gear and the unique shape of the spool base. It is used in most lightweight and medium-frame engines.

The governor gear shaft is pressed into the mounting flange or cover to a specific dimension. To install, lightly tap the shaft with a soft hammer to start the shaft into the shaft boss. Refer to the OVRM engine and exposed shaft length of 1 5/16-inch length and press the shaft into the boss using a press or vise.

The solid link is always connected from the throttle of the carburetor and the outermost hole in the governor lever. The linkage with the spring attached is connected between the control lever and the lower hole in the governor lever. When servicing, record the linkage attachment points prior to disassembly and reinstall in the same way.

With the engine stopped, adjust the governor by loosening the screw holding the governor clamp and lever. Turn the clamp counterclockwise on vertical shaft engines and clockwise on horizontal shaft engines, then push the governor lever connected to the throttle to a full wide-open throttle position. Hold the lever and clamp in this position, then tighten the screw.

Rewind starters

There are several types of rewind starters found in OVRM engines. The standard rewind starter has a different type pulley than the stylized rewind starter. The standard rope starter is the easiest to repair.

Standard rope starters To disassemble standard rope starters, pull the knot in the rope and slowly release the spring tension. Remove the retainer screw, retainer cup (cam dog on snow-proof type), starter dog and spring, and bake spring. Lift out the pulley and turn the spring and keeper assembly to remove. Replace all worn or damaged parts.

To assemble the standard starter, place the rewind spring and keeper assembly into the pulley. Turn to the lock position. Place a light coat of grease on the spring. Place the pulley into the starter housing. Now, install the brake spring, starter dog, and dog return spring. Replace the retainer cup (cam dog on snow-proof type) and retainer screw. Snug tightly all screws.

Stylized rewind starters To disassemble stylized rewind starters, remove the rewind from the engine blower housing, and release the tension on the rewind spring. Place a 3/4-inch, deep-reach socket inside the retainer pawl. Set the rewind on a bench, supported on the socket. Drive out the center pin with a 5/16-inch roll pin punch. Replace all defective parts. Use care when handling the pulley because the rewind spring and cover is held by the bosses in the pulley.

To reassemble starter, reverse the preceding procedure. Remember that the starter dogs with the dog spring must snap back to the center of the pulley. Always replace the center pin with a new pin on reassembly. Also, place the two new plastic washers between the center leg and the retainer pawl. The new plastic washers are provided along with the new center pin.

Check the retainer pawl. If it is worn, bent, or damaged, replace it. Tap the center pin in until it is within 1/8 of an inch of the top of the starter. Be careful not to drive the pin in too far; it might cause the retainer pawl to bend and the starter dogs will not engage the starter cup.

12-volt electric starters

To service 12-volt electric starters, first check the pinion gear parts for wear or damage. If the gear does not engage or slips, it should be washed in solvent (rubber parts cleaned with soap and water) to remove dirt and grease, and dried thoroughly. Replace any parts that are damaged. The numbered list of parts of the electric starter are shown in FIG. 10-20.

Remove, inspect, and replace parts as necessary. Reverse the procedure for reassembly. For ease of assembly, assemble armature into brush end frame first. Place a small amount of light grease between the drive nut and helix on the armature shaft. Do not apply lubricant to the pinion driver. Replace brushes.

Check the brushes before removing armature for excessive wear. Make sure brushes are not worn to the point where the brush wire bottoms out in the slot of the brush holder (FIG. 10-21). Brush springs must have enough strength to keep tension on the brushes and hold them against the commutator. Replace the entire cap assembly if brushes need replacement.

If the commutator bars are glazed or dirty, turn them down on a metal lathe (FIG. 10-22). While rotating, hold a strip of 00 sandpaper lightly on the commutator, moving it back and forth. Do not use an emery cloth.

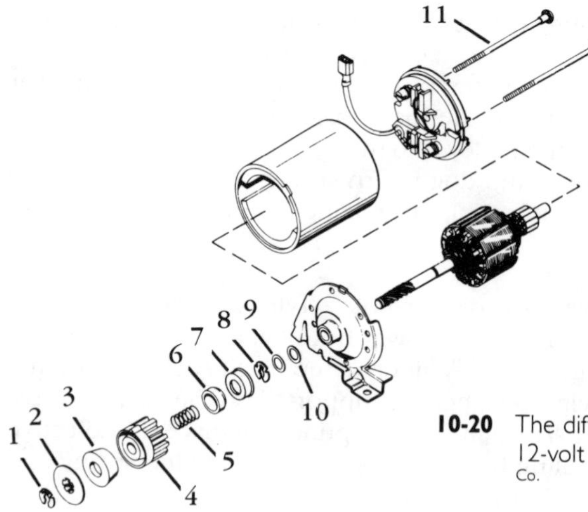

10-20 The different parts that make up the 12-volt electric starter. Tecumseh Products Co.

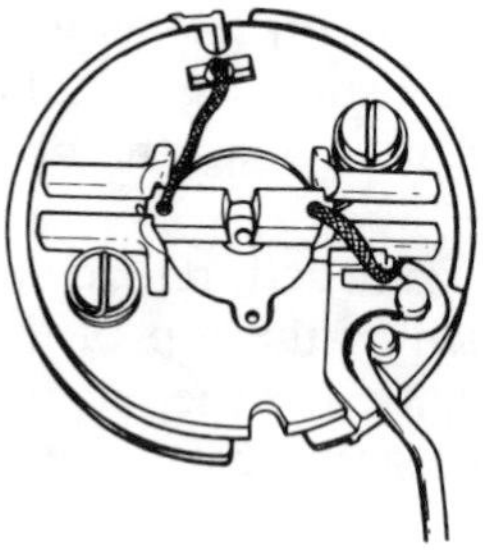

10-21 When an electric starter will not rotate, check the brakes for a worn or broken connection. Tecumseh Products Co.

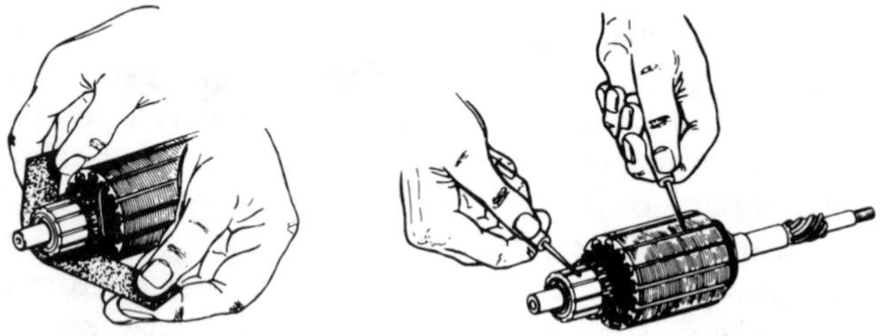

10-22 Clean up the armature with sandpaper. Check continuity between each bar. Tecumseh Products Co.

Recut the grooves between the commutator bars to a depth equal to the width of the insulators.

Check the continuity between copper bars with a VOM or DMM ohmmeter so no measurement exists between each bar. Rotate the ohmmeter to the high range (RX100) and check for grounds between copper bars and the metal area of the armature. No continuity should be made on either measurement.

Overheat valve rotary mower ignition

The solid-state ignition of the Tecumseh's OVRM engine has a capacitor discharge ignition (CD1) in an all electronic ignition system. The CD1 ignition is encapsulated in epoxy to protect it from dirt and moisture.

The solid-state ignition starts as the magnets on the flywheel rotate past the change coil and electrical energy is produced in the module. This energy is transferred to the capacitor where it is stored until needed by the spark plug (FIG. 10-23). The magnet continues rotating past a trigger coil where a low-voltage signal is produced and closes an electronic switch (SCR).

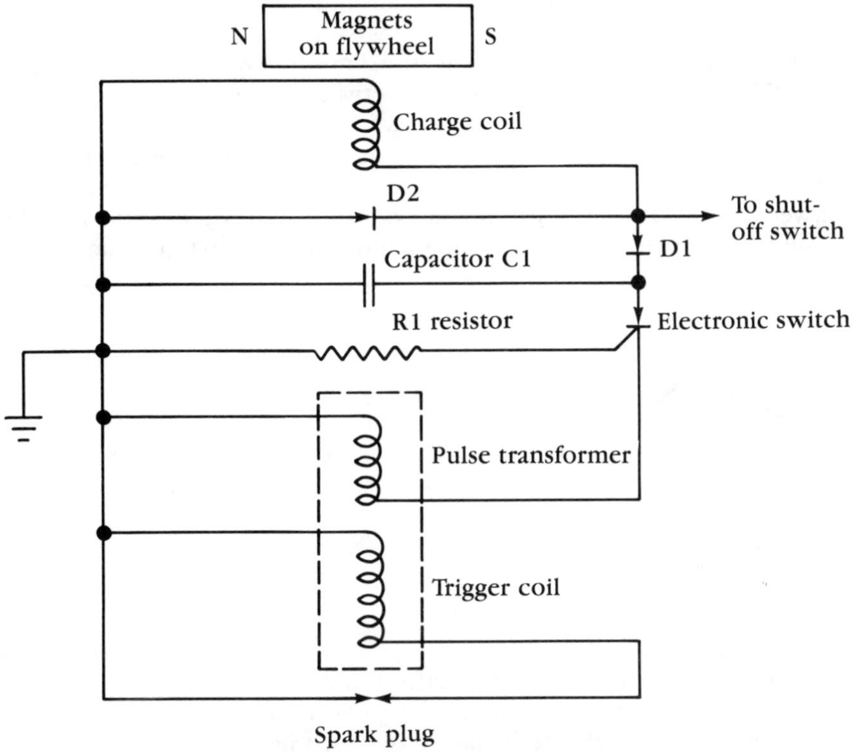

10-23 The solid-state ignition system of Tecumseh OVRM engines. Tecumseh Products Co.

The energy that is stored in the capacitor passes through the SCR switch to a transformer where the voltage is increased from 200 volts to 25,000 volts. This high voltage is fed through the high-tension lead to the spark plug, which arcs across the electrodes of the spark plug and ignites the fuel-air mixture.

Periodically check the spark plugs. Check the electrode gap with a wire feeler gauge and adjust the gap. Replace if electrode is pitted, burned, or porcelain is cracked. Make sure the clean plug is free of all foreign material. Use a spark plug tester to test for spark. If the spark plug fouls up or fires intermittently, check for the following conditions:

1. Incorrect spark plug.
2. Poor grade of gasoline.
3. Breather plugged.
4. Oil level too high.
5. Engine using excessive oil.
6. Clogged air filter.

The electronic ignition system is sealed in a module located outside the flywheel, and components are not located under the flywheel (FIG. 10-24). Note that the module has two holes on the one leg of the laminations to secure the 350-milliamp charging system. The proper air gap setting between magnets and the laminations on CD1 systems is .0125. Place a .0125 gauge (part number 670297) between the magnets and laminations and tighten the mounting screws to a torque of 30 to 40-inch pounds. Recheck the gap setting to ensure there is proper clearance between the magnets and laminations. Note that because of variations between pal shoes, the air gap might vary .005/.020 when the flywheel is rotated. There are no further timing adjustments on external lamination systems.

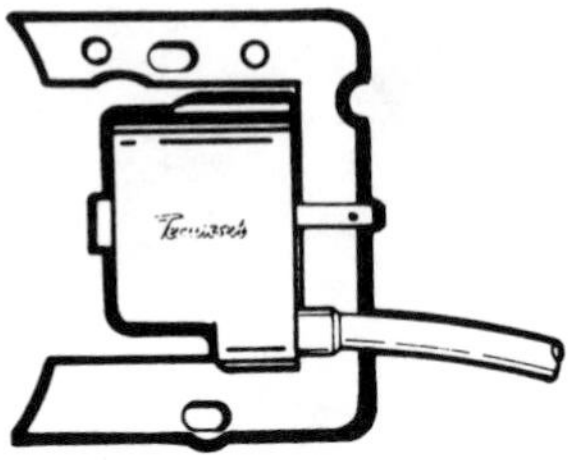

10-24 The solid-state ignition components located inside the epoxy module. Tecumseh Products Co.

Leave the disassembling and assembling of the flywheel, valves, pistons, connecting rods, and crank shafts to the professional mechanic. Follow the manufacturers literature closely if you want to make any repairs. The exact Tecumseh engine literature is a must item.

OVM FOUR-CYCLE ENGINES

The four-cycle overhead-valve medium-frame engine is similar to the overhead valve rotary mower engine. Servicing OVM carburetors, rewind starters, and 12-volt electric starters is described in the following sections. Leave the flywheel, pistons, rings, connecting rods, and crank shaft repairs to the professional mechanic.

Carburetors

More carburetors are rendered useless by neglect and abuse than all operational ills combined. A carburetor has but one task to perform, to mix fuel with air and feed it into the combustion chamber—at all speeds. The operational efficiency of a carburetor can be compromised by any foreign material (solid or liquid) that retards this flow of air or fuel. There are only three areas of carburetor malfunction: it is too lean; it is too rich; or it leaks.

Tecumseh carburetors are identified by a model number and code date stamped on the carburetor (FIG. 10-25). When servicing carburetors, use the engine model number on the carburetor and the correct section in the Master Parts Manual. Figure 10-26 lists the OVM carburetor parts.

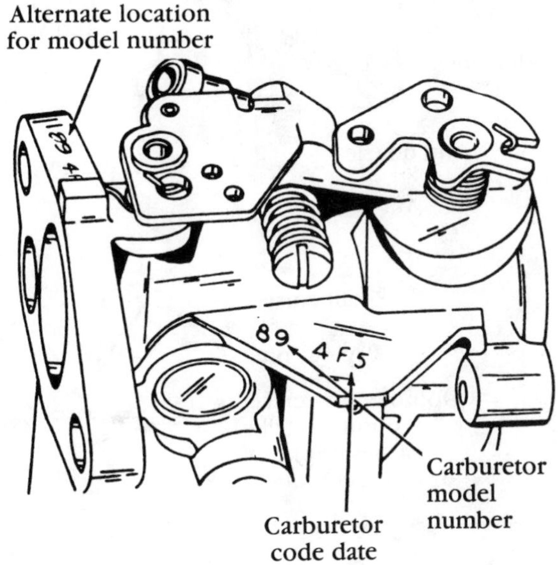

10-25 The OVM carburetor identification numbers on the engine. Tecumseh Products Co.

Clean all metallic parts with solvent, 00 commercial carburetor cleaner, no longer than 30 minutes. To properly clean, remove the welch plug to expose drilled passages. To remove the welch plug, sharpen a small chisel to a sharp-wedged point. Drive the chisel into the welch plug, push down, and pry the plug out of position (FIG. 10-27). When all shafts and accessories are removed, soak the carburetor in carburetor cleaner for about 30 minutes. Blow out all passages with compressed air in the opposite direction of normal fuel flow or use a soft tag wire. Clean out idle fuel chamber with solvent and compressed air, if handy.

Install a new welch plug after cleaning. Place the welch plug into the receptacle with raised portion up. With a punch the size of the plug, merely flatten the plug. Do not dent or drive the center of the plug below the top surface of the carburetor.

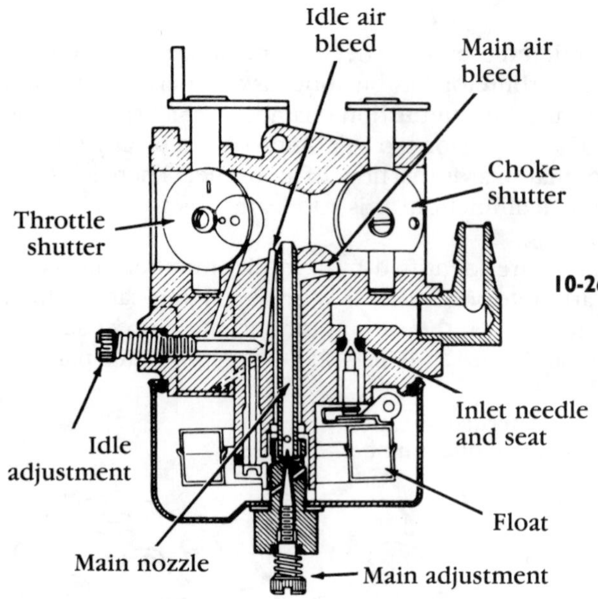

10-26 OVM carburetor parts. Tecumseh Products Co.

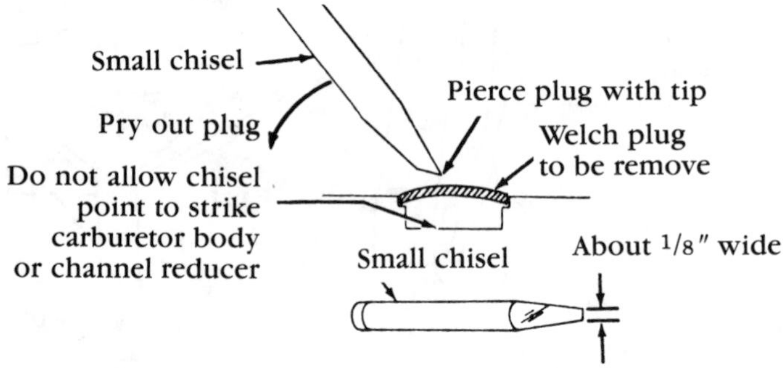

10-27 To clean out the carburetor passage, remove the welch plug. Tecumseh Products Co.

When removing choke and throttle shafts, check shafts and bearings in carburetor for wear. Any looseness in these areas can cause dirt to enter the engine and cause premature wear. If dust seals are present, these should be positioned next to the carburetor body (FIG. 10-28).

The carburetor body contains a main nozzle tube pressed into the carburetor body to a predetermined depth and positioning within the venture of the carburetor. Do not attempt to remove this main nozzle. Any movement of this nozzle will seriously affect the metering characteristics of the carburetor.

Clean the accelerating well surrounding the main nozzle with compressed air and carburetor cleaning solvents. With the choke plate and shaft removed, compressed air can be blown in through the high-speed

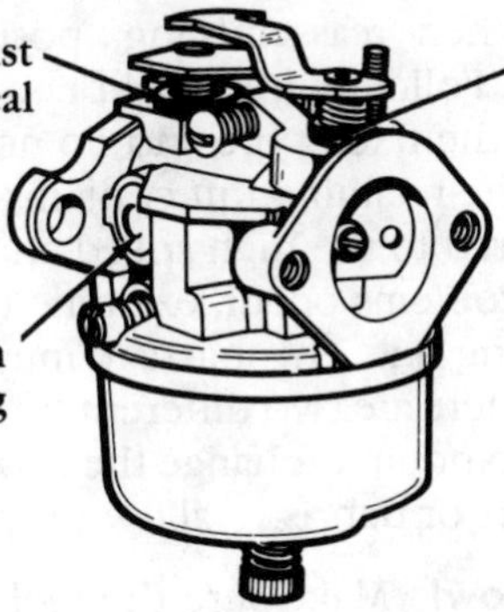

10-28 Clean out all loose dirt in the carburetor. Check shaft and bearings for extreme wear.
Tecumseh Products Co.

air bleed located just behind the lower choke shaft bearing, in front of venture, to remove any dirt that might have accumulated.

To service, examine the three throttle levers and plates before disassembly. Replace any worn or damaged parts. Remove the screw in the center of the throttle plate and pull out the throttle shaft lever assembly.

When assembling, it is important that the lines on the throttle plate are facing out when in the closed position. Position the throttle plate with two lines at the twelve o'clock and three o'clock positions. If there is only one line on the throttle plate, position it at three o'clock on series IV carburetor (found on 8.10 and 12 HP engines). If binding occurs, correct by loosening screws and repositioning throttle plate.

Next, examine the choke lever and shaft at the bearing points and holes in which the linkage is fastened. Replace if worn or damaged. The choke plate is inserted into the air horn of the carburetor in such a position that the flat surface of the choke is down. Note the direction of the choke plate movement before disassembling. These choke plates will operate in either direction.

Idle adjustment Remove the idle screw from the carburetor body and examine the point for damage to the seating surface on the taper. Replace if damaged. Tension is maintained on the screw with a coil spring. Examine and replace O ring seal if damaged. Check the adjusting screw point for damage. Replace the screw retaining assembly if damaged. Examine the sealing O ring on the screw (FIG. 10-29). Replace if any wear or cuts are indicated.

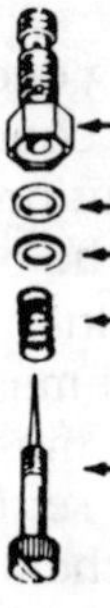

10-29 Reassemble the high-speed adjustment screw on the OVM carburetor as shown here.
Tecumseh Products Co.

When reassembling, position the coil spring on the adjustment screw. Follow with small brass washer and O ring seal. Some carburetors are of the fixed type and do not have a high-speed adjustment screw.

The retaining nut contains the transfer passage through which fuel is delivered to the high-speed and idle fuel system of the carburetor. When idle problems occur, examine the small fuel passage in the groove of the retaining nut. This passage must be clean for proper transfer of fuel.

There are two different bowl nuts that are used in float-type carburetors. Do not interchange the bowl nuts. The fuel-inlet parts must be free of any dirt or debris to allow proper fuel flow.

Fuel bowl Make sure the fuel bowl is free of dirt and corrosion. When tearing down the carburetor for repair, replace the fuel bowl O ring. Before installation, lubricate the O ring with a small amount of oil for easier insulation. The fuel bowl's flat surface must be repositioned on the same side of the carburetor as the fuel inlet fitting and parallel with the float hinge pin to ensure full travel of the float.

Float element Check the condition of the float assembly by pulling out the float hinge pin. Lift the float away from the carburetor body, (FIG. 10-30). This will also lift the needle out of the seat, because a small clip on the inlet needle hooks on the float tab. Check the float for damage. Examine the float hinge bearing surfaces for wear. Check tab that contacts the inlet needle. Replace if worn or damaged.

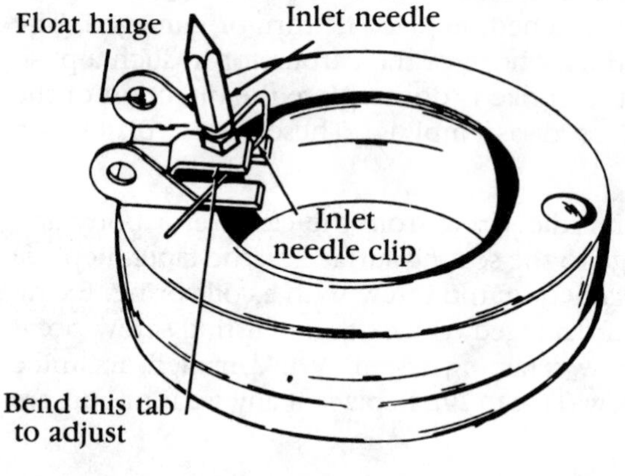

10-30 Check the float hinge for damage at bearing surfaces. Remove the float to make adjustments. Bend the tab shown to adjust. Tecumseh Products Co.

If float sticking occurs, due to deposits or when the tank is filled for the first time, this condition can quickly be corrected by loosening the carburetor bowl nut one full turn. Turn the bowl 1/4 inch in either direction. Then return the bowl to its original position and tighten bowl nut.

Check the position of the float with a float setting tool as in FIG. 10-31. The toe of the float must be within the tolerances of the float setting tool (670253A). The toe must be under step (1) and can touch step (2), without gap for the proper setting. If the float is too high or too low, adjust the height by moving the float and bend tab accordingly.

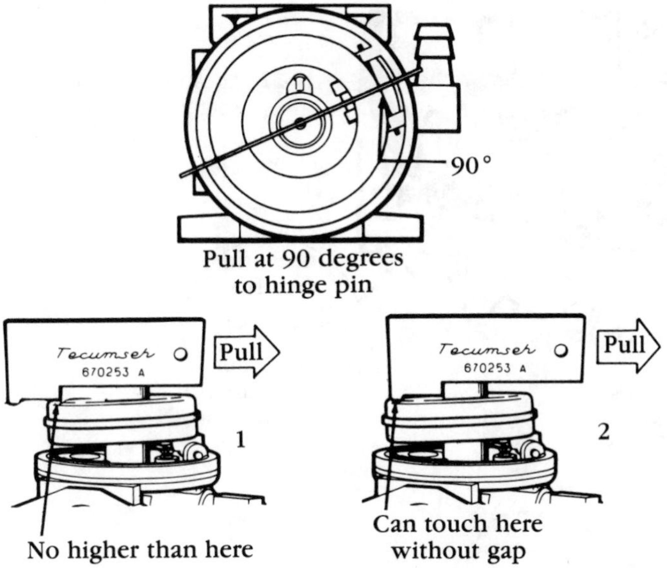

10-31 Level the carburetor float with a setting tool (#670253A).
Tecumseh Products Co.

If the required adjustment is minor, the tab adjustment can be made without removing the float and carefully inserting a small-bladed screwdriver to bend the tab. Be careful not to affect other parts. Note on carburetors equipped with a fiber washer between the bowl and casting, use the fiber washer with the float setting tool.

Inlet needle and seat position The inlet needle seats on a synthetic rubber seat in the carburetor body (FIG. 10-32). To remove the seat, pull out with a short piece of hooked wire to force it out with a short blast of compressed air. To reinstall, moisten the seat with oil, insert with smooth side toward needle or grooved side down into the carburetor. Press into the cavity with a flat punch and seat firmly. The inlet needle hooks onto the float tab by means of a spring clip (FIG. 10-33). To prevent binding, the long straight end of the clip should face the choke end of the carburetor.

The inlet fitting can be removed by pulling and twisting (FIG. 10-34). Be sure to install in the same position. When installing the fitting, insert the tip into the carburetor body. Coat the exposed portion of the shank with Locite Grade A, then press it in until the shoulder contacts the carburetor body.

To adjust the carburetor, allow the engine to warm up 3 to 5 minutes. With the engine in the high-speed position, find the lean drop-off of the main and open the mixture screw one turn for OVM120 and 3/4 turn for OVX120. Bring the engine down to the idle position. Find the lean drop-off, then find the rich drop-off. Set midway between the two extremes. Bring the engine back to the high-speed position and find the high-speed setting as before. Repeat the same procedure for the idle adjustment.

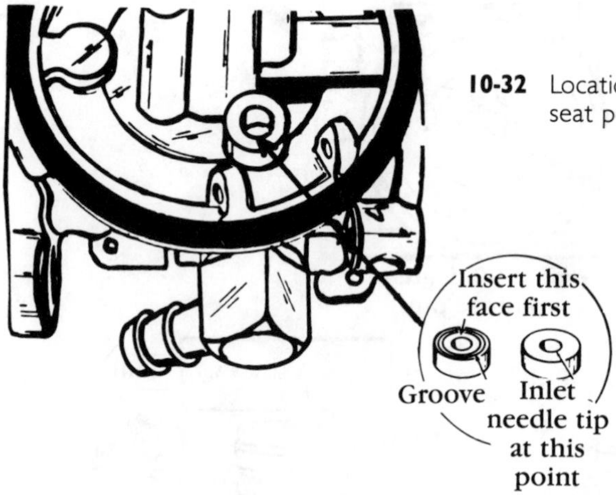

10-32 Location of the inlet needle tip and seat position. Tecumseh Products Co.

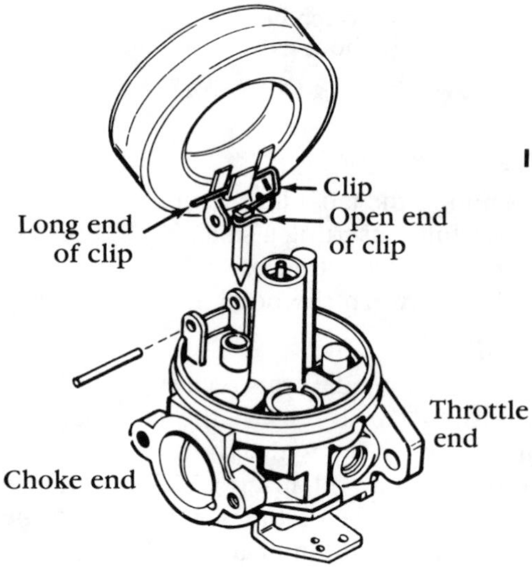

10-33 Notice how the small pin is inserted into the float clip end. Tecumseh Products Co.

Complete carburetor servicing procedures for OVM engines are found in FIG. 10-34.

Starters

There are two different types of rewind starters—stamped-steel rewind starters and cast-metal rewind starters—and a 12-volt electric starter. The inside parts are not interchangeable.

Stamped-steel rewind starters To disassemble a stamped-steel rewind starter to replace a broken cord or defective part, pull out the rope, untie the knot, and slowly release the spring tension. Place the rewind on a 1-inch-deep well socket and drive out the pin with a $^{1}/_{4}$-inch punch. Place

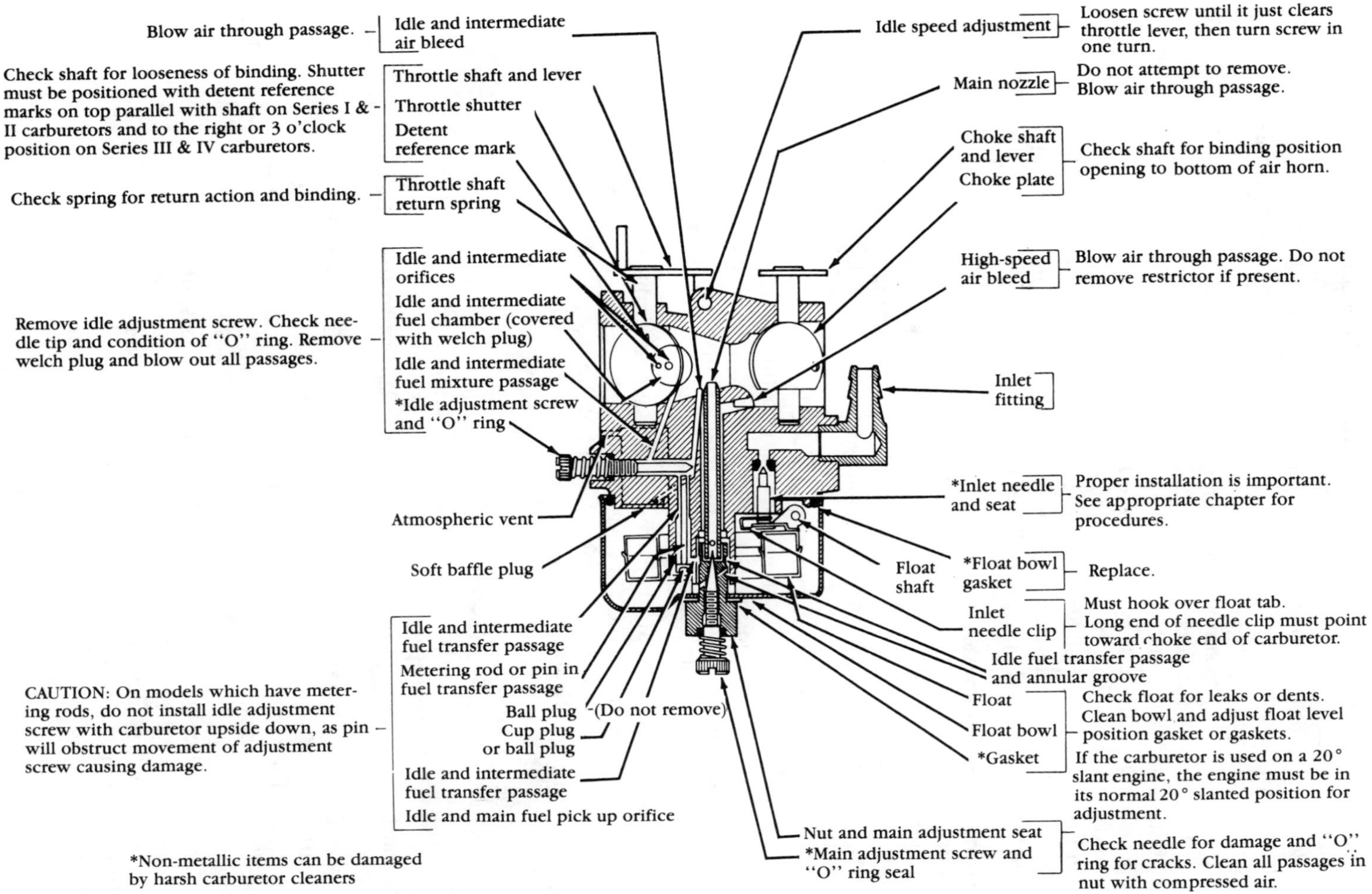

10-34 Carburetor servicing procedures for OVM engines. Tecumseh Products Co.

the punch through the center hole of the rewind until the edge of the center pin can be felt. Keep the roller pin straight when driving it out.

Remove the roll pin, brake spring, spring retainers, dog house, nylon washer, dogs, (notice that dog tips point outward), dog springs, and pulley with spring and spring keepers.

If it is necessary to service the main spring, remove the spring canister, replace, and grease assembly. Replace all worn parts. Also, replace the roll pin and add additional nylon brake spring washers.

Reassemble parts as they are replaced. Place the rewind on a flat surface and drive in the roll pin squarely until seated to the shoulder on the starter body. Wind the pulley clockwise until tight. Release, and turn until the holes in the pulley and housing line up. Feed the rope through, to left-handed knot and slowly release pulley tension.

Cast-metal rewind starters To service a cast-metal rewind starter, untie the knot in the rope and slowly release the spring tension to disassemble the rewind starter. Remove the retainer screw, retainer cup (cam dog on snow-proof type), starter dog and spring, and brake spring. Lift out the pulley. Turn the spring and keeper assembly to remove. Replace all worn or damaged parts.

To reassemble, place the rewind spring and keeper assembly into the pulley. Turn to the lock position. Apply a light coating of grease. Place the pulley into the starter housing, and install the brake spring and starter dogs and dog return springs. Replace the retainer cup (cam dog or snow-proof type) and the retainer screw. Snug up tightly.

12-volt electric starters Most procedures for servicing the 12-volt and 120-volt starters are the same. To disassemble, remove the two lock nuts on the drive end of the starter. Grasp the end of the starter and remove it from the housing assembly. Remove the dust cover, retaining ring, spring retainer, anti-drift spring, and gear and engaging hut. Remove the drive cup from the armature.

To remove the end cup assembly, loosen the nut on the terminal post. Remove the lock nuts and thin bolts from the starter housing. Remove the brushes or brush card separately. Care must be exercised when removing and reinstalling brush springs to eliminate any damage to the spring or brushes.

Visually check the starter motor before checking electrically. Remove the starter motor and check for freedom of operation by rotating the shaft. Check for worn brushes with brush springs and dirt on commutator bars. Check for armature binding that might be caused by dirt or bushings being gummed up.

Check the field of the starter with a continuity measurement with a VOM or DMM. All field coils should have a continuity measurement. Now, test between each field coil connector and starter housing with an RX100 ohm scale. No measurement is normal. Check the armature the same way as in the overhead valve rotary mower engine.

Inspect all brushes on the starter brush coil. Make sure brushes are not worn to the point where brush wire bottoms out in the slot of brush holders. Brush springs must have enough strength to keep tension on the brushes and hold them against the commutator.

If brushes need replacement, remove by unhooking terminals or clipping connections and resoldering. If the brush card is warped from overheating, replace the brush card assembly.

To replace the starter brush card, loosen the two nuts on the starter terminal post, but do not remove them. Just remove the nuts holding the starter and cup in place. Remove the starter end cap. Note the brush washer on the end of the armature.

With pliers or a vise-grip tool, grasp the through-bolts as close to the flange end as possible (away from the threaded end). Remove the two nuts retaining the driving end cap of the starter. Remove the armature and driving end cap assembly. Remove the two through-bolts, noting the position of the brush ground eyelet under the through-bolt flange.

Note the position and the connections of the brush wires. Clip the solid field wires as close to the connections as possible. Now, remove the brush card from the starter. Clean up the starter and any accumulated dust or dirt. Scrape the insulating varnish off the solid field wires about 1/2 inch from the ends.

Insert the new brush card into position, guiding the solid field wires through the proper slots in the brush card. Solder or use a crimp connector on the remaining field wires and brush leads. If a crimped connector is used, place shrink tubing over the connector. Position the wires to prevent shorts or grounding of the starter.

Spread the brushes and insert the armature into the housing. Replace the starter through-bolts through the ground brush eyelet terminals. Tighten securely. If they are tightened too tight, they might warp the new brush card and impair brush movement.

Replace the thrust washer on the end of the armature and replace the starter end cap. Install the starter end cap locking nuts and tighten securely. Tighten the nut on the starter terminal post. Test out the starter before installing it in the engine.

Ignition

The solid-state (CD1) ignition system is quite similar to the OVRM engine except two internal solid-state modules are used on different engines and are not interchangeable. The module with two holes is a 350 milliamp charging system for rotary lawn mowers (FIG. 10-35). The module on the right has different mounting hole spacing and will not accept the 350 milliamp charging system (used in OVM 120 engines).

The spark plug Check the spark plug on the OVM engine the same as on the OVRM engine. Note that the reach on the OVM spark plug is longer than a standard L-head spark plug because of the style of the head and

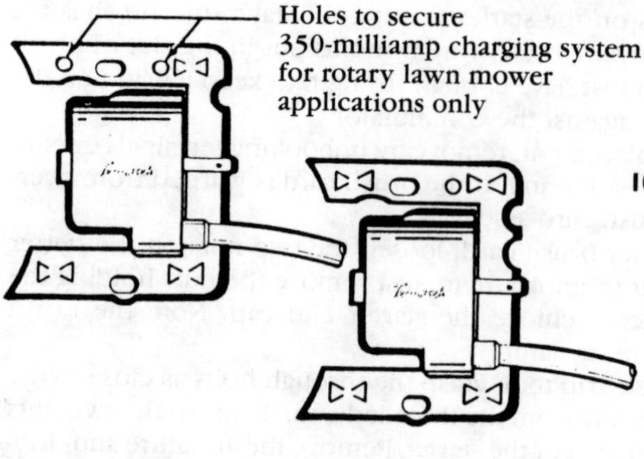

10-35 The two hole solid-state ignition module is for the 350-milliamp charging system of rotary lawn mowers. Tecumseh Products Co.

spark plug location. The wrong spark plug can cause performance problems.

The side-mounted breather The side-mounted breather mounts over the valve compartment and has a read-type check valve that allows pressure to escape through the element and out to the atmosphere. Clean the filter element with solvent. Apply oil to the check valve when installing the assembly.

Possible causes of trouble and probable remedies are provided in the four-cycle engine troubleshooting chart in TABLE 10-4. The Craftsman engine numbers are given in TABLE 10-5.

Table 10-4 Troubleshooting four-cycle engines.

ENGINE FAILS TO START OR STARTS WITH DIFFICULTY

Cause	*Remedy and Reference*
Incorrect spark plug.	Use the recommended spark plug.
Improper valve clearance.	Reset valve lash to specifications.
No fuel tank.	Fill tank with clean, fresh fuel.
Obstructed fuel line.	Clean fuel screen and line. If necessary, remove and clean carburetor.
Tank cap vent obstructed.	Open vent in fuel tank cap.
Loose or defective ignition wiring.	Check ignition wiring for shorts or grounds; repair if necessary.
Spark plug fouled.	Clean and regap spark plug.
Spark plug porcelain cracked.	Replace spark plug.
Poor compression.	Overhaul engine.
Improper ignition air gap.	Reset the air gap to .0125".
No spark at plug.	Disconnect ignition cut off wire at the engine. Crank engine. If spark at spark

Table 10-4 Continued.

	plug, ignition switch, safety switch or interlock switch is inoperative. If no spark, check solid state module. Check wires for poor connections, cuts or breaks.
Electric starter does not crank engine.	See 12 volt starter troubleshooting chart.
ENGINE KNOCKS	
Improper valve clearance.	Set valve lash to specifications.
Carbon in combustion chamber.	Remove cylinder head and clean carbon from head and piston.
Loose or worn connecting rod.	Replace connecting rod. Check crankshaft bearing surface to determine if crankshaft must be replaced.
Loose flywheel.	Check flywheel key and keyway; replace parts if necessary. Tighten flywheel nut to proper torque.
Worn cylinder.	Replace cylinder or short block the engine.
ENGINE MISSES UNDER LOAD	
Incorrect spark plug.	Use the recommended spark plug.
Spark plug fouled.	Clean and regap spark plug.
Spark plug porcelain cracked.	Replace spark plug.
Improper spark plug gap.	Regap spark plug.
Improper valve clearance.	Adjust valve clearance to specifications.
Weak valve spring.	Replace valve spring.
ENGINE LACKS POWER	
Incorrect spark plug.	Use the recommended spark plug.
Improper valve clearance.	Set valve lash to specifications.
Worn rings.	Replace rings.
Lack of lubrication.	Fill crankcase to the proper level.
Air cleaner restricted.	Replace or service air cleaner.
	Valves leaking. Grind or cut valves and cut the seats.
ENGINE OVERHEATS	
Air flow obstructed.	Remove any obstructions from air passages in shrouds.
Cooling fins clogged.	Clean cooling fins.
Excessive load on engine.	Check operation of associated equipment. Reduce excessive load.

Table 10-4 Continued.

Carbon in combustion chamber.	Remove cylinder head and clean carbon from head and piston.
Lack of lubrication.	Fill crankcase to proper level.
ENGINE SURGES OR RUNS UNEVENLY	
Incorrect spark plug.	Use the recommended spark plug.
Governor parts sticking or binding.	Clean, and if necessary repair governor parts.
Carburetor throttle linkage or throttle shaft and/or butterfly binding or sticking.	Clean, lubricate, or adjust linkage and deburr throttle shaft or butterfly.
Intermittent spark at spark plug.	Disconnect ignition cut-off wire at the engine. Crank engine. If spark, check ignition switch, safety switch and interlock switch. If no spark, check solid state module. Check wire for poor connections, cuts or breaks.
Air leak at carburetor.	Replace carburetor gaskets.
Dirty carburetor.	Clean carburetor.
ENGINE VIBRATES EXCESSIVELY	
Engine not securely mounted.	Tighten loose mounting bolts.
Bent crankshaft.	Replace crankshaft.
Lawn mower blade out of balance.	Sharpen and balance the blade.
Associated equipment out of balance.	Check associated equipment.
ENGINE USES EXCESSIVE AMOUNT OF OIL	
Engine speed too fast.	Use tachometer adjust engine RPM to specification.
Oil level too high.	To check level turn dipstick cap tightly into receptacle for accurate level reading.
Oil filter cap loose or gasket damaged causing spillage out of breather.	Replace ring gasket under cap and tighten cap securely.
Breather mechanism damaged or dirty causing leakage.	Replace breather assembly.
Gaskets damaged or gasket surfaces nicked causing oil to leak out.	Clean and smooth gasket surfaces. Always use new gaskets.
Valve guides worn excessively thus passing oil into combustion chamber.	Ream valve guide oversize and install 1/32" oversize valve.
Cylinder wall worn or glazed, allowing oil to bypass rings into combustion chamber.	Bore, hone, or deglaze cylinder as necessary.
Piston rings and grooves worn excessively.	Reinstall new rings and check land clearance and correct as necessary.

Table 10-4 Continued.

Piston fit undersized.	Measure and replace as necessary.
Engine overheating.	Clean cooling system and fins.
Oil passages obstructed.	Clean out all oil passages.
OIL SEAL LEAKS	
Crankcase breather.	Clean or replace breather.
Oil seal hardened and worn.	Replace seal.
Crankshaft seal contact surface is worn undersize causing seal to leak.	Check crankshaft size and replace if worn excessively.
Crankshaft bearing under seal is worn excessively, causing crankshaft to wobble in oil seal.	Check crankshaft bearings for wear and replace if necessary.
Seal outside seat in cylinder or sump cover is damaged, allowing oil to seep around outer edge of seal.	Visually check seal receptacle for nicks and damage. Replace oil seal.
New seal installed without correct seal driver and not seating squarely in cavity.	Replace with new seal, using proper tools and methods.
OIL SEAL LEAKS (cont.)	
New seal damaged upon installation.	Use proper seal protector tools and methods for installing another new seal.
Bent crankshaft causing seal to leak.	Check crankshaft for straightness and replace if necessary.
Oil seal driven too far into cavity.	Remove seal and replace with new seal, using the correct driver tool and procedures.
BREATHER PASSING OIL	
Engine speed too fast.	Use tachometer to adjust correct RPM.
Loose oil fill cap or gasket damaged or missing.	Install new ring gasket cap and tighten securely.
Oil level too high.	Check oil level—turn dipstick cap tightly into receptacle for accurate level reading, DO NOT fill above full mark.
Breather mechanism dirty.	Clean breather body thoroughly. Use new components when reinstalling unit.
Drain holes in breather body clogged.	Clean holes with wire to allow oil to return to crankcase.
Piston ring end gaps aligned.	Rotate gaps so as to be staggered 90° apart.
Breather mechanism loose or gasket leaking.	Install new gasket and tighten securely.
Damaged or worn oil seals on end of crankshaft.	Replace seals.

Table 10-4 Continued.

Rings not properly seated.	Check for worn, or out of round cylinder. Replace rings. Break in new rings with engine working under a varying load. Rings must be seated under high compression, or in other words, under varied load conditions.
Breather assembly not assembled correctly.	See section on breather assembly.
Sump cover gasket leaking.	Replace cover gasket.

Tecumseh Co.

Table 10-5
Craftsman reference chart.

OVM	*OVRM*
143.366012	143.384132
143.366072	143.384142
143.366202	143.384152
143.366212	143.384162
143.366232	143.384182
143.376012	143.384192
143.376032	143.394092
143.376072	143.394102
143.376082	143.394112
143.386012	143.394192
143.386032	143.394202
143.386092	143.394212
143.386102	
143.386152	
143.386162	
143.386012	

Tecumseh Co.

Glossary

AC Alternating current. The power source supplied by power companies to the receptacles in residences.

aerator A tool with tines that fights thatch, loosens soil, and prevents disease.

air gap This is the distance between the stationary laminations and the rotating flywheel magnets in the engine.

amp Ampere. The unit for measuring the electricity flowing through a motor or power tool.

armature The armature rotates and drives the motor pulley. The chuck or motor pulley is connected to the armature.

auger The post hole auger digs a hole for sinking posts into the ground, such as for a fence.

battery A device that provides DC power with a chemical reaction to operate a DC motor. Batteries can be wired in series to acquire a specific voltage.

bearing A sleeve or ball bearing allows the shaft of an armature or gears to rotate without friction.

breaker points Provide energy to the primary winding of a magnet coil.

breathers Allow crankcase pressure to escape from the engine and to admit outside air back into the crankcase without bringing dust or dirt in with the fresh air.

brush A conductive graphite or carbon material that rides on a commutator.

camshaft Can incorporate a centrifugal spark advance in the engine. A worn or malfunctioning camshaft can affect engine starting at all speeds. Breaker points are operated by a cam-driven assembly.

carburetor Mixes fuel with air and feeds it to the combustion chambers, at all speeds.

clutch Engages rotation of the engine to apply power to the cutting operation or drive movement of a mower, tractor, tiller, or shredder.

commutator A part of the armature that rotates in the motor. Carbon or graphite brushes lay against the armature as it rotates.

compression Combustion force. The compression on a one-cylinder engine is very important, and without the required amount, the engine would be hard to start and/or not develop its maximum horsepower.

compost Decayed vegetable matter for the garden or soil.

condenser The condenser, or capacitor, stores up electricity. The instant breaker points open, the capacitor acts as a storage reservoir for electricity during an extremely small fraction of a second before the arc across the breaker points is extinguished in the engine.

CPS Cycles per second.

cylinder The piston chamber in an engine. The piston moves inside the cylinder to develop combustion and energy. The cylinder head, or block, contains the cylinder, piston, and valves.

DC Direct circuit. Batteries provide DC voltage to cordless lawn and garden tools.

diode A rectifying device. Silicone diodes are used in DC battery-charging and solid-state ignition systems.

drive sprocket A toothed pail that drives a saw chain.

electric motor A device that converts electrical energy to mechanical energy.

feeler gauge A tool used to measure and adjust the spark plug gap distance.

flywheel Establishes the magnetism of a magnet system and forms a part of a magnet circuit. Usually, the flywheel has to be removed to check breaker point contacts.

gap The area between electrodes of a spark plug.

gauge A measurement of thickness. The lower the gauge, the larger the wire. A feeler gauge measures the spark plug gap distance.

governor The governor used in engines keeps the engine from overspeeding and controls the engine speed from no-load or full-load.

ground A wire that grounds a motor or equipment and returns the path of the current to the ground, or earth. The ground wire of a power tool is usually green.

horsepower(HP) A unit of electrical power that equals 746 watts. Motors and engines are rated in horsepower.

idler A wheel or pulley that provides tension on belts or chains.

insulation The protective cover over extension cord wires.

magnets Magnets is simply a specialized form of an electric generator that generates electricity. Permanent magnets are used to produce a magnetic field.

ohmmeter A device used to measure the resistance in ohms.

ohms Unit of electrical resistance equal to the resistance of a circuit in which a potential difference of one volt produces a current of one ampere.

piston A device that moves up and down inside a cylinder to produce compression and power for an engine.

polarized When AC power tools or equipment are equipped with three-prong plugs for ground potential, they are said to be *polarized*.

overload protection A device that protects motors when they become overloaded or overheated.

resistance A force that works against the flow of electrical current. A resistor is measured in ohms.

RPM Revolutions per minute. The speed at which a motor or engine shaft revolves.

SPST Single pole, single throw switch. A SPST switch turns power tools OFF and ON.

switch A device that can interrupt an electrical power circuit to a motor.

switch linkage The mechanism that transmits motion from a trigger to a switch.

switch lockout A movable stop that prevents the unintentional operation of a switch until it is manually activated.

torque The measure of a rotating force around an axis. The amount of pressure applied when tightening a bolt or nut with a torque wrench.

voltage The force that moves electrical energy through a circuit.

watt A unit of electrical power. One watt is dissipated by a resistance of 1 ohm through which a current of 1 ampere flows.

winding The conductive coils in a motor. These coils can be wrapped or have enamelled wire in the field and armature windings.

Resources

The following is a list of manufacturers and addresses for your convenience. There is also a list of manufacturers for specific lawn and garden equipment.

ARIENS CO.
655 W. Ryan St.
Bullion, WI 54110

ECHO, INC.
400 Oakwood Road
Lake Zurich, IL 60047

HOMELITE DIVISION OF
TEXTRON INC.
14401 Carowinds Blvd.
Charlotte, NC 28273

HUSQUAINA FOREST
& GARDEN CO.
907 W. Irving Road
Itasca, IL 60143

MCCULLOCH CORP.
P.O. Box 11990
Tucson, AZ 85734

POULAN/WEED EATER
5020 Flouring Road
Shreveport, LA 71129

REDMAX/KOMATSU ZENOAH
AMERICA CO.
1505 Pavilion Place, Suite A
Norcross, GA 30093

SHINDAIWA, INC.
P.O. Box 1090
Tualatin, OR 97062

SOLO, INC.
5100 Chestnut, Box 5030
Newport News, VA 23665

STIHL, INC.
536 Viking Drive
Virginia Beach, VA 23452

TANAKA LTD.
22322 Ioth Ave., SE
Bethell, WA 98033

SHREDDERS/CHIPPERS

AL-KO KOBER CORP.
25784 Borg Road
Elkhart, IN 46514

AMERIND MACKISSIC CORP.
Box 111, Dept. 00039
Parker Ford, PA 19457

BCS AMERICA INC.
13601 Providence Road
Mathews, WI 28105

CRARY CO.
Box 849
West Fargo, ND 58078

CUB CADET CORP.
Box 360930
Cleveland, OH 44136

FLOWTRON OUTDOOR PRODUCTS
2 Main Street
Melrose, MA 02148

GARDNERS SUPPLY
128 Intervale Road
Burlington, VT 05401

TROY-BILT (GARDENS WAY INC.)
102nd St. & 9th Ave.
Troy, NY 12180

GENERAL POWER EQUIPMENT CO.
(LAWN CHIEF)
201 East Brink St.
Harvard, IL 60033

KEMP CO.
160 Koster Road
Lititz, PA 17543

MANTIS MANUFACTURING CO.
1458 County Line Road
Huntingdon Valley, PA 19006

MACKISSIC/MIGHTY MAC
Box 111
Parker Ford, PA 19457

RINGER
9959 Valley View Road
Eden Prairie, MN 55344-3585

ROTO-HOE
100 Auburn Road
Newbury, OH 44065

SCOTCHMEN
RFD #1 - Dept. 0G029
Pottstown, PA 19464

TORNADO PRODUCTS, INC.
N114 W18605 Clinton Drive
Germantown, WI 53022

LAWN AND GARDEN TRACTORS

AMERICAN HONDA MOTOR CO., INC.
4475 River Green Parkway
Duluth, GA 30136

ARIENS CO.
655 W. Ryan St.
Brillion, WI 54110

BCS AMERICA INC.
13601 Providence Road
Matthews, NC 28105

FORD NEW HOLLAND
500 Dilla Ave.
New Holland, PA 17557

GARDEN WAY INC.
102 2nd St. & 9th Ave.
Troy, NY 12180

GENERAL POWER EQUIPMENT
(LAWN CHIEF)
201 East Brink St.
Harvard, IL 60033

CUB CADET CORP.
Box 360930
Cleveland, OH 44136

JOHN DEERE
John Deere Road
Moline, IL 61265

DERITZ-ALLIS LAWN & GARDEN EQUIPMENT
500 N. Spring St.
Port Washington, WI 53074

INGERSOLL EQUIPMENT
122 S. 4th St.
Winneconne, WI 54986

KUBOTS TRACTOR CORP.
550 W. Artesia Blvd.
Compton, VA 90220

LAWN-BOY
Box 152
Plymouth, WI 53073

NORMA OUTDOOR PRODUCTS, INC.
210 American Drive
Jackson, TN 38301

GRAVELY INTERNATIONAL INC.
Box 5000
Clemmons, NC 26012

HOMELITE DIVISION OF TEXTRON, INC.
14401 Carowinds Blvd.
Charlotte, NC 28273

HUSQUAINA FOREST & GARDEN CO.
907 W. Irving Park Road
Itasca, IL 60143

TORO WHEEL HORSE
8111 Lyndale Ave. So.
Minneapolis, MN 55420

WHITE OUTDOORS PRODUCTS
Box 361131
Cleveland, OH 44136

YAMAHA MOTOR CORP.
Box 6555
Cypress, CA 90630

SIMPLICITY MFG. CO.
Box 997 500 N. Spring St.
Port Washington, WI 53074-0997

SNAPPER POWER EQUIPMENT
535 Main Road
McDonough, CA 30253

RIDING MOWERS

AMERICAN HONDA MOTOR CO.
4475 River Green Parkway
Duluth, GA 30136

ARIENS CO.
655 W. Ryan St.
Brillion, WI 54110

BOLENS
102nd St, & 9th Ave.
Troy, NY 12180

CUB CADET CORP.
Box 360930
Cleveland, OH 44136

DIXON INDUSTRIES
Box 1569
Coffeyville, KS 67337

EXCEL INDUSTRIES, INC.
Box 7000, 200 S. Ridge Road
Hesston, KS 67062-2097

FORD NEW HOLLAND
500 Diller Ave.
New Holland, PA 17557

GARDEN WAY, INC.
102nd Street 7-9th Ave.
Troy, MI 12180

JOHN DEERE
John Deere Road
Moline, IL 61265

DUETZ-ALLIS LAWN & GARDEN EQUIPMENT
500 N. Spring St.
Port Washington, WI 53074

HOMELITE DIVISION OF TEXTRON CO.
14401 Carowinds Blvd.
Charlotte, NC 28273

HUSQUIARNIA FOREST & GARDEN CO.
907 W. Irving Road
Itasca, IL 60143

INGERSOLL EQUIPMENT CO., INC.
122 S. 4th St.
Winneconne, WI 54986

LAWN BOY
Box 152
Plymouth, WI 53073

NOMA OUTDOOR PRODUCTS INC.
210 American Drive
Jackson, TN 38301

GENERAL POWER EQUIPMENT CO.
(LAWN CHIEF)
201 East Brink St.
Harvard, IL 60033

THE GRASSHOPPER CO.
Box 637 - One Grasshopper Trail
Moundridge, KS 67107

SIMPLICITY MANUFACTURING CO.
500 N. Spring St.
Port Washington, WI 53074-0997

SNAPPER POWER EQUIPMENT
535 Macon Road
McDonough, GA 30253

TORO WHEEL HORSE
8111 Lyndale Ave. So.
Minneapolis, MN 55420

WALKER MFG. CO.
5925 E. Harmony Road
Fort Collins, CO 80525

WHITE OUTDOOR PRODUCTS
Box 361131
Cleveland, OH 44136

POULAN/WEED EATER
5020 Flourney Lucas Road
Shreveport, LA 71129

WOODS DIVISION OF HESSTON
Box 1000
Oregon, IL 61061

TILLERS/CULTIVATORS

AMERICAN HONDA MOTOR CO., INC.
4475 River Green Parkway
Duluth, GA 30136

ARIENS CO.
655 W. Ryan St.
Brillion, WI 54110

BCS AMERICA INC.
13601 Providence Road
Mathews, NC 26105

CUB CADET CORP.
Box 360930
Cleveland, OH 44136

GENERAL POWER EQUIPMENT
(LAWN CHIEF)
201 East Brink St.
Harvard, IL 60033

HOMELITE DIVISION OF TEXTRON, INC.
14401 Carowinds Blvd.
Charlotte, NC 28273

HUSQUAINA FOREST & GARDEN CO.
907 W. Irving Park Road
Itasca, IL 60143

KUBOTA TRACTOR CORP.
550 W. Artisia Blvd.
Compton, CA 90220

MAINLINE OF NORTH AMERICA
Box 526
London, OH 43140

MANTIS MANUFACTURING CO.
1458 Country Line Road
Huntingdon Valley, PA 19006

HOFFCO INC.
358 NW F St., Dept. FG
Richmond, IN 47374

NOMA OUTDOOR PRODUCTS INC.
210 American Drive
Jackson, TN 38301

POULAN/WEED EATER
5020 Flourney Lucas Road
Shreveport, LA 71129

SNAPPER POWER EQUIPMENT
535 Macon Road
McDonough, GA 30253

TAYLOR MFG. CO.
Box 518
Elizabethtown, NC 28337

TROY-BILT (GARDEN WAY INC.)
102nd St. & 9th Ave.
Troy, NY 12180

WHITE OUTDOOR PRODUCTS
Box 361131
Cleveland, OH 44136

MERRY TILLER INC.
4500 5th Ave. So.
Birmingham, AL 35222

WALK-BEHIND MOWERS

AMERICAN HONDA MOTOR CO.
4475 River Green Parkway
Duluth, GA 30136

AMERICAN LAWN MOWER
Box 369, Dept. FG
Shelbyville, IN 46176

ARIENS CO.
655 W. Ryan St.
Brillion, WI 54110

BLACK & DECKER
10 North Park Drive
Hunt Valley, MD 21030

BOLENS
102nd St. & 9th Ave.
Troy, NY 12180

COUNTRY HOME PRODUCTS
Box 89, Dept. A702
Cedar Beach Road
Charlotte, VT 05445

CUB CADET CORP.
Box 360930
Cleveland, OH 44136

JOHN DEERE
John Deere Road
Moline, IL 61265

GARDEN WAY, INC.
102nd St. & 9th Ave.
Troy, NY 12180

GENERAL POWER EQUIPMENT CO.
(LAWN CHIEF)
201 East Brink St.
Harvard, IL 60033

HOMELITE DIVISION OF TEXTRON, INC.
14401 Carowinds Blvd.
Charlotte, NC 28273

HUSQUAINA FOREST & GARDEN CO.
907 W. Irving Road
Itasca, IL 60143

KINCO MANUFACTURING
170 No. Pascal
St. Paul, MN 53104

KUBOTA TRACTOR CORP.
550 W. Artesia Blvd.
Compton, VA 90220

LAWN BOY
Box 152
Plymouth, WI 53073

NOMA OUTDOOR PRODUCTS INC.
210 American Drive
Jackson, TN 38301

POULAN/WEED EATER
5020 Flourney Lucas Road
Shreveport, LA 71129

SNAPPER POWER EQUIPMENT
535 Macon Road
McDonough, GA 30253

TORO, CO
8111 Lyndale Ave. South
Minneapolis, MN 55420

WEED WIZARD, INC.
Box 275
Dahionega, CA 30533

WHITE OUTDOOR PRODUCTS
Box 361131
Cleveland, OH 44136

WOODS DIVISION OF HESSTON
Box 1000
Oregon, IL 61061

YAMAHA MOTOR CORP.
Box 6555
Sypress, CA 90630

YARDMAN
Box 360940
Cleveland, OH 44136

Index

A

air filters
- Briggs & Stratton engines, 158-160
- chippers/shredders, 92
- cleanup tips, 16, 43
- Clinton engines, 170-172
- grass/weed trimmers, gas-powered, 69
- Jacobsen engines, 185-186, 193-194
- power units/two-wheel tractors, 130
- riding mowers, 138-139
- Tecumseh engines, 207-208, 217-218
- tillers/cultivators, 58, 109, 111
- walk-behind mowers, 83

axes, sharpening, 28

B

batteries, riding mowers, 152
BCS 700 model power unit, 129
bearings, cleanup tips, 17, 19
belts, drive belts, cleanup tips, 17, 18
blades, cleanup tips, 17
Briggs & Stratton engines, 155-161
- air cleaner replacement, 158-161
- carburetor adjustments, 157-158
- control adjustments, 155-158
- cylinder head, 160
- fuel requirements, 155
- governor control adjustments, 157
- maintenance schedule, 158-161
- oil/lubrication, 155
- remote choke control adjustment, 156
- spark arrestor screen, 160
- spark plugs, 160-161
- throttle control adjustments, 157

brush hogs (*see* rear-end mowers)
bulb planters, sharpening dull tools, 30

C

carbon monoxide hazards, 4
carburetors (*see also* engines)
- Briggs & Stratton engines, 157-158
- Carter carburetors, 178-179
- chain saws, 48-54
- Clinton 501 carburetors, 174
- Clinton engines, 173-179
- float element adjustment, 230-231
- fuel bowl, 230
- grass/weed trimmers, gas-powered, 69-70
- idle adjustment, 229-230
- inlet needle and seat position, 231-232
- Jacobsen engines, 187-188, 198-199
- lift-type carburetors, 174-176
- LMB, LMG, LMV-type carburetors, 176-177
- OVM carburetors, 219-220
- rebuild, 211-213, 220-221
- Tecumseh engines, 208-214, 219-221, 227-232
- tillers/cultivators, 59
- troubleshooting chart, 214
- UT carburetors, 177-178
- walk-behind mowers, 83

carts, yard carts, 42
chain saws, 44-55
  carburetor, adjustments, 53-54
  carburetor, Eager Beaver 2.1, 49
  carburetor, fuel pump, 51, 53
  carburetor, MACCAT, 49
  carburetor, metering system, 51
  carburetor, parts assembly, exploded view, 52
  carburetor, servicing, 48-54
  component parts, exploded view, 46, 48
  fuel pump servicing, 51, 53
  guide bar maintenance, 45
  Homelite EL model chain saws, 44-46
  McCulloch 300 series chain saws, 46-49
  muffler screen, 54-55
  oil pump servicing, 54
  sharpening, 45-46
  starter assembly servicing, 47
  starter housing servicing, 47
  tension adjustments, 45
  troubleshooting chart, 49-50
chippers/shredders, 91-101, 246
  air filters, 92
  bolts and shields, tightening, 92-93
  centrifugal clutch, 94, 96-97
  Crary Bear Cat chippers/shredders, 97-98
  cutting blades, sharpening, 97-98
  discharge screen clean-out, 101
  leaf shredders, 63
  lubrication, 93-94, 101
  MacKissic Inc., Model 12PE7 and 12PTE shredders, 94
  maintenance procedures, 98-101
  muffler servicing, 92
  parts layout, exploded view, 95, 99
  parts list, Crary Inc., 100
  parts list, MacKissic Inc., 96
  plugged rotor clean-out, 101
  safety, 10
  starter system, 94
cleanup tips, 15-20, 27-28, 43-44
  air filters, 16, 43
  bearings, 17, 19
  belts, drive belts, 17, 18
  blades, 17
  degreaser solvents, 15
  high-tension wires/leads, 20
  ignition systems, 16-17
  rust removal, 20
  spark plugs, 17-19, 43
Clinton engines, 163-183
  501 carburetors, 174
  air cleaner service, 170-172
  carburetors, 173-179
  Carter carburetors, 178-179
  failure of engine, causes, 167-168
  fuel requirements, 168-169
  hard starting, 164-165
  identification numbers, 163
  impulse starters, 180-183
  knocking or noisy operation, 166
  lack of power under load, 165
  lift-type carburetors, 174-176
  LMG, LMB, LMV-type carburetors, 176-177
  lubrication, 168-170
  maintenance procedures, 170-172
  missing under load, 165
  overheating, 166-167
  recoil starters, 179-180
  spark plug service, 172
  starter servicing, 179-183
  surge, 166
  troubleshooting chart, 164-168
  tune-ups, major and minor, 172-183
  UT carburetors, 177-178
  vibration, 167
coils (*see* ignition systems)
compost tumblers, 55-58
Craftsman tools, Tecumseh engine reference number chart, 240
Crary Bear Cat chippers/shredders, 97-98
cultivators (*see* tillers/cultivators)
cultivators, hand-cultivators, sharpening dull tools, 30-32

D

degreasers, engine cleaners, 15
digital multimeters (DMM), 10-11, 13-14

E

Eager Beaver 2.1 carburetor, chain saws, 49
edgers, electric-powered, 60
electric starters, 223-224, 234-235
electrical safety
  extension cords, 7
  grounding power tools, 5-6
engines (*see also* carburetors), 153-240

air filters, 16, 43, 158-160, 170-172, 185-186, 193-194, 207-208, 217-218
BCS A220 and AL 330 power-unit engines, 129
breather element, side-mount, 236
breather passing oil, 239-240
Briggs & Stratton (*see* Briggs & Stratton engines)
carburetors (*see* carburetors)
choke adjustments, 156
Clinton engines (*see* Clinton engines)
control adjustments, 155-158
degreasers, 15
difficult starts, 164-165, 236-237
electric starters, 223-224, 234-235
exhaust systems, 187, 196
failure of engine, 167-168
fuel requirements, 155, 168-169, 205-206, 217
fuel system, 196-198
governor adjustments, 157, 188-189, 199-200, 222
ignition systems, 16-17, 189-191, 200-203, 225-226, 235
impulse starters, 180-183
Jacobsen engines (*see* Jacobsen engines)
knocking, 166, 237
lack of power under load, 165, 237
leaks oil, 239
lubrication, 21-22, 205-206, 217
misses under load, 165, 237
oil/lubrication requirements, 43, 155, 168-170
overheating, 166-167, 237-238
recoil starters, 179-180, 187, 194-195, 214-215
rewind starters, 222-223, 232, 234
spark plugs, 17-19, 43, 160-161, 172, 191, 202-203, 235-236
starter servicing, 179-183
surging, 166, 238
Tecumseh engines (*see* Tecumseh engines)
throttle adjustments, 157
tune-up procedures, 172-183, 208, 218-219
uses oil, 238-239
vibration, 167, 238
equipment and supplies, 244-250
exhaust systems, Jacobsen engines, 187, 196
extension-cord safety, 7

F

filters (*see* air filters)
forks, spading forks, sharpening dull tools, 33
fuel
Briggs & Stratton engines, 155
Clinton engines, 168-169
grass/weed trimmers, gas-powered, 68-69
Jacobsen engines, fuel system, 196-198
regular vs. unleaded gas, 22
riding mowers, 134
safety tips, 4-5
Tecumseh engines, 205-206, 217
tillers/cultivators, 59-60
fuel bowl, carburetor, 230

G

gas (*see* fuel)
governors
Jacobsen engines, 188-189, 199-200
Tecumseh engines, 222
grass shears/trimmers, 63-77
air filters, gas-powered trimmers, 69
battery charging, 64, 65-66
blade sharpening, 30, 65, 77
carburetors, gas-powered trimmers, 69-70
cordless, hand-held trimmers, 63-66
fuel requirements, gas-powered trimmers, 68-69
line-type trimmers, electric-powered, 66-67, 70-71
line-type trimmers, gas-powered, 71-76, 78
line-type trimmers, line adjustment, 67-68
recoil starters, gas-powered trimmers, 73-75
starter rope replacement, gas-powered trimmers, 75, 76
troubleshooting, gas-powered trimmers, 71-72, 78
grounding electrical power tools, 5-6

H

hand cultivators, sharpening, 30-32
hand mowers, sharpening blades, 32
handle replacement, 23-24
hatchets, sharpening blade, 33
hedge trimmers, 60-61
cordless, 60-61

hedge trimmers (*cont.*)
electric-powered, 61
sharpening dull tools, 33
high-tension wires/leads, cleanup tips, 20
hoes, sharpening, 34
Homelite EL model chain saws, 44-46

I

idle adjustment, carburetor, 229-230
ignition systems
cleanup tips, 16-17
Jacobsen engines, 189-191, 200-203
Tecumseh engines, 225-226, 235
impulse starters, Clinton engines, 180-183
inspections, 81-82

J

Jacobsen engines, 185-203
123V two-cycle engines, 185-191
A984H two-cycle engines, 191-203
air cleaner servicing, 185-186, 193-194
carburetors, 187-188, 198-199
exhaust system, 187, 196
fuel systems, 196-198
governors, 188-189, 199-200
ignition systems, coil and gap, 189-191, 200-203
interlock module, 201-202
push (stop engine) button, 202
recoil starters, 187, 194-195
spark plugs, 191, 202-203
TCI module, 201

K

Kinco Mountain Goat power weed cutters, 118-125
knives, sharpening dull tools, 36-37

L

lawn and garden tractors (*see also* riding mowers), 246-247
lawn spreaders, maintenance tips, 34
leaf blowers, 61-63
leaf shredders, 63
loppers/pruners, sharpening, 29-29, 32-33, 38-39
lubrication, 20-22
Briggs & Stratton engines, 155
chippers/shredders, 93-94, 101
Clinton engines, 168-170
engines, 21-22
power units/two-wheel tractors, 129
power weed cutters, 124-125
rear-end mowers, 125-126
riding mowers, 134, 135
Tecumseh engines, 205-206, 217

M

MACCAT carburetor, chain saws, 49
MacKissic Inc. Model 12PE7 and 12PTE chippers/shredders, 94
Mainline Rotary VMC90 tillers/cultivators, 113-116
manufacturers and suppliers, 245-250
McCulloch 300 series chain saws, 46-49
mowers (*see* hand mowers; rear-end mowers; riding mowers; walk-behind mowers)

O

oil changes, 43
overheat valve rotary mower ignition, Tecumseh engines, 225-226

P

planting-type hand tools, 35
post hole diggers, sharpening, 36
power units/two-wheel tractors, 129-132
air filter maintenance, 130
BCS 700 model power unit, 129
BCS A220 and AL 330 engines, 129
bolt tightening, 130
engine maintenance, 129
maintenance procedures, general maintenance, 130
mower bar maintenance, 131-132
oil and lubrication, 129
PTO attachments, coupling procedures, 131
rotary mower blade maintenance, 132
power weed cutters (*see also* power units/two-wheel tractors), 117-125
belt replacement, wheel belt, 123
bolt tightening procedures, 120
chain maintenance, 120
inspection procedures, 121, 123

Kinco Mountain Goat power weed cutter, 118-125
knife and wear-plate adjustments, 120-121
knife assembly, adjustments, 121, 124
knife clutch idler adjustments, 120
lubrication, 124-125
noisy operation, 121
parts layout, exploded view, 119, 122
sharpening blades/knives, 124
vibration excessive during operation, 121
wheel belt tension adjustments, 120
wheel-clutch lockouts, 118
pruners, pruning shears (*see* loppers/pruners)
PTO attachments, power units/two-wheel tractors, 131

R

rakes, 37
rear-end mowers, 125-132
belt maintenance/replacement, 125-126
belt troubleshooting guide, 128
blade sharpening, 126
cutting-height adjustment, 125
gearbox maintenance and lubrication, 127
lubrication, 125-126
maintenance procedures, general maintenance, 127
spindle servicing, 126
universal joint service, 127
recoil starters
Clinton engines, 179-180
grass/weed trimmers, gas-powered, 73-75
Jacobsen engines, 187, 194-195, 214-215
rewind starters, 222-223, 232, 234
riding mowers, 132-152, 247-248
after-mowing cleanup, 133
air cleaner cleaning, 138-139
battery servicing, 152
belt maintenance, 139
belt replacement, 143, 145-148
blade sharpening, 140-142
blower screen cleaning, 138
brake pedal linkage adjustment, 142
drive belt guide adjustment, 148-152
fuel filter change, 137-138
fuel requirements, 134
fuse replacement, 143
grease, 134, 135
leveling the mower, 132-133
lubrication, 134, 135
maintenance/service schedule, 135
oil changes, 134, 135, 136
oil filter change, 137
safety tips, 8
spark plugs, 139-140
speed control linkage adjustment, 142
tire maintenance, 138
troubleshooting chart, 144
rototillers (*see* tillers/cultivators)
rust removal, 20, 25-27, 44

S

safety, 3-14
carbon monoxide safety, 4-5
chippers/shredders, 10
extension-cord safety, 7
fuel safety, 4-5
general safety guidelines, 3-4
grounding and electrical safety, 5-6
mowers, riding and walk-behind, 8
snowblowers, 8
tillers/cultivators, 10
weather conditions and safety, 7-8
scythes, sharpening, 37
sharpening dull tools, 10-11, 24, 77-79
axes, 28
bulb planters, 30
chain saws, 45-46
chippers/shredders, blade sharpening, 97-98
cordless weed-trimmer blades, 65
files, 79
forks, spading forks, 33
grass shears/trimmers, 30
grass-weed trimmers, blade-type, 77
hand cultivators, 30-32
hand mowers, 32
hatchets, 33
hedge trimmers, 33
hoes, 34
knives, 36-37
loppers, pruners, and tree saws, 28-29, 32-33, 38-39

sharpening dull tools (*cont.*)
post hole diggers, 36
power weed cutters, blades or knives sharpening, 124
rear-end mowers, blade sharpening, 126
riding mowers, blade sharpening, 140-142
scythes, 37
shovels and spades, 37-38
snow shovels, 37-38
tillers/cultivators, tine sharpening, 113
walk-behind mowers, blade sharpening, 87-91
weeding-type hand tools, 34-35, 40
whetstones, 41
yard carts, 42
shovels and spades, sharpening, 37-38
shredders (*see* chippers/shredders)
snow shovels, 37-38
snowblowers, 101-108
chute jammed, 104, 107
chute will not rotate, 106-107
gear-shifting, 106
inspection procedures, 101-102
noisy blade operation, 107
parts layout, exploded view, 102
safety tips, 8
starter rope replacement, 106
troubleshooting chart, 103
sod planters, 38
spades (*see* shovels and spades)
spark plugs
Briggs & Stratton engines, 160-161
cleanup tips, 17-19, 43
Clinton engines, 172
Jacobsen engines, 191, 202-203
riding mowers, 139-140
Tecumseh engines, 235-236
walk-behind mowers, 83
wires/leads, 20
spreaders (*see* lawn spreaders)
starter-rope replacement
grass/weed trimmers, 75, 76
snowblowers, 106
starters, 179-183, 232-235
electric starters, 223-224, 234-235
impulse starters, 180-183
recoil starters, 179-180, 187, 194-195, 214-215
rewind starters, 222-223, 232, 234
suppliers, 245-250

T

Tecumseh engines, 205-240
air cleaner service, 207-208, 217-218
breather element, side-mount, 236
breather passing oil, 239-240
carburetors, 208-214, 219-221, 227-232
carburetors, rebuild, 211-213, 220-221
carburetors, troubleshooting chart, 214
Craftsman reference number chart, 240
difficult starts, 236-237
electric starters, 223-224, 234-235
float element adjustment, 230-231
four-cycle engines, 216-226
four-cycle engines, OVM, 226-240
fuel bowl, 230
fuel requirements, 205-206, 217
governors, 222
identification numbers, 216-217
idle adjustment, 229-230
ignition systems, 235
ignition systems, overheat valve, 225-226
inlet needle and seat position, 231-232
knocking, 237
lack of power under load, 237
leaks oil, 239
misses under load, 237
oil/lubrication requirements, 205-206, 217
overheating, 237-238
OVM carburetors, 219-220
recoil starters, 214-215
rewind starters, 222-223, 232, 234
spark plugs, 235-236
starters, 232-235
surging, 238
troubleshooting chart, 236-240
tune-up procedures, 208, 218-219
two-cycle engines, TVS/TVXL840, 205-215
uses oil, 238-239
vibration, 238
tillers/cultivators (*see also* power

units/two-wheel tractors), 108-116, 249
air filter, 58, 109, 111, 109
BCS power units, 129
belt adjustments, 112-113
carburetor servicing, 59
cleaning the tiller, 109
clutch controls, 115
fuel requirements, 59-60
height adjustment, mowing bar attachment, 114
inspecting the tiller, 109
knife-holder adjustment, mowing bar attachment, 116
Mainline Rotary VMC90 tillers, 113-116
maintenance, 115
mower bar attachments, 113-116
safety tips, 10
throttle lever adjustment, 115
transmission service, 115
wheel service, 113
tools for repair, 10-14
digital multimeters (DMM), 10-11, 13-14
sharpening dull tools, 10-11
storage and organization, 12
voltage-ohmmeter (VOM), 10, 13-14
tractors (*see* lawn and garden tractors; power units/two-wheel tractors; riding mowers)
tree pruners and saws (*see* loppers/pruners)
trowels, 39
two-wheel tractors (*see* power units/two-wheel tractors)

V

voltage-ohmmeters (VOM), 10, 13-14

W

walk-behind mowers, 82-91, 249-250
air filters, 83
blade sharpening, 87-91
carburetor, 83
forward speed, inoperative, 84
forward speed, no adjustment, 84
front wheel adjustments, 87
fuel tanks, 83
lock bar does not release, 87
minor repairs, 83
rear wheel adjustments, 87
safety tips, 8
spark plug servicing, 83
throttle control repairs, 84
weather conditions and safety, 7-8
weed trimmers, 63-77
air filters, gas-powered trimmers, 69
battery charging, 64, 65-66
blade sharpening, 65, 77
carburetors, gas-powered trimmers, 69-70
cordless, hand-held trimmers, 63-66
fuel requirements, gas-powered trimmers, 68-69
line-type trimmers, electric-powered, 66-67, 70-71
line-type trimmers, gas-powered, 67-71, 71-76, 78
line-type trimmers, line adjustment, 67-68
recoil starters, gas-powered trimmers, 73-75
starter rope replacement, gas-powered trimmers, 75, 76
troubleshooting, gas-powered trimmers, 71-72, 78
weeding-type hand tools, 34-35, 40
wheelbarrows, 40-41
whetstones, 41
wires, cleanup tips, 20

Y

yard carts, 42

Other Bestsellers of Related Interest

GARDENING FOR A GREENER PLANET: A Chemical-Free Approach—*Jonathan Erickson*

Control pests in your lawn and garden with these environmentally safe methods. Using a technique known as "integrated pest management," this book shows you how to protect food and foliage from destructive insects without contamination from toxins found in chemical pesticides. He explains, in easy-to-follow steps, the correct way to use natural methods such as beneficial insects and organisms, companion planting, minerals and soaps, and botanical insecticides in the war against garden-hungry bugs. 176 pages, 108 illustrations. **Book No. 3801, $13.95 paperback, $21.95 hardcover**

BRICKLAYING: A Homeowner's Illustrated Guide—*Charles R. Self*

In this handy do-it-yourself guide you'll learn the basics of bricklaying: how to create different pattern bonds, mix mortar, lay bricks to achieve the strongest structure, cut bricks, finish mortar joints, and estimate materials. You'll also find out how to mix, test, and pour concrete to create foundations and footings for your brickwork. With the step-by-step instructions and illustrations found here, you can build any project with little difficulty. 176 pages, 146 illustrations. **Book No. 3878, $14.95 paperback, $22.95 hardcover.**

CREATIVE GARDEN SETTINGS
—*John D. Webersinn and G. Daniel Keen*

Look at the ways you can landscape your property and turn your house into a panorama of outdoor creativity, at the same time increasing the value of your home. Whether you want to build a deck, a patio, a stone fence, or a trickling fountain—nothing is beyond your reach. Keen and Webersinn combine their skills to bring you a well-written guide to everything from building permits to outdoor lighting. 200 pages, 100 illustrations. **Book No. 3936, $14.95 paperback, $24.95 hardcover**

PSYCHED ON BIKES: The Bicycle Owner's Handbook—*B. Andrew Renton*

Select, ride, maintain, and repair your own bike. This guide covers all types of bikes—one speed, three speed, and derailleur—and is not brand, make, or speed specific. Plus, it offers valuable advice on what to look for when buying a bike and shows you how to get the best value for your money. 192 pages, 135 illustrations. **Book No. 3668, $14.95 paperback only**

MAKING SPACE: Remodeling for More Living Area—*Ernie Bryant*

After you've developed your remodeling plan, this book gives you the step-by-step instructions and diagrams you need to complete your project. You'll find easy-to-follow techniques for constructing space-enhancing attic, garage, basement, full-room, and porch/deck conversions. Plus, easy-to-understand instructions highlight all the important steps of construction, and lead you through the entire process. 248 pages, 262 illustrations. **Book No. 3898, $12.95 paperback, $22.95 hardcover**

CERAMIC TILE SETTING—*John P. Bridge, Photography by Robert A. Bedient*

Discover how easy it can be to install your own ceramic tile floors, walls, and counters for a fraction of what you'd spend to hire a pro. From initial layout to floating and leveling, this easy-to-use guide contains all the information you need to start and finish a professional-looking project. Projects are arranged in order of difficulty and include step-by-step instructions. 244 pages, 165 illustrations. **Book No. 4053, $14.95 paperback, $24.95 hardcover**